W9-BRR-740

1st

O.P.

4 00

THE RISE OF THE RIGHT

By the same author

Special Counsel
Amnesty? Now! Never! If . . .
        (with Arlie Schardt and Mark O. Hatfield)
The Making of the New Majority Party
How to Win Arguments

THE RISE OF THE RIGHT

BY WILLIAM A. RUSHER

William Morrow and Company, Inc.

New York   1984

Copyright © 1984 by William A. Rusher

All rights reserved. No part of this book may be reproduced
or utilized in any form or by any means, electronic or mechanical,
including photocopying, recording or by any information storage
and retrieval system, without permission in writing from the
Publisher. Inquiries should be addressed to William Morrow and
Company, Inc., 105 Madison Avenue, New York, N.Y. 10016.

Library of Congress Catalog Card Number: 84-60207

ISBN: 0-688-01936-6

Printed in the United States of America

First Edition

1 2 3 4 5 6 7 8 9 10

BOOK DESIGN BY ALLEN MOGEL

This book is
DEDICATED
to
my colleagues at National Review,
living and dead.

They fought a good fight.
They finished their course.
They kept the faith.

Contents

Introduction

Shortly after President Reagan's election in 1980 I decided the time was ripe for a narrative history of the conservative movement in the United States from its origins in the early 1950s down to the present. The intellectual history of the movement had been ably described by George H. Nash in his *The Conservative Intellectual Movement in America Since 1945* (Basic Books, 1976). But its political history, both as a separate matter and in its relation to the movement's intellectual development, had never been addressed comprehensively. Worse yet, there had been a large number of books and articles about separate aspects and episodes of the political story, many of them hostile to conservatism and most of them misleading in important respects. I felt that having served for a quarter of a century as publisher of *National Review* and participated personally in most of the major conservative political activities that took place during that period, I was well qualified for my self-assigned task.

What has emerged from my pen is something different and less pedantic: an account of the birth, growth, and triumph of the conservative movement as they were witnessed by one observer-participant from a front-row seat. The disadvantage of such a personal perspective, of course, is that no one individual can possibly witness everything that happens on so broad a stage over so long a period of time. I watched or took part in most of the major events, and I have added descriptions of others wherever I felt this was necessary to give the reader an adequate understanding of the story as it unfolded. But I regret that this does not do justice to the contributions of many intrepid battlers for conservatism who deserve extended and grateful recognition. When the definitive history of modern American conservatism is written, there will be entire chapters in it concerning the accomplishments of an array of conservative organizations and individuals far too numerous to mention here. Meanwhile, let this brief acknowledgment of their existence and their achievements serve as my apology—and my salute.

That the modern conservative movement is on balance a "success story" admits, it seems to me, of little argument. As far as my own involvement in it is concerned, however, I have tried to be entirely frank, recounting the efforts that failed as well as those that succeeded, and not only the many moments that are delightful to recall but certain others that were positively painful to describe. As for a theme, careful readers will note my conviction that ideas must precede effective political action. And they will also have no trouble tracing the strategic conviction that underlay my own efforts almost from the start: America's conservative majority is comprised of both economic and social components and will produce political victory only when both components are appealed to successfully.

Like most books, this one is the beneficiary of far more devotion than simply that of the author. Let me record my heavy debt of gratitude to Dorothy McCartney, who patiently researched and responded to my incessant factual inquiries, and above all to Claire Wirth, who suffered through repeated manuscript revisions and all the other agonies of bringing the whole project to fruition yet still manages—so kind and forgiving is her nature—to wish it well.

Despite its shortcomings, for which I alone am responsible, I trust that this book will be useful to readers of many kinds. It is, I believe, the first book that has tried to tell the story of the modern conservative movement in sequence from its inception and as such ought to prove interesting to anyone concerned with the major trends in American politics. It should appeal with particular force to those who consider themselves conservative and who would like to know more about the origins, history, and leaders of American conservatism. Finally, I trust it will not be wholly disregarded by historians of the future, when at last they turn to this subject. For it boasts, at least, the supreme advantage of the eyewitness: I was there.

—WILLIAM A. RUSHER

New York City, August 23, 1983

The Early Fifties

It was in 1950 that Lionel Trilling, one of America's leading intellectuals, made his famous remark that "In the United States at this time liberalism is not only the dominant but even the sole intellectual tradition. For it is the plain fact that there are no conservative or reactionary ideas in general circulation."

Trilling was using the word *liberalism* in its twentieth-century American sense: as signifying that broad series of reformist, interventionist, collectivist, and redistributionist impulses, to be implemented within the free-enterprise system, that were associated with Franklin Roosevelt's New Deal. Beginning with Wendell Willkie's victory over Robert Taft in the Republican convention of 1940, and continuing with the nomination victories of New York Governor Thomas E. Dewey in the conventions of 1944 and 1948, the GOP had signaled its readiness to accept many of the New Deal's reforms and innovations as permanent and to compromise on most of the rest.

This is hardly to say that America in 1950 was short of political controversies. It was merely that the controversies tended to take place within a broader context of agreement on fundamentals, and those fundamentals, as Trilling correctly noted, were overwhelmingly liberal.

There were, to be sure, the makings of something very like conservative positions on one major subject with both domestic and international implications. When the presidential campaign of 1952 got under way, the basic lines of the Republican attack on the Truman administration in both the domestic and foreign fields were clear: With the addition, largely for its alliterative value, of an allusion to various scandals involving administration figures, the issues, as the Republicans saw them, were "COMMUNISM, CORRUPTION, and KOREA."

There is a tendency, especially among liberals, to refer to the

11

whole period of the early 1950s as the McCarthy era and to sub-
sume the entire issue of domestic communism, and even the problem of how to end the Korean War, under that heading. It is true
that the controversy over the activities of domestic Communists
did, in its later stages, come to be identified with the fortunes of
the Wisconsin senator who plunged into it in February 1950 with
his celebrated speech to the Republican Women of Wheeling,
West Virginia. But Republican interest in the subject had been
high from the opening days of the Eightieth Congress in 1947. The
famous "Hiss case," which captured the nation's attention and for
many people on both sides epitomized the issue, had come to public attention in 1947 with Whittaker Chambers's first appearance
before the House Un-American Activities Committee and ended
for all practical purposes with Hiss's conviction in his second trial
for perjury in January 1950—*prior* to McCarthy's Wheeling
speech. Moreover, the creation by the Senate in December 1950 of
a permanent Subcommittee on Internal Security, headed by the
chairman of the parent Judiciary Committee, Nevada Senator Pat
McCarran, insured that Senate attention to any problems posed by
the activities of domestic Communists would be in bipartisan but
vigorously anti-Communist hands—vested there, moreover, quite
independently of whatever investigations might be undertaken by
Senator McCarthy, who was simply the ranking Republican on the
Government Operations Committee and its Permanent Investigations Subcommittee.

In addition, the Truman administration's unwillingness to
force the Korean War to a satisfactory conclusion by bombing the
Chinese sanctuaries north of the Yalu River concerned many people who were not involved in the controversies over domestic
communism. The towering figure of America's greatest warrior,
Douglas MacArthur, visiting the front, devising and conducting
the historic Inchon landing, or directing the war and meanwhile
governing Japan from "the headquarters of the Supreme Commander" in Tokyo's Dai Ichi Building, created an alternative center of authority, power, and information with which the Truman
White House found it increasingly, and exasperatingly, difficult to
cope. One day the press would carry the remarks of an anonymous
"White House spokesman" on the war; a day or two later it would
report those of an equally anonymous "Dai Ichi spokesman," who

would coolly contradict and refute everything the White House spokesman had said. In April 1951 President Truman's patience—never his strongest suit—gave way under the pressure of this tacit defiance of his authority, and he dismissed MacArthur, recalling him to the United States.

MacArthur's subsequent return to American soil (he had not been home since before World War II), the welcoming parades, his dramatic address to a joint session of Congress, his subsequent series of speeches to state legislatures (he would talk in no lesser forum), and finally his keynote address at the 1952 Republican National Convention in Chicago, where his old aide-de-camp, Dwight Eisenhower, was ultimately nominated for the presidency, exerted a powerful impact on American public opinion. MacArthur's age (seventy-two) and his imperious personality made him personally a less than ideal presidential candidate in the democratic atmosphere of mid-century America, but the principles he enunciated so superbly—above all, perhaps, his reminder to Congress that "in war there can be no substitute for victory"—were deeply lodged in the voters' minds. Harry Truman, who had reveled in being the underdog in 1948, declined even to seek reelection in 1952. He knew all too well what the outcome would be.

Eisenhower's razor-thin defeat of Taft in the 1952 convention in Chicago, and his subsequent massive triumph over Adlai Stevenson that November, swept the GOP into control of both the House and Senate and thereby returned the federal government fully to Republican management for the first time in almost a quarter of a century. It also put an end to the long feud between Taft and Dewey, resolving it, at least in theory, in favor of the latter. In fact, however, the political life of both men was over. Taft, majority leader of the Senate at last, was dead of cancer within a year. Dewey stepped down as governor in January 1955 and effectively retired from politics altogether, returning to the private practice of law. Inevitably, the policies of the Republican party in the years following 1952 were shaped in the luminous but nebulous image of Dwight Eisenhower.

In electing Eisenhower as its president, most of the nation probably intended to move, to some moderate degree, in the relatively conservative directions suggested by the Republican campaign slogan: toward a tightening of the nation's internal security system and a satisfactory conclusion of the Korean War. But these cautious impulses toward the right hardly seemed to contradict in a serious way the observation Trilling had made in 1950. Domestically the country's differences were still largely narrowed to a matter of degree concerning the need for various alleged improvements in the free-enterprise economic system. Internationally the Cold War was under way in full force, but both major parties were broadly agreed on the need to wage it vigorously, and the United States was comfortably ahead of the Soviet Union in almost every department, with no evidence that this situation would change in the foreseeable future. Oil was being imported at $1.70 a barrel. Even the United Nations was practically trouble-free: The Third World would scarcely come into being as a separate major entity until 1960.

Liberalism of the modern twentieth-century variety seemed, and for the moment was, still comfortably dominant.

Chapter I

A Personal Word

Since this memoir of the growth of the conservative movement in the past third of a century is based largely on my own observations of it from a seat in the front row, as it were, it may be appropriate at this point to sketch briefly my own background and my frame of mind as the early 1950s unfolded. This process will also shed light on influences that were affecting many others as the decade got under way.

I was born in Chicago in 1923 and moved to New York with my parents when I was seven. There I attended various public schools, most of them in the suburbs of New York City. Entering Princeton in the autumn of 1940, I had the poor judgment to turn eighteen less than five months before Pearl Harbor. On the "accelerated" program prescribed for members of Princeton's Field Artillery ROTC, I received my degree (AB) in May 1943, in what is now Princeton's Woodrow Wilson School of Public and International Affairs. Poor eyesight barred me from a wartime commission as an artillery officer, but I was deemed qualified for Air Force Administration OCS. After slightly less than three years on active duty, including administrative jobs at Air Force Headquarters, India-Burma Theater, in Calcutta, I was discharged in February 1946 with the rank of captain and entered Harvard Law School that June. Once again the academic program was accelerated, this time for the convenience of veterans: I graduated in October 1948 and promptly went to work as an associate in the Wall Street law firm of Shearman & Sterling & Wright, New York City's largest.

My parents were Republicans, and my early inclination in that direction is probably attributable to that simple fact—massively aided by the coincidence that the Republican presidential nominee in 1936, when I was thirteen and just becoming precociously interested in politics, was Alfred M. Landon, who hailed from my mother's hometown, Independence, Kansas (population about 12,000), and knew my family casually.

Landon's overwhelming defeat that November by Franklin Roosevelt was a blow for which my childish pride was unprepared. (My father was equally surprised: Trusting the *Literary Digest*'s famous poll, he had wagered a hat on Landon in a bet with a business acquaintance.) It is impossible to know all the critical influences on a growing youngster, but it is at least conceivable, in my case, that an unconscious determination to avenge Landon's trouncing provided a good share of the psychic energy that has fueled the rest of my life. If so, there are ironies aplenty: Landon, though himself a midwesterner, was the handpicked candidate of the eastern Republicans who still dominated the GOP in 1936—and whose final defeat by a southern and western coalition it was my pleasure to help contrive more than a quarter of a century later. Moreover, Ronald Reagan, whose 1980 election as president slaked at last and in full the burning thirst that first developed in me in 1936, himself voted for Roosevelt all four times FDR ran for president. Nonetheless, there is a sense in which, for me at least, 1980 was the year in which H. V. Kaltenborn's famous prediction at last came true: The "rural vote," figuratively speaking, finally came in.

At least one other psychogenic influence, however, was at play in the shaping of my political attitudes. My family had moved from Chicago to New York at a key moment in their son's development. At age seven a boy identifies culturally with what he has known and may cling to it as a defense against new and implicitly threatening experiences. As a very young midwesterner in the East, probably teased (though I have no recollection of this) by classmates for my nasal twang, I became self-consciously a midwesterner-in-exile—swelling with pride when we studied Chicago in geography class, rooting for the Cubs though I was largely uninterested in baseball. I have no doubt at all that even if nothing else had, Alf Landon's quintessential midwesternism would have endeared him to me, especially as against the squire of Hyde Park.

This anti-eastern and specifically anti-New York bias (in cultural terms only, and at a rather superficial level—actually I soon became quite happy in the East) lay dormant until I had an opportunity to play politics at the state and national levels of the Young Republican organization sponsored by the GOP.

I had led the Republican forces in the Princeton Model Senate before going off to war; I had founded and became the first president of the Harvard Young Republican Club while at law school afterward. Going to work for my Wall Street law firm late in 1948, therefore, I promptly joined the New York Young Republican Club, a large and prestigious organization to which many young Wall Streeters and other Manhattan businessmen belonged. During the next few years I served on its board of governors with such contemporaries as John V. Lindsay and President Reagan's secretary of housing and urban development, Samuel Pierce. But as early as 1949 I forged an alliance between a minority faction of the club and a group of its ancestral rivals loosely designated as "upstate," and tasted victory in the state YR convention of 1950 as one of the leaders of the anti-New York City coalition.*

In terms of intellectual content, the Republican loyalties I displayed prior to 1953 were comprehensive but shallow. I had no coherent world view and no religious beliefs: My attitude toward religion might have been described as one of respectful agnosticism. My Republican politics adequately expressed my position on most subjects in which I was really interested.

In terms of the GOP's internal conflicts, my Republicanism at that time was rather distinctly of the moderate or "progressive" variety. For all my latent pro-midwesternism, living in New York and reading the *Herald Tribune* in the years from 1936 to 1940, I had unconsciously imbibed and enthusiastically adopted that newspaper's brand of eastern Republicanism: concessive on domestic issues where New Deal reforms were concerned and broadly internationalist, as well as rather specifically Anglophile, in foreign affairs. As World War II approached, I grew steadily more convinced of the need for the United States to make common cause with Britain and France in stopping Hitler; when it broke, I became a passionate "interventionist," eager for America to wade into the fray. In the summer of 1940 I joined William Allen White's Committee to Defend America by Aiding the Allies; then, finding that rather pallid stuff, I signed up with Herbert Agar's Fight for Freedom Committee when that militant organization was founded in 1941. In 1940 I followed the *Herald Tribune* in

* The leader of the coalition was F. Clifton White, a Young Republican from Ithaca, five years my senior, who was elected president of the state YRs that year. I became chairman of his board of governors and have remained his friend and ally ever since.

supporting the candidacy of Wendell Willkie, the only implicit interventionist among the competitors for the Republican nomination that year. If he had not been nominated, I think it is quite likely that I would have supported Roosevelt on the basis of the war issues. But Willkie's nomination kept me loyal to the GOP, and three years later I wrote my senior thesis at Princeton on *The Progressive Element in the Republican Party from 1938 to the Present* and dedicated it to Willkie.

On domestic issues, having no really firm grounding in classical-liberal economic principles, I tended to agree with the leaders of eastern Republicanism that Roosevelt's New Deal displayed dangerous tendencies toward big government and dubious economics, but that in the political circumstances compromise was inevitable and probably desirable. I remember, in particular, thinking that the vaunted Social Security program was fiscally unsound, but that the United States was probably wealthy enough to afford it anyway.

I did have one brush with doctrinaire libertarianism in the spring of 1943, but it was not destined to lead anywhere. As a finalist in the National Intercollegiate Radio Prize Debates (sponsored by the American Economic Foundation), I gave a perhaps too defensive talk in support of free-enterprise principles. The broadcast was heard by Rose Wilder Lane, a noted libertarian author of the day, who promptly initiated a correspondence with me that lasted until I was shipped off to India as an air force officer in the summer of 1944. Her defiant contempt for the Leviathan state was something wholly new in my experience and made a powerful impression on me. But her greatest intellectual enthusiasm at that time was reserved for the Arab culture of the Saracens, about which she had just written a book. (She compared the Saracens favorably to the Christian Crusaders.) All this was somewhat beside the point that might have made a decisive impact on me.

With the war's end, I might have turned my attention more closely to domestic economic issues, and arrived at conservative conclusions on those subjects sooner, if the wartime emphasis on foreign affairs had not been followed so promptly by the Cold War. Here my principal tutor was *Time* magazine, another pillar of the Republican party's eastern leadership. When I graduated from law school in 1948 and entered that large Wall Street law firm, my political loyalties—having survived a mercifully brief law school interest in the possibilities of Harold Stassen—swung easily to New York Governor Thomas E. Dewey.

Dewey was the leader of the eastern, anti-Taft wing of the GOP, but it would be seriously misleading to conclude on this account that he was a "liberal," in the modern usage of the word, in any but the most purely relative sense. Dewey, Henry Luce, and the other eastern Republicans of the late 1940s were well to the right of the Democratic party of that day on domestic issues and firmly committed to the successful prosecution of the Cold War against the Soviet Union. In fact—and this cut distinctly in their favor as far as I was concerned—their tendency to involvement in world affairs, which they inherited from Willkie and the other "interventionists" of 1940–41, dovetailed with Cold War activism rather better than the views of Robert Taft and his followers, who were the heirs of such isolationist sentiment as there was in the Republican party.

Meanwhile, from 1946 to 1953 I watched, largely through the prisms of *Time* and the *Herald Tribune,* the developments on the domestic and foreign scenes that I have already described: the investigations into domestic communism, the Korean War, Truman's recall of MacArthur, etc. I had been as surprised as everybody else by Truman's defeat of Dewey in 1948 and was as eager as many other Republicans to enlist the popularity of General Eisenhower in the high cause of putting the Democrats out of office at last in 1952. My Republicanism was catholic enough at that point to embrace even Senator Taft among its objects of admiration, but 1952, I felt, was no year to take chances—especially after the GOP's surprise defeat in 1948. Accordingly, attending the Republican convention in Chicago as a Young Republican observer, I rooted enthusiastically for Eisenhower, and that November, when he was elected and the Republican party carried both houses of Congress, I experienced a sense of joy I had not previously known in my sixteen years of attention to the nation's political controversies.

By the time Dwight Eisenhower was sworn in as president in January 1953, therefore, I was just under thirty years old; a Wall Street attorney, contentedly active in Young Republican affairs at the state and national levels; inclined to a conventional political career, either as a political manager or as a candidate for public office; delighted at the upsurge in my party's fortunes; deeply concerned over the problems presented by both domestic and international communism; reconciled to the need to compromise with the still-dominant liberal impulses in the domestic sphere; and intrigued by the occasional whiff of conservative political theory that crossed my nostrils.

Involved as I was during these years in the partisan struggle and in the internal controversies of the Republican party, I was aware of the more theoretical dimensions of political thought only dimly. And yet, by comparison with most of my Young Republican colleagues, I almost qualified as an intellectual. I had after all been exposed at Princeton, in the School of Public and International Affairs (where I chose American politics as my special field), to the works of Charles E. Merriam, Harold D. Lasswell, and other leading political scientists. In my early (1949) encounters with my Young Republican ally Clif White, who was then an instructor in political science at both Ithaca College and Cornell University, this common fund of knowledge and interest cemented our friendship and supplied the ingredients for many a wide-ranging bull session on his visits to New York City. We both viewed politics as at least potentially a science, and we thought and talked long and hard about how to conduct scientifically the bid for political leadership that we were—of course—planning to make.

On political principles, however, I cannot recall that we often dwelt very long. We understood their importance—in fact, when they came up at all, we treated them with reverence—but the Dewey dispensation in Republican politics was common ground between us, and it was more or less tacitly understood that a victory for the Republican party, if one could only be achieved, would conduce handsomely to the public weal.

I had, however, read and been powerfully impressed by Friedrich von Hayek's *The Road to Serfdom* not long after its publication in 1944. At Harvard Law School in 1947 I encountered it again, as required reading in Lon Luvois Fuller's wide-ranging course on jurisprudence. Also required was Barbara Wootton's formal book-length reply to Hayek, entitled *Freedom Under Planning* (Chapel Hill, 1945), and I recall being vividly impressed by how honestly, yet withal how unsuccessfully, the noted British socialist strove to refute Hayek.

Hayek's book, which became the Bible and battle cry of post-war classical liberals, had been published by the University of North Carolina Press at the end of World War II, just when the nature of the economic systems that would dominate the postwar world was up for discussion and decision. As one reviewer remarked at the time, Hayek's assault on socialism and economic planning was "no mere sortie from the castle: It is a full-scale attack, with horse, foot, and artillery."

Hayek began by noting: "According to the views now dominant, the question is no longer how we can make the best use of the spontaneous forces found in a free society. We have in effect undertaken to dispense with the forces which produced unforeseen results and to replace the impersonal and anonymous mechanism of the market by collective and 'conscious' direction of all social forces to deliberately chosen goals." In a series of trenchant chapters that struck as hard at postwar American liberal thought as they did at European socialism, he then argued that the kind of economic planning that aims at the replacement of competition is, necessarily, not only economically but politically authoritarian and that the resulting state inevitably becomes the enemy first of virtue, then of truth, and ultimately even of peace. He concluded with a ringing call for the revival of classical nineteenth-century liberalism:

> If we are to build a better world, we must have the courage to make a new start—even if that means some *reculer pour mieux sauter*. . . . The young are right if they have little confidence in the ideas which rule most of their elders. But they are mistaken or misled when they believe that these are still the liberal ideas of the nineteenth century, which, in fact, the younger generation hardly knows. Though we neither can wish nor possess the power to go back to the reality of the nineteenth century, we have the opportunity to realize its ideals—and they were not mean. . . . The guiding principle that a policy of freedom for the individual is the only truly progressive policy remains as true today as it was in the nineteenth century.

Hayek was not, of course—nor did he pretend to be—the first author to speak up in favor of classical liberal economics. His own

bibliography in *The Road to Serfdom* lists twenty-one books published between 1934 and 1943, including volumes by such important writers as W. H. Chamberlin, Élie Halévy, W. H. Hutt,
Walter Lippmann, Ludwig von Mises, Wilhelm Röpke, and F. A.
Voigt. But Hayek's book, perhaps by the happy accident of its
timing and certainly to some extent thanks to its vigor, attracted
wide public attention. It was my own first introduction to rigorous
classical liberalism, and I was duly impressed.

Other early books and publications of a conservative nature,
however, escaped me as thoroughly as they escaped Trilling. I remember reading reviews of William F. Buckley, Jr.'s *God and
Man at Yale*, which appeared in 1951 and was certainly one of the
earliest comprehensive condemnations of the regnant liberal mentality as then on display at Yale, but I don't believe I read the book
itself at the time. Perhaps my background at Princeton and Harvard led me to assume that whatever the situation up at Yale, it
had no direct relevance to my concerns. In that belief I was, of
course, sadly mistaken.

The years 1953 and 1954, however, were to advance my political education spectacularly. In the first place, it rapidly became
apparent that Eisenhower's election was no panacea for the nation's problems, even from the standpoint of a fairly moderate Republican. The basic reforms and innovations of the New Deal
were left intact—not, to be sure, that any realist had expected
anything else. The Democratic party's more recent redistributionist and collectivist tendencies too, however, were nowhere
squarely challenged. Abroad, the Korean War was promptly settled on a basis that amounted to acceptance of a stalemate and
which might well have led to a serious effort to impeach Harry
Truman if he had arranged it. Considerably worse yet from my
personal standpoint, the Eisenhower administration showed little
stomach for pursuing the GOP's long-standing interest in the issue
of domestic communism.

It is not yet possible to discuss the problem of domestic communism, as it presented itself in the late 1940s and early 1950s,
with any hope of an objective reception. Too many of the key pro-
tagonists—at this writing even Alger Hiss—are still alive; too
many fragile but important reputations still have passionate defenders; too much sheer effort has been invested by liberals, during
the last thirty-five years, in establishing and maintaining a highly

tendentious version of what the situation actually was and of what happened as a result. Suffice it to say, therefore, that like many other Americans, I had become convinced, by the disclosures of the late 1940s, that during the Roosevelt administration an impressive number of American Communists and fellow travelers had penetrated both government and various other aspects of our national life and that this state of affairs required both recognition and counteraction.

From 1950 onward this viewpoint was casually equated by the media with "McCarthyism" and burdened with condemnations based on the particular style, tactics, and activities of Senator Joseph McCarthy. But while McCarthy certainly identified himself with the issue, and played a leading role in investigating the subject, he was far from the only congressional investigator of communism, and by no means the ablest or most effective. The House Committee on Un-American Activities had been on the scene since the late 1930s and had played a key role in disclosing the espionage activities of Alger Hiss in 1947 and 1948. And as already noted, the Senate, while still under Democratic control in 1950, had created an Internal Security Subcommittee of its Judiciary Committee under the latter's own chairman, the formidable Pat McCarran, a former chief justice of the Supreme Court of Nevada.

There was, therefore, no need for one to be a particular disciple of Joe McCarthy's, or even a supporter of his much-execrated "methods," to be seriously concerned over the issue of domestic communism or an advocate of congressional investigations of the subject. Certainly I, for one, was perfectly able to make the relevant distinctions—although as the battle over McCarthyism rolled toward its climax, I found myself, simply as a lawyer, far more revolted by the misrepresentations and other tactics being used against McCarthy than by anything of which he himself was in fact guilty.

In addition, by 1952 I had met, through mutual friends in Manhattan Republican politics, Robert Morris, the New York attorney who had served in 1950 as Republican (minority) counsel to the Tydings committee investigating McCarthy's early charges. Morris had gone on to become in 1951 the first chief counsel to Senator Pat McCarran's Internal Security Subcommittee and then late in 1953 retired from that post upon winning election as a judge of New York City's Municipal Court. He kept in touch with his numerous friends in the broad field of Communist investigations, however, and I met many of these in the course of visits to his brownstone apartment on Manhattan's East Sixty-fourth Street in 1954 and 1955.

Strongly reinforcing my conviction that my new concerns were not imaginary—that international communism, in all its guises, was indeed a foe that America must confront and overcome and that there was a respectable philosophical basis on which it could be confronted—was Whittaker Chambers's *Witness* (Random House, 1953). In retrospect one can see that this powerful book drew together, in superb prose, all of my major new preoccupations at this critical point in my life: my latent interest in the philosophical challenge of communism, my fascination with Communist espionage and related subjects, and my concern for U.S. victory in the Cold War with the Soviet Union.

Witness did for postwar American anticommunism what Hayek eight years before had done for classical liberal economics. The story of Whittaker Chambers's conversion to communism, his service as a Communist espionage courier, his break with the party, his 1948 confrontation with his old party comrade Alger Hiss, and Hiss's two subsequent trials and ultimate conviction (in 1950) for perjury are too well known to require recounting here. But *Witness*, which dealt with all those subjects, also defined the philosophical case against communism and in so doing marked an epochal step in the history of modern American conservatism.

Chambers first impinged on America's consciousness in 1947 as a not especially attractive figure emerging from the shadows of communism and espionage to confess to an evil past. But in the course of his long public struggle with Hiss, Chambers became an authentic hero to those who believed that communism was embarked on a program of world conquest and that its American agents—including outright spies like Chambers—were objects of legitimate concern. The heart of *Witness* lies, of course, in its account of Chambers's relationship with Hiss, but in many ways its most powerful pages are those entitled "Foreword in the Form of a Letter to My Children." In those pages, Chambers (a former editor of *Time* who was a superb writer) expressed, as well as it is ever likely to be expressed, the fundamental clash between communism and the root principles of Judaeo-Christian civilization. *Witness* made it brilliantly clear why a thoughtful individual might well devote his life to resisting the triumph of communism. To many of those whose attention had been riveted by the outbreak of the Cold War in 1946 and the subsequent revelations concerning Communist infiltration in the United States, the book provided the philosophical capstone to a passionate commitment. Listen as Chambers explains what he conceives to be the real significance of the Hiss case:

On a scale personal enough to be felt by all, but big enough to be symbolic, the two irreconcilable faiths of our time—Communism and Freedom—came to grips in the persons of two conscious and resolute men. . . .

[Communism] is not new. It is, in fact, man's second oldest faith. Its promise was whispered in the first days of the Creation under the Tree of the Knowledge of Good and Evil: "Ye shall be as gods." It is the great alternative faith of mankind. Like all great faiths, its force derives from a simple vision. Other ages have had great visions. They have always been different versions of the same vision: the vision of God and man's relationship to God. The Communist vision is the vision of Man without God.

It is the vision of man's mind displacing God as the creative intelligence of the world. It is the vision of man's liberated mind, by the sole force of its rational intelligence, redirecting man's destiny and reorganizing man's life and the world. . . .

The crisis of the Western world exists to the degree in which it is indifferent to God. It exists to the degree in which the Western world actually shares Communism's materialist vision, is so dazzled by the logic of the materialist interpretation of history, politics and economics, that it fails to grasp that, for it, the only possible answer to the Communist challenge: Faith in God or Faith in Man? is the challenge: Faith in God.

Economics is not the central problem of this century. It is a relative problem and can be solved in relative ways. Faith is the central problem of this age. The Western world does not know it, but it already possesses the answer to this problem—but only provided that its faith in God and the freedom He enjoins is as great as Communism's faith in Man.

In these remarkable paragraphs Chambers was proclaiming that opposition to communism, foreign and domestic, was not merely a journalistic by-product of America's Cold War with Russia but a bold stand against the latest and deadliest form of the atheist materialism so often associated with the eighteenth-century Enlightenment: the last chance for the Western world to regain its bearings and save itself from moral—and therefore ultimately physical—destruction.

In *Witness,* Chambers demonstrated that philosophical anti-communism was a full and worthy partner of classical liberalism in the arsenal of the American right.

It was through Bob Morris that I was sounded out, when the new (Eighty-third) Republican Congress took over in January 1953, as a possible member of the legal staff of the Internal Security Subcommittee or the House Un-American Activities Committee. I was powerfully tempted, but my law firm had no policy permitting a young associate to take a lengthy leave of absence for such a purpose, and I was at that time unwilling to break my ties with the firm for what would inevitably be only a few years' employment in Washington at best. Moreover, my own decisive break with Eisenhower Republicanism—the event that ultimately made me willing to abandon both private law practice and partisan politics altogether—had not yet occurred, and was not to occur for another year. When it did occur, however, it was—not surprisingly—Eisenhower's policy on the issue of domestic communism that brought it about.

Unquestionably it would have been possible for Eisenhower to take public charge of the important job of investigating and where necessary eliminating Communist influences in government and vest it in deputies of his own choosing. He could, in other words, effectively have bypassed McCarthy, made the issue his own, and laid it to rest in due course after appropriate action—leaving McCarthy the choice of accepting a *fait accompli* or defying a president of his own party.

But the president and his advisers, watching the controversy grow as McCarthy assumed the chairmanship of the Government Operations Committee in the new Republican Senate, did none of these things. Eisenhower was alive to the extremely tender sensibilities of many liberals on this whole issue—sensibilities inflamed, in not a few cases, by a realization that their possessors had acquiesced all too easily in the presence of Communists among their colleagues in earlier (and different) times. Rather than undertake the painful job of drawing negative political conclusions—and consequences—from this whole history, Eisenhower elected to ignore it: to let the liberals off altogether and insure only that so far as security measures made it possible, no Communists or fellow travelers remained in government posts in his own administration.

This decision, which many people hailed as an act of the highest statesmanship, had, unfortunately, the effect of leaving the "Communist issue" to the only too willing McCarthy—and also put the administration in a position of potential, perhaps even inevitable confrontation with him. The confrontation duly came to pass in January 1954 over the issue of McCarthy's alleged browbeating of Brigadier General Ralph Zwicker, the man ultimately responsible for the promotion of an officer who was a security risk. As a former general himself, Eisenhower took personally McCarthy's treatment of Zwicker—not pausing to note that Zwicker had behaved in a fashion quite contumacious enough to warrant the response he actually drew from McCarthy. Vice President Nixon was instructed by the cautious president (who in public remained typically aloof from the matter himself) to make a speech implicitly criticizing McCarthy. On March 13 Nixon obeyed in a national radio broadcast, asserting, "When you go out to shoot rats, you have to shoot straight, because when you shoot wildly . . . you might hit someone else who is trying to shoot rats, too." The implication, though circumspectly indirect, was clear, and the media, of course, hastened to spell it out: The Eisenhower administration was condemning McCarthy.

Nixon's speech on Eisenhower's behalf completed my own emotional break with the Eisenhower administration. It was not a matter of being, in any deep personal sense, "pro-McCarthy." It was rather that more than any other single factor, my growing preoccupation with the subject of communism had separated me emotionally from the routine interests of a politically active young Republican and prompted me to invest my efforts in the arena of more explicitly anti-Communist activities. Nixon's speech was bound, therefore, to be a bitter blow.

I can remember, with the clarity that so often characterizes our recollection of the great climacterics of our lives, the precise circumstances under which I heard that speech, recognized its significance, and accepted what that implied for my own past and future. I was one of several passengers in a car returning to Manhattan that Saturday evening from a day and dinner in Westhampton, Long Island. It was a political bunch, as friends of mine usually were, and somebody turned on the car radio so that we could listen to Nixon's talk as we sped westward along the parkways. To the others, it was little more than just another political speech. My response, however, was to fall uncharacteristically silent. Usually, on those long car rides, I was a dependable source of entertainment, often leading the conversation with a series of jokes, anecdotes, and more serious discussion topics. But that night, when Nixon had finished, I settled into a silence not so much gloomy as utterly empty. My friends did their best to rouse me, but without success. To me, the speech seemed to say clearly that my whole eighteen-year commitment to the Republican party had been a mistake, that I would have to cut deeper, and altogether elsewhere, if I wanted to influence my country's destiny in the ways I believed to be desirable.

The relatively few but important serious books of conservative political philosophy that I had read or heard about suggested a possible new direction for my efforts. I have already described the impact that *Witness* had had on me. Further back, I could recall, and still admired, Hayek's rocklike defense of the principles of classical liberal economics in *The Road to Serfdom.* In addition, recently—in 1953, in fact—a powerful spokesman for yet another aspect of conservatism had appeared on the scene.

I do not recall whether I read Russell Kirk's *The Conservative Mind* (Chicago) when it was published or only absorbed its thrust through *Time's* long and favorable review, but in either case its influence on me was considerable. Absorbing as the battle against foreign and domestic communism might be, it was at least subliminally dissatisfying to be only "against" something. Communism was no doubt eminently worth being *against,* but what was I *for*? The Republican party was all too plainly not the answer, if the postelection Eisenhower was to be its leader and the shaper of its policies. Kirk introduced me to the traditionalist heritage of Burkean conservatism, which dovetailed neatly with my instinctive hostility to the scientistic, programmatic bent of all forms of Marxist socialism, including communism. He also endowed me—

no small gift—with a new and deeper understanding of the meaning of the word *conservatism.*

Kirk was a youthful professor of history at Michigan State University with a doctorate in letters from St. Andrews University in Scotland. Nailing to his mast the flag of Edmund Burke, the eighteenth-century British statesman and political thinker, Kirk proclaimed: "Taken as a whole, Burke's accomplishment is the definition of a principle of order. . . . Men are saved from anarchy by adherence to the principles of a just order. They are saved by reverence toward God and toward the prescriptive ways of man."

Kirk then traced nineteenth-century conservative thought in the words and deeds of such men as the Adamses, Coleridge, Calhoun, Disraeli, and many others, and concluded with summaries of the viewpoints of the woefully few important conservative writers of the first half of the twentieth century: Irving Babbitt, Paul Elmer More, George Santayana, etc. His very chapter headings, however, as he approached the twentieth century ("Conservatism Frustrated: America, 1865–1918"; "English Conservatism Adrift: the Twentieth Century") proclaimed the low estate of his "traditionalist" faith at the time, and his impressively detailed bibliography was sadly short of works first published after 1900.

But Kirk knew what he believed, and he retreated not at all from what he defined at the outset as the "six canons of conservative thought":

(1) Belief that a divine intent rules society as well as conscience, forging an eternal chain of right and duty which links great and obscure, living and dead. Political problems, at bottom, are religious and moral problems. . . .
(2) Affection for the proliferating variety and mystery of traditional life, as distinguished from the narrowing uniformity and equalitarianism and utilitarian aims of most radical systems. . . .
(3) Conviction that civilized society requires orders and classes. The only true equality is moral equality; all other attempts at levelling lead to despair, if enforced by positive legislation. . . .
(4) Persuasion that property and freedom are inseparable. . . .
(5) Faith in prescription and distrust of "sophisters and calculators." Man must put a control upon his will and his appetite, for conservatives know man to be governed more by emotion than by reason. . . .

(6) Recognition that change and reform are not identical, and that innovation is a devouring conflagration more often than it is a torch of progress. . . .

He was equally sure, and witheringly scornful, of what he considered the common denominators of "radicalism": the perfectibility of man, contempt for tradition, and the impulse toward political and economic leveling. He defied them and would continue to do so regardless of the political outcome: "If a conservative order is indeed to return, we ought to know the tradition which is attached to it, so that we may rebuild society; if it is not to be restored, still we ought to understand conservative ideas so that we may rake from the ashes what scorched fragments of civilization escape the conflagration of unchecked will and appetite."

Other books that influenced me profoundly in these years were James Burnham's *The Web of Subversion* (John Day, 1954) which put the facts of important Communist penetration of American life beyond serious doubt, regardless of one's opinion of Joseph McCarthy, and Kirk's *Academic Freedom* (Regnery), a 1955 discussion of that vexed issue in the light of traditionalist conservative values. I have never forgotten the sweep and power of the latter book's concluding paragraph:

> To what truths, then, ought the Academy to be dedicated? To the proposition that the end of education is the elevation of the reason of the human person, for the human person's own sake. To the proposition that the higher imagination is better than the sensate triumph. To the proposition that the fear of God, and not mastery over man and nature, is the object of learning. To the proposition that quality is worth more than quantity. To the proposition that justice takes precedence over power. To the proposition that order is more lovable than egoism. To the proposition that to believe all things, if the choice must be made, is nobler than to doubt all things. To the proposition that honor outweighs success. To the proposition that tolerance is wiser than ideology. To the proposition, Socratic and Christian, that the unexamined life is not worth living. If the Academy holds by these propositions, not all the force of Caesar can break down its walls; but if the Academy is bent upon sneering at everything in heaven and earth, or upon reforming itself after the model of the market-place, not all the eloquence of the prophets can save it.

Now I had a new sign under which to conquer. By mid-1954 I could no longer be satisfied merely with being a "Republican"—whatever that meant. I was something else: something with a longer tradition, a richer heritage, a deeper significance.

I was a *conservative.*

Chapter II

The *Freeman* and *National Review*

There is little doubt that Hayek's *The Road to Serfdom*, Kirk's *The Conservative Mind*, and Chambers's *Witness* were the three most powerful philosophical contributions to the conservative movement that was stirring intellectually in the early 1950s, but they were not the only ones. Small and fragmented as it was, the world of conservative thinkers toward which I began to turn, in and after 1954, was not quite so negligible as it had been when Lionel Trilling made his observation in 1950—nor was it totally insignificant even then. Dr. George Nash's comprehensive work *The Conservative Intellectual Movement in America Since 1945* is the definitive study of this subject, and it is not necessary to duplicate or summarize it here. One major episode in the early 1950s deserves special mention, however, because it was so clearly in the main line of conservative developments and led so directly to yet another. That was the founding of the *Freeman*.

The *Freeman* was in many respects, in terms of both philosophy and personnel, a sort of journalistic John the Baptist—a precursor of *National Review*—and its existence after 1950 would to some extent have invalidated Trilling's dictum if he had uttered it in any later year.

The name of the publication was borrowed from a still earlier magazine published by Albert Jay Nock in the 1920s, and it was launched in 1950 under the joint editorship of three classical liberals: a former editor of *Life* named John Chamberlain; Henry Hazlitt, a *Newsweek* columnist who had written an influential book entitled *Economics in One Lesson;* and Suzanne LaFollette, one of Nock's editors. They had the financial and editorial support of a large and variegated board of directors that included Leonard Read, a former head of the Los Angeles Chamber of Commerce; Jasper Crane, a Du Pont executive; Joseph N. Pew, Jr., the Sun Oil heir; a New York businessman named Lawrence Fertig; and

Alfred Kohlberg, another businessman, who willingly transferred
the financial backing he had been giving to the anti-Communist
monthly *Plain Talk* to a publication of wider scope.

A fortnightly from the start, it was the *Freeman*'s avowed aim
to do for what it stubbornly insisted on calling "liberalism"
(meaning, of course, classical liberalism) what journals of opinion
like the *Nation* and the *New Republic* had done for twentieth-
century liberalism, and for the left more generally, in previous
decades.* Declaring that "True liberalism rests on the common
law, on clear and definite statute law, and on a government of limited powers," the new publication challenged the powerful tide of
twentieth-century political opinion by calling for "local autonomy
and the decentralization of political power." As for economics,
The *Freeman* was equally uncompromising: "Economic freedom,
as embodied in the free market, is the basic institution of a liberal
society."

To the *Freeman* were quickly drawn many of the individuals
who, then and later, constituted the intellectual leadership of the
nascent conservative movement. Among them were Willi
Schlamm, a protégé of Whittaker Chambers's at *Time*, who edited
the "Arts and Manners" section; Frank Meyer, a former Communist and Oxford-educated philosopher; Frank Chodorov, a devoted
libertarian; the Hollywood humorist and screenwriter Morrie Ryskind; Forrest Davis, a diplomatic reporter for the *Saturday
Evening Post*; Anthony Harrigan, a South Carolina newspaperman; and a covey of recent Yale graduates: William F. Buckley,
Jr., L. Brent Bozell, and M. Stanton Evans.

Unfortunately, if perhaps inevitably in the disorderly every-
man-for-himself intellectual atmosphere of early-1950s conservatism, strains soon developed, both among the editors and within
that large board of directors. One faction—the purer classicists,
loosely identified with Pew and having the sympathy of Henry
Hazlitt—was reluctant to have the *Freeman* engage in what it regarded as unseemly journalistic battles. The other, which very definitely included Schlamm and directors like Alfred Kohlberg and
reflected the combative temperaments of Chamberlain and La-
Follette, was eager to project the magazine into such controversies

* For an excellent account of the *Freeman*'s founding, see John Chamberlain's newly
published autobiography, *A Life with the Printed Word* (Regnery Gateway, 1982).

as the one over Joseph McCarthy and the 1952 battle between Eisenhower and Taft—in favor of Taft, naturally. Matters came to a head not long after Forrest Davis, a strong Taft partisan and a rather quarrelsome personality, became one of the publication's editors: The board of directors failed to back Davis over Hazlitt on certain key issues; Chamberlain, LaFollette, and Davis resigned; so did Schlamm; and Leonard Read sorrowfully bought the shell of the *Freeman*, converting it into a monthly commentary on economic philosophy under the auspices of his Foundation for Economic Education, at Irvington-on-Hudson. As such, it could, of course, no longer be the feisty journal of opinion its founders had envisioned.

How important is it, in any case, for a coalition of political philosophers and theoreticians to have a "unified field theory," as it were—a comprehensive world view incorporating their various insights? It is clearly not always essential to political victory and at times may even be a handicap: Twentieth-century liberalism dominated American politics for half a century without one, cheerfully admitting and even boasting of its eclecticism.

But the test of liberalism may only be coming now, in the 1980s. Perhaps a unifying fundamental philosophy is essential, not for victory in the good days but for survival in the bad ones. When the victorious coalition falls apart; when the clarion call no longer works; when the inspirational vision fails to exert its old appeal—where then shall the faithful turn for consolation and renewal? Inward, surely; but then there must be something *there*—something more than simply a noble impulse, an admirable emotion, or a willingness to sacrifice. Karl Marx set Europe ablaze, not with his denunciation of capitalism, or even with his remedy for its evils, but with an allegedly scientific analysis of the laws of history: an analysis that purported not only to explain observable reality but to predict, with scientific precision, the future course of events. He claimed to be giving his followers both an explanation of what had happened and what was happening and a means of foreseeing, and thereby guiding, manipulating, and profiting from, what would inevitably happen next. A movement that convincingly asserts such capacities has a staying power out of all proportion to its size or to transient circumstances.

Just how self-confident in this respect, however, were the protoconservatives of the early 1950s entitled to feel? The three political forces—traditionalism, classical liberalism, and anticommunism—that came together in the early 1950s under the rubric of "conservatism" were readily distinguishable and by no means self-evidently complementary. On the contrary, they were at least potentially inconsistent and had in fact a historical record of conflict. Classical liberalism had arisen in the eighteenth century as the challenger and nemesis of the old feudal order; Burkean traditionalism was, quite simply, a shocked response to the excesses of the new liberal dispensation, tapping deep roots in the very centuries the social order of which liberalism had overthrown. Anti-Communists, on the other hand, were often all too willing to make common cause with states and movements that no classical liberal could conscientiously endorse and with which traditionalism has few bonds or none. Left to themselves, the three constituent parts of the modern conservative movement would no doubt have disagreed vigorously.

But, of course, they were not left to themselves. By 1950 they all perceived in twentieth-century liberalism the principal threat to the realization of their separate purposes. The new liberalism had embraced and vastly extended the Enlightenment's rejection of the traditional bases of social order; it had accepted the socialist concept of the dominant role of the state in human affairs and, both by these concessions and by a conscious, if intermittent, policy of appeasement, was fatally undermining the strength of the West at the moment of its deadliest peril at the hands of communism. Not for the first time in human history, a powerful alliance was hammered together under the pressures of a common foe.

And as the three components of modern conservatism began to draw together, they discovered that their views were actually more complementary than contradictory. In point of fact, each addressed a different level of the problem of politics. Traditionalism is primarily concerned with *philosophical* questions: the nature of man and the universe; the structure and obligations of social order; the rights and duties of men. Classical liberalism is essentially a grand *strategy* for the design of the good society within those parameters, brilliantly conceived to liberate the titanic energies within the minds of men. And anticommunism is at base a well-designed system of military, political, and economic *tactics* for coping with this century's principal challenge to the true progress and happiness of mankind as perceived by traditionalism and engineered by classical liberalism. In the light of hindsight, at least, it is clear that the three basic components of 1950s conservatism were potentially capable of being conjoined in a comprehensive political philosophy.

Despite, or perhaps precisely because of, the collapse of the *Freeman*, it seemed to many people in 1954 that the times called urgently for a new journal of opinion to carry on its work and lay the foundations for political action of a sort that would do for the principles of conservatism what the Republican party under Dwight Eisenhower was so spectacularly failing to do.

The new journal would be militantly engagé—dedicated to waging political war against the liberals, rather than merely restating conservative principles in some safely abstract form. To avoid the fratricidal strife that had brought down the *Freeman*, it seemed clear to many who pondered the matter that power over the publication—which meant, in practice, ownership of its voting stock—ought to be vested in a single individual rather than a warring board of directors. But who, or what, could bring the prickly components of the conservative movement together and induce it to speak with a single journalistic voice? Who could proclaim and refine conservatism's fundamental principles, resolve or compromise disputes on internal issues, promote intellectual and political spokesmen, and lead the philosophical battle against both communism and modern liberalism? Who—to descend to more practical matters—had or could raise the necessary money, recruit the writers and editors, referee the inevitable quarrels, and bring the whole enterprise into being? Who (we now know History's answer) but William F. Buckley, Jr.?

Buckley was the third of four sons in his generation, and if there is a family tradition as to why his parents named their first son John and their second James, reserving the father's own name for the third, I don't know what it is. But this particular youngster seemed early aware that he was destined for some sort of special distinction. He shared in full the sense of total security and loving familial acceptance that was the elder Buckleys' greatest and most enduring gift to their brood and added to it a brash assertiveness that complemented the quieter virtue nicely. At age five, according to a story the younger Bill devoutly wishes he had never heard, he dashed off a letter to King George V of England caustically suggesting that His Majesty pay Britain's overdue war debt to the United States. But the story lingers, because it precisely limns the author of that letter.

Roman Catholic traditionalism, love of country, devotion to free enterprise, perhaps a certain Anglophobia inherited from Irish ancestors: These were among the values that the elder Buckley sought, successfully, to inculcate in his children. In 1940, when I was joining William Allen White's militantly "interventionist" Committee to Defend America by Aiding the Allies, the Buckley family was a pillar of its great adversary, the "isolationist" America First Committee. In all other respects the Buckleys shared my otherwise total aversion to FDR and his policies.

William, Jr., like his brothers and sisters in the younger half of the family, was educated in private schools in the United States—and then in Britain, when their father decided that the speaking of English was in danger of becoming a lost art among his progeny. Thus did the ancestral patois of Texas and Louisiana come to be overlaid by the cultivated accents of the King's English—a rare and improbable combination that has fascinated Bill Buckley's American listeners for decades. Other cultural accretions also attributable to his English education will be readily apparent to anyone who has ever seen or heard him.

Buckley turned sixteen less than two weeks before Pearl Harbor and served in the infantry (in this country) before the war ended. Thereupon he entered Yale with the class of 1950—his path there smoothed by the legend of his elder brother James, an immensely popular member of the Yale class of 1943. Bill, like Jim, became a member of Skull and Bones, Yale's most prestigious secret society, and set about impressing his forceful personality upon the university in various ways. Soon he was editor of the *Yale Daily News* and a chronic thorn in the side of Yale's liberal faculty and administration. The year after his graduation, as a sort of going-away present, he dropped on them his first book: *God and Man at Yale* (Regnery, 1951).

GAMAY, as it is called nowadays around our office, was focused narrowly on the situation Buckley knew best from personal observation: the relentless liberalism of the Yale faculty and its supporters in the university administration. The department of economics, he demonstrated, not to mention those of politics and sociology, was awash with "collectivists" and all but devoid of advocates of "individualism," while the departments of religion and philosophy were largely in the grip of avowed atheists and agnostics. Taking perhaps too literally the university's fund-raising rhetoric about the central importance and leadership functions of Yale's alumni, Buckley openly suggested that if Yale was indeed supposed to be a fundamentally Christian institution and a pillar of the free-enterprise system, its alumni were not, to put it mildly, getting their money's worth.

"Individualism" (i.e., free-enterprise economics) and the Christian tradition! Here, in this first book by a twenty-five-year-old graduate of Yale, one sees an early example of the meshing of two of the three principal strands of postwar conservative thought: traditionalism and classical liberalism. And anticommunism was not really missing, for various references in the book made it clear that Buckley was well aware of and thoroughly committed to the struggle against communism. (As a matter of fact, soon after *GAMAY* was published, Buckley joined the CIA at the solicitation of his Yale mentor and professor Willmoore Kendall and spent well over a year in "deep cover" in Mexico, keeping various politicians in his father's old stamping ground well supplied with U.S. dollars.)

As early as 1951, then, Buckley had combined and deployed in a single book the three central themes of what was to become the modern conservative critique of liberalism. He did not yet regularly refer to the amalgam as conservatism, and he confined his critique, modestly but perhaps unfortunately, to the Yale context. (It would certainly have applied equally well to the country as a whole, whose dominance by liberalism Trilling had noted only the year before.) But for all that, *GAMAY* caused a most gratifying splash, and well beyond the borders of Yale. *Time* and *Newsweek* ran news stories about it; *Life* published an editorial. Louis Filler, writing in the *New England Quarterly*, described it as "a phenomenon of our time," adding: "It could hardly have been written ten years ago, at least for general circulation"—an interesting hint that perhaps the time was growing ripe for attacks on liberalism.

Yale's defenders, however, were by and large in no mood to concede that Buckley had a point. Herbert Liebert of Yale Library told readers of the *St. Louis Post-Dispatch* that ". . . the book is a series of fanatically emotional attacks on a few professors who dare to approach religion and politics objectively." Buckley's old bailiwick, the *Yale Daily News,* looked forward editorially to a day "When the Buckley book has succeeded in turning the stomachs of its readers." Yale Law professor Fred Rodell, writing in the *Progressive,* was sure that ". . . most Catholics would resent both the un-Christian arrogance of [Buckley's] presentation and, particularly, his deliberate concealment—throughout the entire foreword, text, and appendices of a highly personalized book—of his very relevant church affiliation." McGeorge Bundy, whose article-length attack on *GAMAY* for the *Atlantic* was unofficially adopted by the Yale administration as its answer to the book, elaborated on this latter theme: "Most remarkable of all, Mr. Buckley, who urges a return to what he considers to be Yale's true religious tradition, at no point says one word of the fact that he himself is an ardent Roman Catholic. In view of the pronounced and well-recognized difference between Protestant and Catholic views on education in America, and in view of Yale's Protestant history, it seems strange for any Roman Catholic to undertake to speak for the Yale religious tradition."

Aside from the fact that Buckley's Roman Catholicism was, to say the least, well known in the Yale community and that he could therefore hardly have hoped to keep this supposedly devastating secret from the alumni for very long, the truth was that his plea for a pro-Christian and pro-individualist Yale had not the slightest parochially Catholic taint. Dwight Macdonald, in his essentially hostile article for the *Reporter,* recognized and acknowledged this, writing that "Buckley is indeed a Catholic, and an ardent one. But, oddly enough, this fact is irrelevant, since his book defines Christianity in Protestant terms, and his economics are Calvinist rather than Catholic."

Certainly a lot of Catholics thought so. The Jesuit magazine *America,* well known for its liberal bias, editorialized that Buckley "unwittingly succeeds in contravening Catholic moral doctrine as applied to economics and politics on almost every topic he takes up" and concluded that "Mr. Buckley's own social philosophy is almost as obnoxious to a well-instructed Catholic as the assaults on religion he rightly condemns."

But such criticisms were relatively mild. Buckley was to learn that in 1951 serious attacks on an intellectual establishment as powerful as modern liberalism could expect the Full Treatment. Robert Hatch, writing in the *New Republic,* perhaps American liberalism's premier journal of opinion at the time, sounded the basic theme: "It is astonishing, on the assumption that Buckley is well-meaning, that he has not realized that the methods he proposes for his alma mater are precisely those employed in Italy, Germany, and Russia. An elite shall establish the truth by ukase and no basic disagreement shall be tolerated." (It is amusing, nearly a third of a century later, to note how closely the liberal reception of *GAMAY* followed the prescription in that last sentence.)

Hatch, however, was being relatively polite. Professor T. M. Greene, master of Yale's largest residential college, was rather more feline in the *Yale Daily News:* "Mr. Buckley has done Yale a great service, and he may well do the cause of liberal education in America an even greater service, by stating the fascist alternative to liberalism. . . . What more could Hitler, Mussolini, or Stalin ask for?" (Bear in mind that this was only six years after the end of World War II and at the very height of the early Cold War with the Soviet Union.)

And, incredibly, here is Frank Ashburn, headmaster of the prestigious Brooks School and a Yale trustee, writing in the highly respected *Saturday Review of Literature:* "The book is one which has the glow and appeal of a fiery cross on a hillside at night. There will undoubtedly be robed figures who gather to it, but the hoods will not be academic. They will cover the face."

As Buckley commented after quoting Ashburn in his 1977 introduction to the new edition of *GAMAY,* "Gee whiz."

I have dwelt at some length on the critical reaction to *GAMAY* for two reasons. In the first place, those who cannot recall the intellectual atmosphere of the early 1950s may want to savor this illustration of the behavior of liberals in their days of near-total power. Buckley, of course, was not by a long shot the only person to be given a bouncing around for having the temerity to tangle with liberal orthodoxy. Quite independently, for the moment, of the merits (if any) of Senator Joseph McCarthy's case, it is a fact that he had wandered into the sights of liberalism's mighty guns just one year previously, with his speech to the Republican Women of Wheeling, West Virginia, on February 9, 1950, and, as a result of his charges and his reckless disinclination to retract them, was the recipient of a barrage that lasted nearly four solid years and resulted in his political destruction and (in all likelihood) his death at forty-eight in 1957. To adopt Mr. Dooley's pithy formulation regarding politics, challenging the power of a dominant political and intellectual elite "ain't bean-bag."

In the second place, the reception accorded to *GAMAY* was a major factor in the "blooding" of William F. Buckley, Jr., and therefore in the history of modern American conservatism. If America's regnant liberals assumed, after the treatment they gave *GAMAY*, that so clever a young man would draw the appropriate conclusions and behave more prudently thereafter, consider their emotions when just two years later Buckley (who had returned from Mexico in April 1952, left the CIA, and briefly written political articles for William Bradford Huie's *American Mercury*) teamed up with his brother-in-law and Yale classmate L. Brent Bozell to bring forth a detailed and largely sympathetic analysis of Senator McCarthy's probings into the issue of domestic communism, entitled *McCarthy and His Enemies* (Regnery, 1954).

The Yale controversy could be dismissed as a tempest in a teapot. But when Buckley strode into the ongoing national brawl over McCarthy's involvement with the Communist issue, he could no longer be dismissed as merely a precocious Ivy Leaguer with some amusingly old-fashioned ideas. What made matters far worse was the fact that Buckley and Bozell (the latter of whom had just graduated from Yale Law School) had produced an extremely careful and closely reasoned examination of the charges both by and against McCarthy. From that moment forward, Buckley was both a special target of America's dominant liberals and a rapidly rising spokesman for its minuscule minority of self-aware and combative protoconservatives.

Partly through *GAMAY* and partly through other connections, Buckley was soon personally acquainted with many of the leading conservative personalities. He had persuaded the already well-known libertarian journalist John Chamberlain to write an introduction to *God and Man at Yale*. Willmoore Kendall, too, an original political thinker and a Catholic convert, was already a friend. It was through Kendall, moreover, that Buckley about 1950 met James Burnham, then a high-ranking CIA official as well as a towering figure in academic circles and an outspoken leader of the anti-Communist activists. Check DIAMOND.

It was none of these major figures in the early *National Review*, however, but another middle-aged friend of young Buckley's who first suggested starting a magazine. Willi Schlamm, the dominating figure in a small circle of journalistic protoconservatives, was at loose ends after his participation in the mass resignations from the *Freeman*. Buckley had met him socially a year or so earlier and had prevailed on him to provide the introduction to *McCarthy and His Enemies*. Now, in mid-1954, Schlamm told Buckley that the collapse of the *Freeman*, the sad condition of the *American Mercury* (which Huie had been forced to relinquish to Russell Maguire, who was steering it toward the swamps of anti-Semitism), and the parlous state of the nation all called for a new publication: a true journal of opinion, such as many (but, alas, not all) of the *Freeman*'s editors had hoped it would be—combative, "journalistic," and, above all, uncompromisingly conservative right across the board.

One imagines that Buckley (probably encouraged by Bozell, who was in on the discussions) was not all that hard to convince. At any rate he left for an early-autumn vacation in Europe "knowing that when I came back [in October] I would be devoting myself full-time to raising money for *National Review*."

It was to be a busy year for Buckley before the magazine's first issue appeared. First, the basic nature, structure, and control of the publication had to be decided on. Schlamm, in what may well have been his most important single contribution to the magazine and even the conservative movement, insisted that full editorial and policy control be assumed by Buckley, as editor in chief. As noted earlier, the experience of the *Freeman* was too recent and too painful to permit anyone to forget the ghastly peril of divided counsels. So the corporation that would own the magazine was set up with two classes of stock: Class A common stock, with no par value but with voting rights; and Class B, nonvoting but with a par value of $1 a share. These latter were sold in sets of twenty, together in each case with a debenture (face value $100, market value $80), which package was priced at $100 in the fond hope that it would be worth $120 at maturity. Class B was designed to be sold to the public; the Class A shares—all of them— were purchased by and vested in Buckley alone.

It is almost impossible to overrate the importance and beneficent effect of this arrangement. In subsequent years, as strong personalities clashed at the magazine and difficult new issues arose to torment and divide the conservative movement, the knowledge that final and total power of decision regarding *National Review*'s editorial policies was vested in a single individual proved a priceless asset. It not only made clear the source of all final decisions but by virtue of that very fact made it possible for individuals who would otherwise feel obliged to wage war *à outrance* for their opinions to acquiesce gracefully in decisions that went against them. One could yield to Buckley, in other words, without for a moment acknowledging that he was in any metaphysical sense necessarily "right": He merely owned the stock. And if Buckley, aware of his own impressive powers in the black arts of argumentation, sometimes too readily assumed that his colleagues had been persuaded, or at least vanquished, by these, when in fact they were merely being outvoted, he had the grace not to insist publicly on his interpretation. By such nuances were faces often saved all around.

The corporation was called National Weekly, Inc.—that being the name chosen also for the magazine, in recognition of its intended frequency. A search of the relevant public records, however, revealed that somebody else had a persuasive prior claim on the magazine title *National Weekly*, so the publication's name was changed (before the first issue ever came out) to *National Review*. The corporation remained National Weekly, Inc., however, for several years.

Recruitment of personnel went forward along with the job of raising the necessary money. Under Buckley, who assumed the titles of editor in chief and publisher, there were to be, at first, four senior editors: Willi Schlamm, Willmoore Kendall, James Burnham, and Jonathan Mitchell. Mitchell was the last-added and least-enduring of these, being signed on at Schlamm's urging as a general authority on publishing journals of opinion. (He had at one time worked for the *New Republic*.) Schlamm and Mitchell, as well as Buckley, of course, were to devote full time to the magazine; Burnham and Kendall both agreed to give it specific and substantial portions of their time.

For the job of managing editor, also with the rank of senior editor, Buckley obtained the valuable services of another veteran of the *Freeman*, Suzanne LaFollette. To cope with the business aspects of the publication, such as they were, he hired Arthur W. D. Harris, who was given the title of business manager.

Buckley had wisely decided to make it a rigid requirement that any person, to qualify for the rank of senior editor, must have an independent reputation of his own. Schlamm, Burnham, Kendall, Mitchell, and LaFollette all qualified in this respect. To the rest of his prospective editorial staff Buckley gave the collective title associates and contributors. In this category were John Chamberlain (whose work for other publications prevented him from taking on the obligations of a senior editor), Brent Bozell, Frank S. Meyer, Russell Kirk, Forrest Davis, Eugene Lyons, Gerhart Niemeyer, Karl Hess, Max Eastman, and E. Merrill Root, among others. F. A. Voigt agreed to be the magazine's correspondent in London; Wilhelm Röpke (the noted economist), in Geneva; and Erik von Kuehnelt-Leddihn, in Vienna.

The year 1955 was also inevitably devoted to raising the necessary money for the venture. Buckley took to the road, selling a good many thousands of dollars' worth of shares and debentures to like-minded conservatives—notably businessmen who could afford to lose the money.

In addition, of course, the publication could and did draw on the Buckley family's own considerable wealth, which at this point probably aggregated several million dollars—not all of it readily realizable and not all of it expendable on this journalistic project of what the family sometimes good-humoredly called "the Young Mahster." Broadly speaking, it has been the tendency of outsiders to overestimate the financial resources of the Buckley family—a tendency the family has not always discouraged. Certainly, in any case, external (i.e., non-Buckley) support for the magazine was important from the start and has been absolutely essential over the years.

The corporation's prospectus, of course, projected an operating loss in the first year or two, followed by a break-even point and a triumphant breakthrough into the black in two or three years, and Buckley's innate optimism probably persuaded him to believe the projections. But it seems unlikely that many in his audiences did so: There had been all too many "Volume I, No. 1's" in publishing history, but notably fewer "Volume I, No. 3's," and, in relative terms, a shockingly short list of "Volume II's."

In view of all the talk about "Texas oil money's" role in funding the right, it is worth noting that Texas was, despite his family's origin there, almost completely a dry hole for Buckley. Perhaps his devout Catholicism struck an uncongenial chord among Texas's largely Protestant conservatives. At any rate, not a single one of the really big Texas moneymen—Hunt, Richardson, or Murchison—ever contributed a nickel toward the founding or maintenance of *National Review*. One independent Texas oilman, Lloyd H. Smith, did contribute generously to the publication from the start and served on the corporation's board of directors for many years, but Smith was almost the exact opposite of the Texas stereotype. A Yale graduate himself (class of 1929), he had served as an editor of the *Yale Daily News* in his undergraduate years, and his enthusiasm for Buckley dated from the latter's days as editor of the publication.

The first issue of *National Review* was dated November 19, 1955, and rolled off the presses about a week earlier. There was considerable eagerness in conservative circles to see what it would be like. My own introduction to the publication which would dominate the rest of my life was deceptively casual. Over a drink in the bar of the University Club during the summer of 1955 Lyle Munson, a former CIA agent who had tangled with John Paton Davies, and whom I had met through our mutual friend Robert Morris, mentioned that "Bill Buckley is starting a magazine, you know." I didn't know, but I took care to become a charter subscriber.

The thirty-two-page first issue is now undoubtedly best remembered for its "Publisher's Statement," in which Buckley flung down the gauntlet and practically dared his opponents to pick it up. It quite simply declared war on "the Liberals, who run this country." (For several years *National Review* continued to capitalize the word *Liberal*, simply for the sake of emphasis.) The magazine, Buckley asserted, "stands athwart history, yelling Stop."

Since the instruments of evaluation were practically all in the liberals' hands, it was hardly to be expected, in the circumstances, that the critical reception of the new publication would be very friendly. As Buckley remarked in an early issue, "Liberals do a great deal of talking about hearing other points of view, [but] it sometimes shocks them to learn that there *are* other points of view."* As matters turned out, only three liberal publications— *Harper's, Commentary,* and the *Progressive*—deemed *National Review* worthy of extensive attention.

John Fischer, editor of *Harper's,* fired the first salvo from his "Easy Chair" in the March 1956 issue. He sounded what was, predictably, the liberals' basic theme in regard to the early *National Review:* America badly needed a conservative journal of opinion, but this one, alas, wouldn't do:

> Last November, newsstands throughout the country offered the first issue of a new magazine, *National Review,* which described itself as "frankly, conservative." A good many people bought it with sympathetic curiosity, feeling that a conservative journal of opinion would be a remarkably useful addition to the American scene.
>
> It is true that the overwhelming majority of our newspapers and magazines are basically conservative, and have been for decades. Yet in all these years they have failed to perform one function which is essential, both to the conservative interest and to the health of society. They have never developed a lucid, coherent body of conservative doctrine.
>
> By and large, their conservatism has expressed itself merely in lopsided news coverage, invective, and in the kind of blind, automatic opposition which provokes accusations about "the one-party press." As a consequence, a reader has no difficulty in discovering what our conservatives are against; but he has great trouble in finding out what they are for. . . .
>
> In these circumstances, many people welcomed *National Review* with considerable hope. Here, maybe, was the long-awaited voice. . . .
>
> These hopes did not survive the first half-dozen issues. By that

* *National Review* (January 11, 1956), p. 24.

time it was plain that the new magazine was an organ, not of conservatism, but of radicalism.

Its radicalism is of the Right, rather than the Left—but the distinction is not very important. In its editorial policy, emotional attitude, and even its format, it strikingly resembles its brethren at the opposite end of the political spectrum: the *Nation*, the defunct *New Masses*, and (in Britain) the *New Statesman* and the *Tribune*, spokesmen for the Bevanite wing of the Labor party. It exhibits all the classic stigmata of extremist journalism. . . .

Like most of the extremist little magazines, it seems to be aimed primarily at an audience of True Believers. As Eric Hoffer noted in his classic work on this species, they are emotional people who throw themselves frantically into a cause—often to make up for some kind of frustration in their private lives. They form the hard core of many religious, nationalist, and revolutionary movements: they have great capacity in Hoffer's words, for "enthusiasm, fervent hope, hatred, and intolerance . . . blind faith and single-hearted allegiance." They are the precise opposite of conservatives.

Maybe all of this should have been expected. The symptoms were foreshadowed in two books by William F. Buckley, Jr., editor of the new magazine: *God and Man at Yale* and *McCarthy and His Enemies*. Moreover, some of his editorial associates have, themselves, long been True Believers. Yet it is sad to see an opportunity missed. . . .

No doubt *National Review* will serve a useful purpose in feeding the emotional hungers of a small congregation of the faithful, and it will have a certain interest for students of political splinter movements. But the far greater need for a journal to express the philosophy of modern American conservatism still remains unfilled.

The article published a month later in *Commentary*'s April issue, written by Dwight Macdonald, would in itself have constituted sufficient notice that liberalism expected no serious opposition, would brook none, and either believed, or intended to pretend to believe, that *National Review* provided none. Macdonald, who had founded the journal called *Politics*, served as an editor of both *Fortune* and *Partisan Review*, and was at the time of this article on the staff of the *New Yorker*, was a politico-literary heavyweight, and he bore down on *National Review* like a British man-o'-war bearing down on a miscreant fishing smack:

On November 19, 1955 [he wrote],* the first issue of *National Review* appeared without causing undue public agitation. Nor have the ten following issues I have seen set any rivers aflame.

However, *NR* seems worth examining as a cultural phenomenon: the McCarthy nationalists—they call themselves conservatives, but that is surely a misnomer—have never before made so heroic an effort to be intellectually articulate. Here are the ideas, here is the style of the *lumpen*-bourgeoisie, the half-educated, half-successful provincials (and a provincial may live within a mile of the Empire State Building as well as in Kokomo or Sauk Center) who responded to Huey Long, Father Coughlin, and Senator McCarthy. Anxious, embittered, resentful, they feel that the main stream of American politics since 1932 has passed them by, as indeed it has, and they have the slightly paranoiac suspiciousness of an isolated minority group. For these are men from underground, the intellectually underprivileged who feel themselves excluded from a world they believe is ruled by liberals (or eggheads—the terms are, significantly, interchangeable in *NR*) just as the economic underdog feels alienated from society.

Warming to his task, Macdonald then focused his attention on the pestiferous William Buckley: "Buckley is a debater—his mind is quick, clear, plausible, and shallow—and he would rather argue than eat, a trait I find endearing. Had he been born a generation earlier, he would have been making the cafeterias of 14th Street ring with Marxian dialectics. He is a lively and engaging fellow, and would be an excellent journalist if he had a little more humor, common sense, and intellectual curiosity; also if he knew how to write."

After similar compliments to the rest of the magazine's editorial staff, Macdonald then unveiled the predictable centerpiece of any serious attack on this new conservative journal of opinion: America greatly needed such a journal—but this wasn't it.

"We have long needed," he acknowledged, "a good conservative magazine. (We have also long needed a good liberal magazine.) This is not it, any more than its predecessor, the LaFollette-Chamberlain *Freeman*—which deployed much the same forces—was. And for the same reasons: because it is neither good nor conservative."

* *Commentary*, (April 1956), p. 367 et seq.

Macdonald thereupon described what all true liberals in 1956 believed an authentic conservative was really like and why *National Review* failed so spectacularly to measure up to their paradigm: "Culturally a conservative is someone like Irving Babbitt or Paul Elmer More, not always the liveliest company in the world but a respecter and defender of tradition. The *NR*'s editorials—as I shall presently show—are as elegant as a poke in the nose, as cultivated as a camp meeting, as witty as a prat-fall."

But Macdonald was not satisfied to dismiss *National Review* as a failure on its own terms. Regarded purely as a diversion, it was equally disappointing: "Journalistically, the *National Review* actually manages to be duller than the liberal weeklies. It is even more predictable, much more long-winded, and a good deal less competent. Considering that its editors are by no means journalistic neophytes, it is a remarkably amateurish job."

Macdonald liked one of his earlier phrases so much that he used it yet again near the end of his article: "This is indeed the voice of the *lumpen*-bourgeoisie." The right had no intellectual future, he declared, and for the most fundamental of all reasons:

[T]he left—to use *NR*'s quaint terminology—has a set of ideas and ideals in which they can believe, which seem to them intellectually consistent and morally attractive, while the right does not. (For myself, I no longer find the left ideology either morally or intellectually satisfying, but that is another question; the point is that it is a far more plausible doctrine than the right's crude patchwork of special interests.) One of *NR*'s few literate letters-to-the-editor, from Frank S. Meyer of Woodstock, N.Y., comments on "the insistence [of other readers] that the magazine publish nothing that makes serious intellectual demands upon the reader," and continues: "But we are an opposition, and we have to fight conformity. . . . It is ideas they [the dominant liberal "social engineers"] fear, for in the end it is ideas which are decisive. It was ideas developed in the *Nation* and the *New Republic* and the *Masses* thirty and forty years ago that seduced a generation and laid the foundations for the New Deal and what has followed. The circulations of these magazines were not large, but they spoke to the younger generation, in and out of the universities, and won them—with devastating effect." Ideas however, or even sufficient journalistic skill to conceal their lack, are just what *NR* lacks.

The *Progressive* waited until July to weigh in, and when it did, it gave the job to Murray Kempton. This may have been a mistake, for Kempton, though certainly liberal enough for anybody's taste, is at heart a kind man, spectacularly unsuited to the commission of infanticide. Nevertheless, he shouldered the task and managed to discharge it adequately, if without Macdonald's obvious zest:

William F. Buckley's *National Review* has used up nine months of life and presumably settled into its desired mold as expression of conservative dissent from the liberal rhetoric which dominates our time. Under this theory, the Editor of *The Progressive* has sent along its first 27 issues with a request for an extended analysis of its content and tendency. . . .

I think I know Buckley well enough to feel that I could pronounce to him nothing crueler than the judgment that his magazine is a bore. He is a young man capable of considerable *esprit;* as a companion, he can be preferable to the average assistant professor of political science who regards him as an enemy of the light. I do not wish him to fail, except in the superficial sense of dying an old man without ever seeing the kind of America he thinks he wants; and, if I did, I could not wish him the emptiness of this particular failure.

Kempton rambled on in a similar vein for several pages, making it clear that *National Review* offered nothing that the Republic needed.*

Such were the Millsian raptures—the warm fraternal greetings—with which in 1956 some of America's most prominent liberals hailed, in three of liberalism's flagship publications, the advent of that long-awaited "other point of view."

If the liberals imagined that *National Review* was likely to fold up and die as a result of their anathemas, however, they were doomed to disappointment. Responding to his critics in the August 1 issue of the magazine, Buckley lashed back at them individually, then summed up with the following unrepentant overview:

* Happily Kempton has grown wiser over the decades and in recent years has not felt it beneath him to publish a number of shrewd commentaries on offbeat subjects in the journal he was once so ready to condemn.

The kind of criticism levelled at *National Review* by Messrs. Fischer, Macdonald and Kempton leaves little doubt, it seems to me, as to the nature of our offense. *National Review* is neither supine nor irrelevant. It does not consult Arthur Schlesinger, Jr., to determine the limits of tolerable conservative behavior, nor does it subsist on mimeographed clichés describing The Plot to Destroy America. It has gathered together men of competence and sanity who have, quietly and with precision, gone to work on the problems of the day and turned over many stones, to expose much cant and ugliness and intellectual corruption. It is to be expected that They should set the hounds on us.

For several years, the dominant intellectual agitators in the United States have got away with the fiction that those who substantially disagree with them do so because they suffer from serious diseases of one kind or another. The theory holds that not intellection, but social or psychic difficulties are responsible for the perversity of Right-wing dissent. . . . Tactically, the theory is wonderfully useful, and the Liberals will continue to live off it as long as they can get away with it. *National Review*, in that its neuroses are not so very easy to identify—witness the failure of three of their most expensive assassins—inconveniences that thesis, and hence becomes a high-priority target.

So be it. The magazine suffers from many imperfections, which we hope, little by little, to move in on. We shall continue to be grateful for counsel from our allies. Liberals, however, should submit their recommendations in self-addressed, stamped envelopes.

For their part, having weighed *National Review* and pronounced it wanting, America's liberals abruptly shifted their tactics and subjected it to a treatment that threatened to be far more effective: silence. *Time*, which was probably best described in those days as moderate Republican, had noted its advent in its November 21, 1955, issue with a three-inch item in the "Press" section. ("The first issue combines a conservative line [far to the right of the Eisenhower Administration] with a chip-on-shoulder, fiercely partisan tone reminiscent of left-wing weeklies in the '30's.") *Newsweek* didn't mention the new magazine at all. And according to a search of the indexes of both magazines, there was exactly one more reference to it in *Time*, and two in *Newsweek*, between its founding and the decade of the 1960s.

Such elaborate disregard by the major newsmagazines inevitably set the tone for *National Review*'s reception—or rather lack of reception—by the intellectual community as a whole. There was no conspiracy involved. These people were, as we have seen, almost without exception liberals, attuned to detect the slightest tremor in their own network of leftist causes, colleagues, and contretemps, but singularly unaware of—and, let it be said, sublimely indifferent to—developments outside that royal enclosure. But whether they ignored *National Review* deliberately or not, the effect was of course devastating: The battle would not merely be fought without quarter; there would, if the liberals could help it, not even be a battle. That decision, however, was—happily—not quite altogether up to the liberals.

There is much more that could be said about the founding of *National Review*, and about its early years and personalities, and no doubt it will be said someday—perhaps by Buckley himself. There was, for example, a curious plan to publish "regional editions" of the magazine, and one such—"the Louisville edition"— actually appeared for a couple of issues. But this is a history of the conservative movement, not of *National Review*, and central as the magazine unquestionably was to the development of American conservatism, it was only one aspect of the process. We shall leave it for the moment, therefore, and return to it from time to time as it plays out its long and influential part in the drama.

Chapter III

The Mobilization of the Right

The founding of *National Review* was only one, though arguably the most important, of a series of developments that took place during the middle and second half of the decade of the 1950s whereby the conservative movement began to organize itself. The forms of organization varied, and so did the interests and emphases of the organizers—very much so, as we shall see. But the identifying characteristic of the years 1955–59, from the standpoint of the conservative movement as a whole, was growth: in size, in self-awareness, in visibility, and in variety. For the first time in living memory, individuals and whole groups proudly calling themselves conservatives, and evidently representing some new current of opinion, began to make themselves heard in public forums.

Perhaps the most vocal, until 1958 or thereabouts, were those conservatives still chiefly concerned with opposition to communism. The Senate's censure of Joseph McCarthy in December 1954 had been a bone-crunching defeat for these people, constituting a signal that the bipartisan leadership of the American society was unwilling to permit the issue of Communist penetration during the 1930s and thereafter to be carried to the lengths they favored; but they certainly did not abandon the issue on that account. McCarthy himself had lost his committee chairmanship and with it most of his investigatory clout (e.g., the subpoena power) when the Republican party lost control of the Senate in the off-year elections of 1954. But the House Committee on Un-American Activities and the Senate Internal Security Subcommittee, under conservative Democratic chairmen, continued to hold hearings spotlighting the past and present activities of American Communists, and their activities were by no means the only evidence of continued public and political interest in the subject.

For example, in February 1955 I myself obtained a leave of absence from my Wall Street law firm to serve for six weeks as special counsel to the Finance Committee of the New York State Senate. The Finance Committee was the Senate's chief operating subdivision, and my appointment by its chairman, Austin Erwin, had been arranged by the Republican majority leader, Walter Mahoney, through my old friend Robert Morris, then a judge of New York's Municipal Court. My assignment was to conduct the committee's investigation of two appointees of the newly elected Democratic governor, Averell Harriman: Persia Campbell, his nominee for commissioner of consumer affairs, and Isador Lubin, his choice for commissioner of labor and industry. A decision was soon reached to focus our inquiry on Lubin, whom the Senate ultimately confirmed (over Mahoney's steadfast opposition) although substantial evidence connecting Lubin to both Communists and Communist causes had been developed in the course of our investigation.

A year later, when Morris resigned from the bench to accept the invitation of chairman James O. Eastland to resume his old job as chief counsel to the Senate Internal Security Subcommittee, I agreed to leave my law firm and go to Washington with him as his associate counsel—the second and only other lawyer on the subcommittee's staff and thus in effect its deputy director. I served in that capacity for seventeen months, from March 1956 to July 1957, and the controversies that swirled about us at the time were sufficient evidence, to me at any rate, that the "Communist issue" was far from dead.*

Certainly *National Review*, and various other spokesmen for the conservative cause, including such political figures as Barry Goldwater and the Senate's Republican minority leader, William Knowland, continued to speak out on the subject. And during the summer of 1957 two new names appeared on *National Review*'s masthead: Whittaker Chambers as a senior editor, and mine as publisher—assurances, if any were needed, that there would be no lack of continuing attention to the subject of communism on the part of the magazine.

But it is true that by 1956 many of the important investigations of the Internal Security Subcommittee involved *past* Communist activities: invaluable for the historical record, like our

* For a detailed account of my year and a half with the subcommittee, see my book *Special Counsel* (Arlington House, 1968).

analysis of the role of Communist agents in the Treasury Department in denying promised gold to wartime China—a deadly blow to the Nationalist Chinese currency in 1944 and 1945, but not a matter of urgency in 1956. The fact was that during (and no doubt largely as a result of) the furious brouhahas of the late 1940s and early 1950s most of the really egregious instances of Communist penetration of the American society had been brought under control or effectively terminated. The sudden and unexpected death of Joseph McCarthy himself in May 1957 was therefore in many ways a truer symbol of the end of that era than his censure two and a half years earlier.

For one group of anti-Communist conservatives, however, the gradual decline in the intensity of the controversy over domestic communism during the middle and late 1950s was merely evidence of the Communists' success in distracting attention from themselves. To these particular conservatives, in fact, Communist machinations were the explanation for just about all the ills afflicting American society. And the success of those machinations was readily explicable, for the Communists had, in their view, quite simply penetrated and largely subverted the nation's leadership.

Conspiracy theories are one of the classic hazards of an interest in politics. During the later 1950s and early 1960s, when attention was focused on conspiracy theorists of the conservative variety, it was widely and solemnly assumed that such people merely demonstrated anew the alleged link between clinical paranoia and rightist politics in general.* It was not until the mid-1960s or thereafter, when the New Left made its appearance on the national scene with all sorts of wild accusations against the Rockefellers, the Council on Foreign Relations, international bankers, multinational corporations, and the CIA, that the conspiracy syndrome was recognized for what it is: a hardy perennial in the garden of political thought, both right and left.

Why is this so? The world is big and complicated, and we, individually, are small and weak. We observe, however, that groups of individuals working together can exert impressive

* See Richard Hofstadter, *The Paranoid Style in American Politics* (Knopf, 1965).

power. If, out of the multifarious flux of events, our attention comes to be focused on a particular series of happenings that is distasteful to us, it is perfectly natural to wonder whether those happenings are not the successive effects of a common cause: whether there is not, somewhere out of sight, a sovereign intelligence manipulating affairs in such a way as to produce those particular results.

If we seek to test this hypothesis, moreover, we soon encounter at a certain low level what appears to be indisputable corroboration: There are indeed conspiracies, or at any rate collective secret efforts, afoot in the world. For example, the Soviet Union is busy in a hundred countries (including the United States) seeking, through agents by no means always identified as such, to shape events in its favor. Or again, the membership of the Council on Foreign Relations consists largely, though not exclusively, of those government officials, businessmen, and lawyers who specialize in the foreign field, and the council serves them as a loose fraternity useful for everything from the exchange of views to the coordination of efforts and high-level job placement. Similarly, international bankers have a lot in common and undeniably cooperate from time to time, however much they may compete on other occasions. If this sort of thing were all the conspiracy theorists were saying, they would be entirely right.

But conspiracy theories are highly addictive, and their devotees go much further. A core conspiracy is identified—the Elders of Zion, or the KGB, or the Rothschilds, or the Freemasons, or the CIA, or the Rockefellers, or the Council on Foreign Relations, or the Knights Hospitalers of St. John of Jerusalem—and a search is conducted for evidence that a long series of historical events is traceable to the manipulations of this particular group of conspirators. The "evidence" is often slender, usually involving common associations (X, who did A, and Y, who did B, are both members of the same organization—from which it is supposed to follow that they acted in concert and that both A and B are aspects of some larger plan, not yet revealed), but the feeble character of the links is supposedly more than compensated by the overwhelming number of them. The long arm of coincidence, it is urged, cannot possibly be so long as all *that*.

By such processes an intricate conspiracy theory can be elaborated, purporting to explain all sorts of events that are otherwise inexplicable, at least as parts of a coherent series. In the later stages of the delusion, virtually anything important that happens anywhere in the world is attributed on the loosest of grounds to the machinations of the supposed conspirators. If President Reagan had been shot and killed in 1981, it would have been because "They" were opposed to him. Since he was shot but survived, it is because "They" wanted him to—the shooting was a warning. If he had never been shot at all, it would have been because—naturally—he is "Their" man.

The amount of emotional satisfaction that can be derived from believing in a malign conspiracy must not be underrated. In the first place, it serves to explain a world that would otherwise be far less intelligible. We fear most of all what we cannot fathom: death, the dark, etc. An unintelligible, chaotic world is frightening to many people. To discover how and by whom it is "really" run is relatively reassuring, no matter how evil its manipulators may be.

In addition, simply to be aware of a conspiracy can be downright gratifying. There is, for one thing, the not inconsiderable satisfaction of being "in the know" and hence superior to other people. Moreover, since one is not only aware of the conspiracy but actively engaged in combating it, there is the excitement of the struggle. However powerful the conspiracy may be, it is never, oddly enough, quite strong enough to obliterate its knowledgeable opponents altogether. Victories for the valorous opposition, then, are possible and do occur from time to time.

In the mid-1950s one American anti-Communist, looking at what had happened to his country in recent years, thought he saw a truly remarkable explanation for it all. Robert Welch was vice-president of the James O. Welch Company of Cambridge, Massachusetts, the family candy manufacturing business. Born in 1899, he had graduated from the University of North Carolina, then spent two years apiece at the U.S. Naval Academy and Harvard Law School. A civic-minded man, he served for seven years on the board of directors of the National Association of Manufacturers and for two years as chairman of the NAM's Educational Advisory Committee. As of January 1, 1957, however, Welch gave up most of his business associations, and most of his income, to devote himself full time to the cause of anticommunism.

As developed in the *Blue Book* of the John Birch Society (the organization Welch soon founded) and other society publications, Welch's interpretation of public events assumed that there was a heavy and direct Communist influence on the contemporary government of the United States—an influence allegedly used not only in support of easily identified Communist causes, both in this country and abroad, but in favor of most of the leftist and liberal programs opposed by all conservatives: increased government spending, governmental overregulation, centralization of power, etc.

In addition to promoting this public analysis, however, Welch was privately developing a still more startling thesis. In a series of two-day seminars for businessmen, begun in or about 1957 and continuing through 1958, Welch took his audiences through a detailed analysis of the military and political career of President Eisenhower, culminating on the second day in the shocking conclusion that Dwight Eisenhower was now, and had been throughout most of his adult life, a conscious agent of the Communist conspiracy.

Incautiously, Welch reduced his argument concerning Eisenhower, and its conclusion, to writing in a book called *The Politician,* a typescript of which was circulated privately among his friends and acquaintances and inevitably reached wider circles.

Welch's basic technique of argumentation was to analyze a whole series of episodes in Eisenhower's career, any one of which was susceptible of explanation on several alternative grounds. Of these possible grounds, only one would involve sympathy for communism or Communist goals; but such sympathy was the *only common ground* that explained the *entire series* of episodes. On the principle of Occam's razor ("entities"—in this case explanations—"are not to be multiplied beyond necessity"), it followed that Eisenhower must be sympathetic to Communist goals.

A typical episode involved the secret Treaty of Halle, under which Eisenhower, as supreme commander of the Allied forces invading Nazi-dominated Europe from the West, agreed to turn over to the Soviet Union those members of "Vlasov's Army" who had surrendered to the advancing Anglo-American forces. Since "Vlasov's Army" was composed of anti-Communist Russians who had chosen to fight beside the Germans against the Soviet Union,

their fate at Stalin's hands was pretty plainly going to be grim, and
Eisenhower's motive in forcibly repatriating them (which he never
subsequently explained) has generated a good deal of speculation.
The agreement was signed, and the transfer effected, just as the
war in Europe was drawing to a close, at a time when Western
sympathy for "Quislings"—nationals of countries overrun by Germany who collaborated with the conquerors—was at a spectacularly low ebb, and when the Soviet Union's prestige in the West,
and the desire to remain on good terms with this wartime ally,
were correspondingly high. Such a combination of sentiments may
well explain Eisenhower's decision, without in the longer perspective excusing it.

But in pure theory one *possible* alternative explanation would
be a secret sympathy, on Eisenhower's part, for communism.
Carefully accumulating such "possibilities" from the long record
of Eisenhower's career, Welch massed them into what he saw as a
probability and finally a certainty. On page 267 of *The Politician*
he declared that "my firm belief that Dwight Eisenhower is a dedicated, conscious agent of the Communist conspiracy is based on
an accumulation of detailed evidence so extensive and so palpable
that it seems to me to put this conviction beyond a reasonable
doubt." On page 268 he went, if possible, even further: ". . . there
is only one possible word to describe his purposes and actions. The
word is treason."

It is well not to be too literal-minded as we contemplate
Welch's extraordinary conclusion and its reception by those who
were privileged to hear or read it in the late 1950s. Many of them,
of course, dismissed it (not necessarily in Welch's presence) as
sheer nonsense. But those invited to attend Welch's little seminars
were carefully selected for their known inclination to believe that
communism had penetrated deeply into the American social fabric in the 1930s and '40s, and no one likely to be skeptical of further dramatic revelations along that line was welcome.* A good
many of Welch's listeners, therefore, were predisposed to accept
whatever he might reveal. In addition, of course, the sheer awful-
ness (if true) of his revelation—that a Communist agent sat right in

* Both the author and Bill Buckley were invited to one such seminar in New York
City—then abruptly disinvited, seemingly because (in Buckley's dry words) "they ran
out of chairs."

the Oval Office, daily committing "treason"—probably seemed to enhance its likelihood. (If it wasn't true, who would dare *say* such a thing?)

Beyond such considerations, however, there is something else that deserves to be said. Verbal communication is a relatively late development in human history, and even after fifty thousand years a statement often has two, or even more, levels of meaning. One is literal; a second is perhaps best described as "poetic": It is the true meaning of the statement but is masked by the statement's nominal form. "I am starving" may, of course, mean exactly that, but we all recognize it as, in the vast majority of cases, just an exaggerated way of saying, "I am very hungry."

Similarly (and I am under no illusion that Robert Welch will thank me for this mildly exculpatory gloss) it may be questioned whether, whatever he would say on the matter, even today, Welch *really* intended to accuse Dwight Eisenhower of consciously betraying his country. Such an accusation is, at the figurative level mentioned above, more truly just a cry of pain: the convulsive attempt of a profoundly distressed individual to call attention to what he considers a shocking state of affairs by saying the very worst thing he can imagine.

And what was this "shocking state of affairs"? To Welch, and to a great many other like-minded Americans in the mid-1950s, it was what seemed to them this country's own *trahison des clercs*: the conscious rejection of America's traditional values by deracinated intellectuals and the substitution of new, unfamiliar, and unpalatable goals for the American society. To Americans of a certain temperament, these developments seemed by the 1950s to have left little indeed of the country in which they had been born, with which they could easily identify, and of which they were naturally, nostalgically, and patriotically proud. Somewhere in the deepest reaches of their souls an alarm bell was ringing, like a crazy klaxon. Their world was badly out of joint, and in the superficially calm and clinical but subliminally outraged conspiratorial analysis of Robert Welch they found practical means of expressing their concern. Not all of them accepted or even knew about Welch's conclusion regarding Eisenhower, but in a broader perspective they shared his dismay at what seemed to be happening to America. In the late 1950s they joined his movement by the tens

of thousands, forming local chapters wherever the numbers justified it, opening bookstores to promote the publications of the John
Birch Society and other approved literature, and working—
usually unobtrusively—in the political arena on behalf of candidates deemed worthy of their support.

Ultimately the growth, policies, and prominence of the John
Birch Society would bring its leadership into public collision with
other elements of the conservative movement. For the moment,
though, in the middle and late 1950s, it shared the growth of the
movement as a whole and existed in uneasy semialliance with organizations and individuals that rejected the "conspiracy theory"
outright and would have no truck whatever with Welch's notions
about Eisenhower.

Much as it disagreed with Welch about Eisenhower's motives, the rest of the conservative movement had its own deep reservations about Eisenhower's policies and actions.

It is difficult nowadays, when conservatives tend to look back
on the Eisenhower years as the Golden Age,* to reconstruct and
understand, let alone sympathize with, the severely critical view
of Dwight Eisenhower and his two administrations that lay very
near the root of 1950s conservatism.

There is, of course, a great deal to be said in Eisenhower's
favor, and most conservatives always knew it. Domestic politics
was not his strong suit, and he cared very little about it; but such
opinions as he had on the subject were broadly conservative ones:
By and large, budgets ought to be balanced, the federal government was spending too much, etc. (Eisenhower is given limitless
credit by liberals for appointing Earl Warren as chief justice of the
United States, but he would probably consider this ironic. Once,
when a friend asked him who had first recommended Warren to
him, Eisenhower snapped, "I wish I could remember, because I'd
like to shoot him.")

Foreign affairs were much more to Eisenhower's taste, and, as
one might expect, here he was—*pace* Robert Welch—very much
the cold warrior. With Secretary of State John Foster Dulles and
his brother, CIA Director Allen Dulles, providing the theoretical

* Cf. Jeffrey Hart's *When the Going Was Good!* (Crown, 1982), a sympathetic conservative look at not only the politics but the popular culture of the 1950s.

justification and the practical support, Eisenhower frequently kept well ahead of the Russians. His approval of the U-2 project— to send spy planes directly over the Soviet Union at altitudes where Russian technology could not reach them—was a daring move in the years before spy satellites became routine on both sides. And in 1958 Eisenhower demonstrated that he had not forgotten the fundamental military principles of speed and superiority when he successfully countered the Soviet destabilization of Lebanon by sending the U.S. Marines ashore there in decisive numbers.

But when all that can be said has been said, the fact remains that Dwight Eisenhower was far more of a conservative in the eyes of America's liberals than he was in those of many conservatives themselves.

No doubt the liberal attitude was partly attributable to the fact that Eisenhower simply left undone many of the things a liberal president would have been doing: increasing spending on welfare, especially as a proportion of the gross national product and in comparison to spending on defense; expanding the role of government, both participatory and regulatory, in the lives of individuals and institutions; reducing military expenditures; pursuing the latest mirage of peaceful coexistence with the Soviet Union; etc.

But consider the Eisenhower record from the standpoint of the conservative activists. At the very outset of his administration he had confronted the question of what to do about the disastrous liberal record on the important issue of internal security and had decided, in effect, to disregard it. This may appear to liberals, in retrospect, to have been an act of high statesmanship—a "healing" process necessary to the nation's psychic well-being. But conservatives, outraged at what had been allowed to happen to this country's internal security, fully aware of who was to blame (and this was primarily the liberals, not the Communists who benefited from their disregard), and mindful of the price liberals had made conservatives pay for their supposed responsibility for the Great Depression—back, presumably, before "healing" was invented— were in no mood to forgive and forget. Worse yet, Eisenhower, after doing his not notably courageous best for several years to avoid any conflict with Senator McCarthy, allowed himself to be drawn into that battle only when its outcome was already apparent, and over a subcontroversy at that (concerning General Zwicker) as to which the merits were far from obvious. Even then, he cautiously signaled his own position indirectly, by instructing Vice President Nixon to make a radio broadcast implicitly critical of McCarthy.

Two and a half years later Eisenhower forced Britain, France, and Israel to abort their courageous attempt to reclaim the Suez Canal from Egypt and then totally ignored the Hungarian rebellion as well as Russia's brutal suppression of it, apparently because at the moment (October 1956) he was hotly pursuing reelection to the presidency on a platform of "Peace and Prosperity" and consequently regarded both of these bold developments as unforgivably ill-timed.

A year later still, America paid the price for Eisenhower's mishandling of the space program when Russia lofted *Sputnik* into orbit atop its biggest military rocket—a propaganda triumph for the Soviet Union that it has never since been able to equal. The United States had for years possessed a military rocket (the Jupiter C) capable of doing the same thing, but Eisenhower had allowed himself to be persuaded that using one of these for such a purpose would alarm "world opinion" and that America's effort to put an object in earth orbit ought therefore to be run exclusively by a civilian agency—the National Science Foundation—as part of this country's contribution to the International Geophysical Year 1957.

The foundation was still dithering around at Cape Canaveral with a smallish rocket called Vanguard when *Sputnik* was blasted into orbit. Hastily Vanguard was launched—and rose about five feet, only to wobble and crash in the Florida sands as millions of TV viewers watched. (President Eisenhower could not be reached for comment; he was "painting a picture of his granddaughter.") Finally Eisenhower got serious—or perhaps desperate—and gave the army the go-ahead. In January 1958 a Jupiter C placed a package of American instruments in space flawlessly on its very first try.

Such was the record that alienated the conservative movement of the 1950s from the Eisenhower administration. By 1957 the break was more or less complete.

As might be expected, conservative sentiment of these dimensions found sympathy and support in many circles in the Republican party—especially on Capitol Hill, where the writ of President Eisenhower commanded less unquestioned obedience than it received in the executive departments. The old Taft organization had lost its leader as well as many of his closest associates and just about all of its steam. But William Knowland of California had become minority leader of the Senate upon Taft's death, and his brand of craggy conservatism appealed mightily to many conservatives on the lookout for a national leader. It is certainly not impossible that if Knowland had remained in the Senate, he would have had a major role to play in this account of the rise of the conservative movement.

Knowland, however, was a man tormented by problems of an essentially nonpolitical nature that simply would not leave him alone. It appeared that his marriage would be jeopardized if he remained in Washington; so, rather than permit that to happen, he challenged the incumbent Republican governor, Goodwin Knight, for the Republican gubernatorial nomination in 1958. To avoid a bruising collision with Knowland, Knight stepped aside and sought the Senate seat Knowland was vacating. Perhaps as a result of this obscure and confusing little ballet, both men were defeated that November by their Democratic rivals—and William Knowland disappeared from the scene as a national conservative leader.*

It was, therefore, to the handsome, silver-haired Senator Barry Goldwater of Arizona that conservatives in the late 1950s increasingly turned as their national political leader and spokesman. It is not merely piquant but highly significant that Goldwater had been a supporter of Eisenhower rather than Taft as a member of the Arizona delegation to the 1952 Republican convention in Chicago. The movement of a major segment of Eisenhower's 1952 support to the right during the 1950s was an important development in the growth of the conservative movement during that decade and—by leaguing the anti-Communists firmly with the classical liberals and the Burkean traditionalists—played a substantial part in determining the movement's ideologi-

---

* Ironically, his marriage ended in divorce anyway. And in February 1974 William Knowland committed suicide.

cal nature. Just for one thing, whereas Taft conservatives inclined toward isolationism (Taft himself, be it remembered, even opposed the United States' joining NATO in 1949), Eisenhower's more conservative supporters such as Goldwater were eager to involve America more deeply in the global rivalry with imperialistic communism.

I myself, as an active Young Republican in the early 1950s, had undergone (see Chapter I) my own swing to the right and did not hesitate to throw my influence behind the new conservative tendencies now developing, far out of sight of the White House, in the GOP. In February 1955, attending a meeting of the Executive Committee of the Young Republican National Federation at the Broadmoor Hotel in Colorado Springs, I heard Senator Goldwater address the group and was promptly fired with enormous enthusiasm for the political possibilities of this craggy Arizonan. In the first place, he clearly represented conservatives like myself, who had supported Eisenhower over Taft in 1952 but now felt acutely unrepresented in the higher levels of the administration. For another—and I doubt I could have articulated this at the time, but I certainly sensed it—he came from the West, where my deepest political instincts told me the future of Republicanism, and in many respects the seedbed of conservatism, lay.

I flew back East, therefore, a dedicated Goldwater enthusiast and promptly astounded and alarmed my YR colleagues in New York by demanding that Goldwater be invited to address our state YR convention that June. In fact, I threatened to resign if he wasn't. (I was the state YRs' general counsel at the time and a sort of elder statesman.) My friends reluctantly agreed, and Goldwater did in fact fly up to Monticello, New York, on June 4 to address the convention. (In a typical gesture of political balance, however, the leaders of the organization also arranged for State Attorney General Jacob Javits to address the convention's concluding banquet that evening.)

Later that same month, at the Young Republican National Federation's biennial convention in Detroit, the chairmanship of the organization was won, for the third time in a row, by the candidate of our still-powerful New York-based national coalition: Charles McWhorter, my friend and political ally since our days at

Harvard Law School, when he had succeeded me as president of the Harvard Young Republican Club. Our victorious combination of states once again bore (as it had borne at the previous YR conventions of 1951 and 1953) a striking resemblance to those assembled by Dewey in support of Eisenhower in 1952. But as in 1953, there were some suggestive additions as well. The YRs of Ohio— Senator Taft's home state—as well as those of several of neighboring states of the old Taft dispensation gave their votes to McWhorter.

This was not chiefly because Ohio, or the Taft troops generally, were becoming acclimatized to Eisenhower Republicanism—though that was undoubtedly a factor—but because Clif White, the architect of our YR coalition, had made it a point for several years past to augment our basic bloc with new allies drawn from the South and West. Moreover, White agreed with my urgent contention that Ohio and its old pro-Taft allies constituted a conservative political element that our coalition should be reaching out to. To symbolize this significant new friendship, McWhorter's first act as national YR chairman was to appoint the leader of the Ohio YRs, John Ashbrook, to head the campaign effort of the YR National Federation in the upcoming presidential election year, 1956. (This appointment gave Ashbrook an early lead in the race to succeed McWhorter as national chairman in 1957, and in fact he did exactly that.)

In September 1955 I called on René Wormser, a New York attorney who had been general counsel to the congressional investigation of tax-exempt foundations chaired by Carroll Reece. I had visited Reece himself in Washington nine years before, when he was Republican national chairman and I was at Harvard Law School, and he had encouraged me to found a Young Republican Club at Harvard; but in the interval we had parted ways—he remaining, of course, a top Taft ally, I to work zealously among the YRs for Dewey and then Eisenhower. In 1955, though, feeling as if I were bearing a white flag of truce, I called on Wormser and told him that I was now a conservative, favored conservative domination of the GOP, and to that end would like to reestablish harmonious relations with Reece.

Wormser accepted my profession as sincere and promised to get back to me. It was some months before he did so: Congressman

Reece, he explained, had been traveling in Europe. But now Wormser had Reece's reply to his message about me, and it was cordial: "Bill Rusher is a good man, and I would be glad to talk with him." In due course, therefore, I called on Reece in Washington, and our friendship was firmly refounded; it was to last until his death in 1961.

From March 1956 until July 1957, as already recounted, I lived in Washington while serving as associate counsel to the Senate Internal Security Subcommittee. While technically Democrat-controlled, the subcommittee was in effect jointly led in an amiable bipartisan spirit by its chairman, Senator James O. Eastland of Mississippi, and its ranking Republican member, Senator William E. Jenner of Indiana, and extracurricular activities of a highly partisan nature, on the part of staff members like myself, were therefore understandably discouraged. Nevertheless, I managed to attend the Republican convention in San Francisco in August 1956 as an observer and to play a lively behind-the-scenes part in the YR national convention that was held in Washington in July 1957, just as my service with the subcommittee was ending.

Ashbrook's election to succeed McWhorter as YR national chairman, with all that implied for the growing conservatism of the Young Republican National Federation, was our chief objective, and Clif White and I both gave it our personal attention: White became Ashbrook's campaign manager, while I served as Ashbrook's floor manager in the convention itself. In addition to naming Ashbrook as chairman, we succeeded in electing as cochairman (the second-highest post) a young lady named Jerri Kent of Tennessee, who just happened to be a member of the congressional staff of Congressman B. Carroll Reece.

As a sort of maraschino on the sundae, I worked successfully with a fellow conservative named Don Bostwick, who was chairman of the convention's platform committee, to persuade the convention to adopt a series of platform planks which implicitly criticized various "moderate" stances of the Eisenhower administration: its policy toward Yugoslavia, toward Section 14(b) of the Taft-Hartley Act, etc. The delegates were willing enough to pass our conservative planks but probably gave the matter relatively little thought, all eyes being trained, naturally, on the Ashbrook and Kent candidacies. The next morning's New York Times, how-

ever, played the platform as the convention's big news, a headline
at the top of page one announcing:

YOUNG GOP HITS IKE

ON 4 OUT OF 5 ISSUES

We later learned that this development caused Ike to lose his
famous temper and that he was prepared at his next press conference with a statement denouncing the YRs for their folly;
but luckily for us no reporter had the poor taste to bring the
matter up!

On the publication front as well as elsewhere, the latter half
of the 1950s was a time of rapid growth for the conservative movement. *Human Events,* under the editorship of Frank Hanighen,
had completed its transition from a newsletter of interest largely
to libertarians to a feisty observer of the Washington scene, with
special reference to such high-octane controversies as the one over
Joseph McCarthy. Among conservative Republican politicians and
staff members on Capitol Hill, *Human Events* was becoming a
weekly whiff of badly needed political oxygen.

In addition, the year 1957 saw the launching, under the editorship of Russell Kirk and with the financial support of Henry
Regnery, of *Modern Age, a Conservative Review,* which George
Nash in his excellent book* correctly calls "the principal quarterly
of the intellectual Right."

The role of a quarterly is radically different from that of a
journal of opinion. The latter is published as often as possible—
weekly, fortnightly, or at the very least monthly—and comments
upon political and other developments from the particular viewpoint it was designed to expound. Quarterlies, on the other hand,
appearing by definition only four times a year, stand far back from
the press of events and rarely comment on them directly. Instead
they deal, from the perspective of their chosen stance, with
longer-range tendencies, concepts requiring lengthier explication,
books of more than ordinary theoretical importance.

Modern Age was squarely in this grand tradition, and—as one
might expect of a quarterly published by Kirk—it tended to stress
heavily the traditionalist panel of the conservative triptych. Liber-

---

* *Op. cit.,* p. 145.

tarian economists and former Communists were in short supply among its editorial advisers, while the list of prominent tradition-alists was impressive, including such scholars as Richard Weaver, Eliseo Vivas, and Frederick Wilhelmsen. It was soon happily edi-fying America's growing conservative community, or at least sev-eral thousand of the more intellectually inclined within it, with symposia on "The Achievement of Ortega y Gasset" and "The Restoration of American Learning."

For its part, *National Review* had undergone its shakedown cruise and was exerting a steadily enlarging influence on the con-servative movement. Willi Schlamm, who had cofounded it with Buckley, ironically became the most spectacular victim of his own insistence that control of the publication be vested in the hands of a single individual. Falling out with Buckley and the other editors over his own role (and theirs), he precipitated a period of enor-mous tension in the upper echelons of the little magazine which was resolved only by his own resignation in mid-1957.

Almost simultaneously Buckley, who had held the titles of editor and publisher since the magazine's launching in November 1955, concluded that the two responsibilities were too heavy for a single individual to shoulder. As it happened, I was at just that moment seeking to return to some law job in the New York area after my stint as Robert Morris's associate counsel at the Senate Internal Security Subcommittee. When I approached Bill (whom I knew slightly, mostly through his brother-in-law and fellow editor Brent Bozell, who had been McCarthy's legislative assistant), thinking that the Buckley family oil business might need another young lawyer, he surprised me by inviting me to become publisher of *National Review*—with the rank, moreover, of a senior editor and the consequent right to full participation in editorial deci-sions.

I took some weeks to mull the offer over—after all, it in-volved leaving my chosen career, in which I had already invested eleven years of training and practice. But by 1957 I was more powerfully inclined than ever to commit myself full time to the conservative movement. In a sense I had already done so, during my year and a half with the subcommittee. My participation in Young Republican politics was coming to a close (I turned thirty-four that summer), and direct participation in senior Republican politics, with all its necessary compromises, held few charms for me. Most important of all, as a charter subscriber to *National Review* I was convinced that its basic analysis of America's problems—i.e., the view that it was not primarily secret Communists but all-too-visible liberals who were ruling and ruining America—was precisely correct. I sensed the kinetic energy of the burgeoning conservative movement and wanted desperately to participate in harnessing and focusing that energy. So, after wrestling for a while with the temptation, I accepted Buckley's offer—and lived happily ever after.

Unfortunately, though, my early years at *National Review* coincided with deepening financial problems that threatened to destroy the publication. The projected advertising revenues failed to materialize. For a time various individual members of the Buckley family chipped in with what one of them bravely called "fives and tens" (—thousand dollars, that is); but in point of fact, the collective family fortune was simply not capable of sustaining indefinitely a magazine that was already losing $100,000 a year. Sales of stock and debentures to "investors" willing to take the predictable capital loss continued to bring in a certain amount of income for a while, but we were soon running afoul of the blue-sky laws of the individual states, which are understandably harsh on money-losing corporations that try to sell securities to their citizens.

In desperation, Buckley turned in 1958 directly to the subscribers. In a long personal letter to each of them, he outlined what we hoped for *National Review* and sketched the financial problems that were threatening its life. In conclusion, he asked for their financial support, suggesting a contribution of $100, over and above the subscription price. Then we sat back and waited—and watched with growing joy and relief as a bar graph set up in the central editorial room of the office inched upward toward our goal. *National Review*'s subscribers had pulled us through—as they have continued to do in every succeeding year, ever since.

We have long since ceased to be apologetic about this annual need for a "fund appeal." A journal of opinion (as I patiently explain to the many free-enterprise enthusiasts who write every year to tell us that we ought to stop begging and sink or swim on straight market principles) is not a commercial venture at all and therefore cannot be judged purely in terms of its survivability in a free market. It exists to expound a point of view and to persist in doing so whether or not that viewpoint is popular or commercially self-sustaining. In this respect it resembles a church, or a university, or a political party; and indeed, a journal of opinion partakes, to some degree, of the nature of all three.

No wonder, then, that it is a historical fact that no journal of opinion in American history has ever made a profit, or so much as broken even, over any significant period of time. Every one of them has found it necessary to develop some kind of external subvention, and the really remarkable thing about *National Review* is that it is the only such publication to base its survival on so broad a numerical base of supporters. There are several thousand people in the United States who have contributed substantial sums of money—$100 or more—to *National Review*, not once but repeatedly, in some cases over a period of many years. At the other end of the financial spectrum is an extremely small handful of wealthy individuals whose contributions have reached five figures; and the largest gift ever made to the magazine at a single time was the bequest, by will, of a section of Kansas farmland which we sold in the early 1960s for $34,000. *National Review*'s survival, then, is directly traceable to the support of several thousand people whose confidence in it never wavered. All honor to them.

The magazine took, in the summer of that same year 1958, one further step that went far toward assuring its survival. It had been founded in 1955 as a weekly; as already recounted, only the merest chance prevented it from being called *National Weekly* rather than *National Review*. By 1958, however, its financial circumstances strongly suggested the wisdom of becoming a fortnightly—a measure that would prevent it from following news developments quite so closely, but that would have the compensating advantage of cutting printing and associated costs (paper, postage, etc.) squarely in half.

A boxed notice in the July 5 issue, accordingly, announced that "NATIONAL REVIEW's summer schedule begins this week. During July and August we will publish only fortnightly. Do not expect an issue next week!" In itself this was (and still is) a common enough practice among magazines, not only during summer's dog days but over the Christmas holidays, in both of which advertising revenues dip sharply—witness those "big double issues" offered at such times by so many publications, discreetly followed by a skipped week. But in September 1958 *National Review* did not return to a weekly publication schedule; it has remained a fortnightly ever since.

That summer's experience in publishing a fortnightly, however, had been a draining one for the editors. It was the summer of the first Lebanon crisis, when President Eisenhower, after a certain amount of dithering, finally sent in the marines; and the editors found themselves suffering dreadfully from the journalistic bends and squeezes on those alternate weeks when they were deprived of their customary pulpit. Moreover, though cutting back to a fortnightly saved on printing and related costs, it, of course, saved nothing on overhead: The staff was still there and had to be paid—and also (no small point) kept busy—every week.

So the back cover of the September 13 issue contained an "ANNOUNCEMENT—Beginning September 27th *National Review* will publish every week of the year. Odd weeks: National Review Magazine—32 pages of news, features, books. Even weeks: National Review Bulletin—8 pages of news—domestic, foreign and business."

The first issue of the Bulletin appeared under date of October 4 and gave its subscription price as "$7.00 a year to subscribers to National Review Magazine; $12.00 a year to all others." The magazine continued to be independently available on the alternate fortnights for $8, but a solid 25 percent of the magazine's readers proved unable to wait two whole weeks for another dose of the True Doctrine and began subscribing to the Bulletin as well. It accordingly netted a small but useful profit.*

The Bulletin was conceived not as a miniature journal of opinion but rather as a sort of highly opinionated newsletter. It always began with a "lead editorial," usually written by the magisterially authoritative James Burnham. Then came a series of editorial paragraphs and longer, titled editorials, not unlike those

---

* The attendant confusion—as well as the increased cost of the combination—prompted the dry-witted Jim McFadden, who was in charge of *National Review*'s promotion efforts, to coin a new sales pitch for in-house delectation only: "You think you're getting less, but remember: You're paying more."

popular features of the magazine. There were also columns, keyed closely to events in Washington and abroad, and a final page of commentary on business trends. The emphasis was squarely on the news and its immediate implications. There were no book reviews, no articles, no columns dealing with longer-range trends. Even the style was sharpened, to exclude any implication of languor. As might be expected, the Bulletin soon developed its own devoted readership, part of which actually preferred it to the magazine. In any case, it was to remain for many years the magazine's bumptious little brother, providing, on those alternate weeks when the magazine didn't appear, a valuable platform for the editors, as well as employment for the editorial staff, and revenues for the parched business department of the joint enterprise.*

That first issue of the Bulletin happened to contain an announcement concerning yet another activity being conducted by *National Review* at the time: the "first Fall program of NATIONAL REVIEW FORUMS," to be held at the Hunter College Playhouse on Thursday, October 2—"Admission $1 (students free)". The forum was to consist of a debate on the topic "Should New York Conservatives Vote for Rockefeller?" (who was running for governor for the first time that autumn). State Senator Earl W. Brydges would take the affirmative, while *National Review*'s own senior editor and columnist Frank Meyer would argue the negative. As it turned out, some 400 people, most of them vociferously anti-Rockefeller, attended the debate. Clearly, Buckley and *National Review* felt that the mobilization of conservative political strength ought to be pursued by all available means and not confined merely to the publication of a journal of opinion.

Midway through Eisenhower's second term another action of his brought conservative resentment of him to a white heat. This was his invitation to Soviet Premier Nikita Khrushchev to visit this country in 1959. I do not know what the State Department working papers on this Communist propaganda triumph (a Soviet premier's first-ever visit to the United States) listed as the possible benefits that might inure to this country; but whatever they were, the subsequent history of our times makes it clear that they were

---

* Publication of the Bulletin was ultimately ended as of December 31, 1979.

not realized. The only lasting effect of the visit was to diminish a little further—as such visits inevitably diminish—the will and inclination of American public opinion, and therefore of America's political leadership, to resist subsequent Soviet demands. Eisenhower himself seemed, belatedly, to recognize the moral hole the visit was tearing in the fabric of the free world's case against communism, for the press reported that the president's usually mobile and broadly smiling features were glum and fixed as he accompanied the beaming Khrushchev in an open car on the traditional ride from the airport to downtown Washington.

I missed that cavalcade, but one memory of an event closely contemporary with the Khrushchev visit has remained with me vividly ever since and hardened my heart on the subject of my onetime hero, Dwight Eisenhower. As part of the spurious spirit of "peaceful coexistence" that characterized Soviet-American relations in 1959, an exhibition of Soviet technology was opened that summer in New York City at the newly built Coliseum on Columbus Circle. One fine afternoon I happened to be strolling up Fifth Avenue. Looking westward along Fifty-ninth Street, I saw flying grandly over the Coliseum a huge flag I had never seen there before—or anywhere else in America, as far as I could remember. It was, of course, the Hammer and Sickle—the flag of the USSR, its bright red folds flapping briskly against the brilliant blue of the New York sky. How many millions of innocent human beings had died, I reflected, under the aegis of that bloody banner! How many proud nations had been ground into dust or puppetry by those who waved it!

National Review was a magazine, not a political party or even a membership organization, but Buckley decided that it should sponsor an anti-Khrushchev rally at Carnegie Hall to symbolize the resentment that at least some Americans felt toward Khrushchev, the system he represented, and the American administration that had no better judgment or taste than to invite him to this country as its honored guest. The episode launched a standing joke around our offices, for Bill, having had the original inspiration, turned its actual execution over to me with the comment that the job would merely require "a couple of phone calls." Ever since, any really major effort around *National Review* is likely to be described sardonically as involving merely "a couple of phone calls."

In point of fact, bringing off the rally consumed the time of most of *NR*'s staff for nearly three weeks. There was the hall to be hired, tickets to be printed, publicity to be obtained, troops to be rounded up. Buckley himself, piqued by hints that he wasn't shouldering his share of the burden, undertook to find an organist to play Carnegie Hall's resident organ. The result, as I ought to have foreseen, was that the crowds flocking into the hall on the evening of September 17 found a noted musician playing not "The Battle Hymn of the Republic" or some similar inspirational air but a Bach fugue.

The program itself, however, over which I presided, was a vintage example of late-1950s conservatism. Speakers included Rabbi Benjamin Schultz, Eugene Lyons, Brent Bozell, Joe McCarthy's widow, Jeanie, and Dean Clarence Manion of Notre Dame Law School. Buckley gave the concluding address, and offered the audience some memorable examples of his style:

> The damage Khrushchev can do to us on this trip is not comparable to the damage we have done to ourselves. Khrushchev is here. And his being here profanes the nation. But the harm we have done, we have done to ourselves; and for that we cannot hold Khrushchev responsible. . . .
>
> I mind that Khrushchev is here; but I mind more that Eisenhower invited him. I mind that Eisenhower invited him, but I mind much more the defense of that invitation by the thought-leaders of the nation. . . .
>
> I have not heard a "reason" why Khrushchev should come to this country that is not in fact a reason why he should *not* come to this country. *He will see for himself the health and wealth of the land?* Very well; and having confirmed the fact, what are we to expect? That he will weaken in his adherence to his maniacal course? . . . One might as well expect the Bishop of Rome to break the apostolic succession upon being confronted by the splendid new YMCA in Canton, Ohio. Does Khrushchev really *doubt* that there are 67 million automobiles in this country? What is he to do now that he is here? Count them? . . . Is he going to encounter that firmness of American resolution which will cause him, when he returns to Russia, to furrow his brow in anxiety on resuming the war against us?
>
> I suggest that this brings us to the major reason why Khrushchev should *not* have been invited. If indeed the nation is united

behind Mr. Eisenhower in this invitation, then the nation is united behind an act of diplomatic sentimentality which can only confirm Khrushchev in the contempt he feels for the dissipated morale of a nation far gone, as the theorists of Marxism have all along contended, in decrepitude. . . . Will he not return convinced that behind the modulated hubbub at the White House, in the State Department, at the city halls, at the economic clubs, at the industrial banquets, he heard—*with his own ears*—the death rattle of the West? . . .

Ladies and gentlemen, we deem it the central revelation of Western experience that man cannot ineradicably stain himself, for the wells of regeneration are infinitely deep. No temple has ever been so profaned that it cannot be purified; no man is ever truly lost; no nation irrevocably dishonored. Khrushchev cannot take permanent advantage of our temporary disadvantage, for it is the West he is fighting. And in the West there lie, however encysted, the ultimate resources, which are moral in nature. Khrushchev is *not* aware that the gates of hell shall not prevail against us. Even out of the depths of despair, we take heart in the knowledge that it cannot matter how deep we fall, for there is always hope. In the end, *we* will bury *him*.

In such terms did conservatism, in that year of Our Lord 1959, defy the conventional wisdom of the day.

The years 1958 and 1959 saw a further hardening of the conservative position now being openly taken by the Young Republican National Federation. John Ashbrook, who had also been elected to the Ohio legislature, and Jerri Kent, through whom we kept in close touch with Reece, were of course both personally and outspokenly conservative. But in New York, which chose Jacob Javits as its senator in 1956 and where Nelson Rockefeller was elected governor in 1958, liberal Republicanism was riding high, and the new masters did not overlook the Young Republicans. White and I had retired from the YR scene, both in New York and nationally, after 1957, but Rockefeller's Republican state chairman, L. Judson Morhouse, cleansed the state YR organization of all leading figures known to be close to us and replaced them with a fresh set beholden to Rockefeller and dedicated to his brand of liberal Republicanism. It was a delegation of Rockefeller Republicans, therefore, that New York sent to the next meeting that would be a reasonably fair test of national Republican sentiment: the YR national convention in Denver in June 1959.

By now these biennial YR national conventions were recognized by most observers as significant straws in the Republican wind, and there seemed no doubt that in 1959 the signal would be for a shift to the right. Popular as Barry Goldwater was, however, it was clear that Vice President Richard Nixon would be the front-runner for the party's 1960 presidential nomination and that his chief rival would be Governor Nelson Rockefeller. Under those circumstances, there was no doubt whatever that most Young Republicans, given their antiliberal bias, would favor Nixon.* The conservatives' choice for YR chairman to succeed Ashbrook, a Kansan named Ned Cushing, who favored Nixon, was therefore duly elected at the 1950 convention in Denver; but the structure of the coalition that backed him had changed in one vital respect.

Ever since 1949, the victorious combination in YR national politics had always included, and been led by, New York—a by-product of Thomas Dewey's long hegemony in the GOP. Under White's leadership the condition had been augmented by new alliances with the Midwest and the South. Now, in 1959, New York had passed into the hands of Nelson Rockefeller, and Cushing's managers calmly put an antiliberal majority together out of the old Taft states (Ashbrook's Ohio and its neighbors) plus the South and the West. This new coalition was to prove of enormous significance for the future of the entire Republican party. For it demonstrated, for the first time in modern memory, that *a convention reasonably representative of the national distribution of forces in the GOP could be controlled by a conservative coalition not including New York and its relatively liberal allies.* Just what that implied would not become entirely clear until July 1964, when many of Ned Cushing's state and regional managers—led by Clif White—nominated Barry Goldwater for president at the Cow Palace in San Francisco.

Most of this conservative growth registered in the middle and late 1950s went unnoticed by the media and therefore by the public as a whole. Certainly this was true of most of the developments

---

* Nixon, incidentally, had not neglected to do what he could to insure this, naming the retiring YR national chairman, Charles McWhorter, as an administrative assistant in his vice presidential office in 1957.

in the Young Republican National Federation, not to mention such events as the founding and survival of *National Review* (the circulation of which hovered around 25,000) and *Modern Age* (which had perhaps 5,000 readers). Not even the John Birch Society, in those early days, received from the media anything like the attention that was to be showered on it—maliciously, to be sure—in the 1960s, when liberals were forced to notice the conservative movement at last.

Only two conservatives, in fact, made much of a dent on the public consciousness prior to 1960, and in both cases their success was largely personal. One was Barry Goldwater, whose position in the Senate guaranteed him a certain audience and who greatly enlarged that audience, and greatly enhanced his own stature as a conservative leader, by an arduous schedule of speeches at Republican and other functions all over the country.

The other was William F. Buckley, Jr., who—not content with hectoring Yale, defending Joe McCarthy, and then founding and editing America's only surviving journal of conservative opinion—was now increasingly being invited to speak or debate before college audiences and even to appear on radio talk shows and television panels. Conservatives had discovered to their delight that in Buckley they had an oratorical champion who could more than hold his own with the best gladiators liberalism could put into the field; and now radio and TV producers found themselves irresistibly drawn—against their own almost always liberal political judgment—by that seductive half-British, half-Southern drawl and the rapier wit that accompanied it. Slowly, reluctantly, many intelligent observers of conventionally liberal opinions found themselves admitting that Buckley was "brilliant" (if not, of course, correct); then every so often "correct" (though only now and then). Some of them, unwilling to concede that he was winning his public arguments with dismaying consistency, settled for just calling him "fascinating"—a faint and equivocal sort of praise that implied a certain damning in important respects left unspecified.

The truth was rather different and a good deal more complex. Buckley was indeed, in public debates, making monkeys out of some of liberalism's most parfait, gentil knights—a circumstance that could be chalked up to glibness, or even to personal skill, only so often before it became necessary to admit that Buckley was winning, in important part, simply because the conservative case was demonstrably better than the liberal one. But worse yet, Buckley was slowly bringing into public focus a personal image the very existence of which did dreadful damage to beliefs that many liberals held dearer, almost, than liberalism itself.

To liberal intellectuals of the 1950s conservatism was not so much invisible as simply beneath notice. It was there, all right, but it was inherently, inescapably *dull*. That was the comfortable conviction that lay behind Dwight Macdonald's sneer, in his 1956 attack on *National Review*, that "Culturally a conservative is someone like Irving Babbitt or Paul Elmer More, not always the liveliest company in the world but a respecter and defender of tradition." That was, in fact, part of the fun of being a liberal: that sense of sure intellectual, even social superiority to one's political adversaries. But Bill Buckley, say what one would, simply did not fit the familiar and innocuous mold of previous conservatives all the way back to Coolidge and Hoover. He was obviously highly intelligent, and most people sensed in him an instinctive fairness as well.* Add to these qualities his quasi-aristocratic English-public-school bearing, his fearsome knowledgeability, and his devastating wit, and one was confronted with a persona that the liberalism of the 1950s was hard put to match, let alone outpoint, with its own large crop of talented spokesmen. The awful fear began to seep into the liberal consciousness that perhaps conservatism, or at any rate a conservative, wasn't *necessarily* dull after all.

It is hard to quantify, let alone evaluate, influences of this sort, but I am confident I am not mistaken in my basic point: Bill Buckley's emergence onto the national stage as a major conservative spokesman and a minor celebrity in the 1950s, and the impact of his striking personality when this began to be brought to bear, caused a lesion in the self-confidence of many liberals that materially influenced the attitudes of both conservatives and liberals thereafter, as well as the ultimate outcome of their long struggle. Buckley was to become far better known during the 1960s and nationally—even internationally—famous during the 1970s. He is

---

* Not everybody. One Long Island woman of liberal bent watched him closely on television for thirty minutes at about this time, then declared solemnly to a friend, "I have seen the devil!"

today a truly national figure by any standard—a major celebrity whose mere presence guarantees the success of any social occasion. His name occurs regularly on lists of the "ten most" thises and thats. But his truly seminal contributions to the conservative movement occurred in the decade of the 1950s, and although the founding of *National Review* is indisputably the greatest of these, I would not hesitate to put second the impact, as described above, of his own remarkable personality.

As one might expect, conservatism in the 1950s was no Garden of Eden in which the lions lay down with the lambs. I have already described the three very different sources (classical liberalism, Burkean traditionalism, and operational anticommunism) from which the conservative movement drew its strength. They did not agree on everything at the outset, and they continued to some extent to disagree—have continued to do so, in fact, to this very day. Certain classical liberals, in particular, tended to feel that their fragile barque of pure libertarian doctrine was being boarded by some very strange customers—traditionalists carrying the ancient baggage of hierarchy and compulsion and anti-Communists all too ready to magnify the state in the cause of global resistance to statism. A particularly bitter and unforgiving description of developments in the conservative movement during the 1950s was published not long ago by Murray Rothbard, a leading spokesman of the most extreme sect of pure libertarians, now openly at war with the rest of the modern conservative movement. Writing in the October 27, 1980, issue of *Inquiry*, his group's own journal of opinion, Rothbard gave this lurid version of the decade of the fifties:

> What happened was this. The political leaders of the Old Right began to die or retire. Taft's death in 1953 was an irreparable blow, and one by one the other Taft Republicans disappeared from the scene. In fact, Taft's defeat in the bitterly fought 1952 convention was to signal the end of the Old Right as a political force. . . . Goldwater was—and is—an all-out interventionist in foreign affairs; it is both symbolic and significant that Goldwater was an Eisenhower, not a Taft delegate to the 1952 Republican convention.
> Meanwhile, the intellectual leaders of the Old Right too were fast disappearing. Nock and Mencken were dead or inactive, and

Colonel Robert McCormick, publisher of the *Chicago Tribune,* died in 1955. *The Freeman,* although the leading right-wing journal in the late forties and early fifties, had never been a powerful force; by the mid-fifties it was weaker than ever. Since the thirties, the Right had suffered from a dearth of intellectuals; it had seemed that all intellectuals were on the left. A disjunction therefore existed between a tiny cadre of intellectuals and writers, and a large, relatively unenlightened mass base. In the mid-1950's, with a power vacuum in both the political and the intellectual areas, the Right had become ripe for a swift takeover. A well-edited, well-financed magazine could hope to capture the dazed right wing and totally transform its character. This is exactly what happened with the formation of *National Review* in 1955.

In a sense Joe McCarthy heralded the shift when, after his censure by the Senate, he feebly changed his focus in early 1955 from domestic Communism to the championing of Chiang Kai-shek. For *National Review,* led by Bill Buckley and William Rusher, was a coalition of young Catholics—McCarthyite and eager to lead an anti-Communist crusade in foreign affairs—and ex-Communists like Frank Meyer and William S. Schlamm dedicating their energies to extirpating the God that had failed them. NR filled the power vacuum, and with Rusher as point man in the political arena, it managed, in a scant few years, to transform the American right wing beyond recognition. By the early 1960s the Rusher forces had captured the Young Republicans and College Young Republicans, established Young Americans for Freedom as their campus arm, and had taken over the Intercollegiate Society of Individualists as a more theoretical organ.

By the 1960 GOP convention, Barry Goldwater had become the political leader of the transformed New Right. By 1960, too, the embarrassing extremists like the John Birch Society had been purged from the ranks, and the modern conservative movement was in place. It combined a traditionalist and theocratic approach to "Moral values," occasional lip service to free-market economics, and an imperialist and global interventionist foreign policy dedicated to the glorification of the American state and the extirpation of world Communism. Classical liberalism remained only as rhetoric, useful in attracting business support, and most of all as a fig leaf for the grotesque realities of the New Right. (This entity is not to be confused with the fundamentalist factions now on the warpath against abortion and ERA.)

In a few brief years the character of the right wing had been totally transformed: Once basically classical liberal, it had become a global theocratic crusade.

Rothbard's account is, as I hope the preceding pages have adequately demonstrated, a grotesque caricature of what really happened, spiced, moreover, with various inaccuracies.* For their part, however, certain of the traditionalists whom Rothbard regards as having usurped the conservative movement have been quick to return his attacks blow for blow. Russell Kirk, for example, writing in the fall 1981 issue of *Modern Age*, probably speaks for most modern American conservatives when he reads the Rothbard types of libertarian out of the movement, bell, book, and candle:

> Any discussion of the relationships between conservatives (who now, to judge by public-opinion polls, are a majority among American citizens) and libertarians (who, as tested by recent elections, remain a tiny though unproscribed minority) naturally commences with an inquiry into what these disparate groups hold in common. These two bodies of opinion share a detestation of collectivism. They set their faces against the totalist state and the heavy hand of bureaucracy. That much is obvious enough.
>
> What else do conservatives and libertarians profess in common? The answer to that question is simple: nothing. Nor will they ever have. To talk of forming a league or coalition between these two is like advocating a union of ice and fire.
>
> The ruinous failing of the ideologues who call themselves libertarians is their fanatic attachment to a simple solitary principle—that is, to the notion of personal freedom as the whole end of the civil social order, and indeed of human existence. . . .
>
> [On the contrary, the] great line of division in modern politics— as Eric Voegelin reminds us—is not between totalitarians on the one hand and liberals (or libertarians) on the other; rather, it lies between all those who believe in some sort of transcendent moral order, on one side, and on the other side all those who take this ephemeral existence of ours for the be-all and end-all—to be devoted chiefly to producing and consuming. In this discrimination

---

* For example, I was not even baptized, let alone a Catholic, in the 1950s or for nearly two decades thereafter, that detail having been neglected in my infancy. And when I finally became a member of the Christian church in 1978, it was as an Anglican, not a Roman, Catholic.

between the sheep and the goats, the libertarians must be classified with the goats—that is, as utilitarians admitting no transcendent sanctions for conduct. In effect, they are converts to Marx's dialectical materialism; so conservatives draw back from them on the first principle of all.

Aside from such major fallings-out, there were, moreover, the usual petty quarrels and rivalries with little or no substantive content. Certain elderly WASPs, who had long considered conservatism their private deer park, took it rather hard that the movement's ablest and most prominent spokesmen were a half-Jewish senator and a young Roman Catholic. *Human Events,* humanly enough, tended for some years to regard *National Review* as a parvenu rival—an attitude that greatly amused the latter's top-lofty editors when they finally became aware of it. At a more serious level, the gulf between the John Birch Society and most of the rest of the conservative movement seemed likely from the start to prove unbridgeable—as it ultimately turned out to be.

But there is simply no gainsaying the spectacular difference, as far as conservatism was concerned, between the beginning of the decade of the fifties and its close. In 1950 Lionel Trilling could say, without serious contradiction, that "it is the plain fact that there are no conservative or reactionary ideas in general circulation" in the United States. By the end of 1959 conservatism was a fast-growing movement with a developing set of coherent ideas, able national spokesmen, its own publishing houses and theoretical journals, firm ties with important leaders and organizational components of the Republican party, and a steadily increasing sense of unity and purpose. It had, in fact, already accomplished most of what any essentially theoretical or philosophical movement can accomplish. The time was fast approaching when conservatism would have to move, in one way or another, onto the brightly lit stage of active politics.

Chapter IV

The Plunge into Politics

The year 1960 was a transitional one for American conservatives. Their movement was now almost fully grown, but it had not taken an active part in politics, nor was it yet altogether ready to do so. Senator Barry Goldwater, its most prominent political spokesman, was not at a point, strictly in party terms, where he could be offered seriously as a presidential candidate—if indeed, he would ever be. Vice President Nixon, the front-runner for the Republican nomination in 1960, had maintained friendly personal and political relations with most of his conservative colleagues in the GOP, and even with the more prominent movement conservatives like Buckley, but had taken care never to become explicitly or exclusively their man. His chief rival for the nomination, however, was New York Governor Nelson Rockefeller, who made no secret of his relative liberalism, and that was quite enough to make Nixon the choice of many conservatives.

Some conservatives questioned whether their movement ought to throw in its lot with the Republican party at all, especially if Nixon was the best it was going to be able to do. I shared this view. As a political personality Nixon had already demonstrated that he evoked powerful emotions, both pro and con; but oddly enough he had always left me simply cold or, more precisely, cool. I thought he was essentially an opportunist and therefore disagreed with those of my conservative colleagues who believed that "at heart" he was one of us. Most of *National Review*'s leading figures were in the latter camp; but Frank Meyer agreed with me, and my recollection is that he joined in my personal refusal to vote for Nixon that November. (I wrote in the name of Barry Goldwater instead.)

I was too much of a realist, however, to take seriously the attempt that a small but stubborn group of conservatives made to nominate Goldwater at the Republican convention in Chicago that July. In fact, I didn't even attend the convention—the first I had missed since 1944.

There was, by this time, simply no questioning Goldwater's political leadership of the conservative movement. His little book *The Conscience of a Conservative* (Victor, 1960), pieced together by Brent Bozell and others out of Goldwater's speeches on a wide range of topics, had appeared earlier that year in a first printing of 10,000 copies. Ultimately more than 3,500,000 hardback and paperback copies were to be sold—powerful testimony, if anybody had been listening, to the tremendous thirst for a statement of conservative principles at a certain level of the literate population of the country in the early 1960s.

Roger Milliken, then Republican national committeeman from South Carolina as well as a hugely successful and wealthy businessman there, and South Carolina's GOP chairman, Greg Shorey, were accordingly determined to put Goldwater's name in nomination for the presidency whether he liked it or not. It is one of the underappreciated ironies of American politics that Barry Goldwater, for all the passionate sincerity of his conservative convictions, was from first to last a thoroughly orthodox party regular who sincerely admired what he called the pros—meaning the nearly value-free mechanics who ran the party machine—and had little use for what he regarded as the amateurs who clustered so noisily around him. He was fond of Milliken and grateful for his confidence, but Goldwater knew that the 1960 nomination was Nixon's and, as the convention approached, was content that it should be so.

He did, nonetheless, allow his own state of Arizona to endorse him as its favorite son candidate, simply to avoid being upstaged by the rambunctious South Carolinians; and he edged a bit closer to a real candidacy when Nixon abased himself in the eyes of many conservatives and flew to New York the weekend before the convention opened to confer with Governor Rockefeller. Out of their conference came the so-called Treaty of Fifth Avenue under which Nixon consented, in return for Rockefeller's withdrawal as a candidate, to various liberal modifications of the platform and promised to name an eastern liberal as his running mate.

The convention's many conservative delegates were furious (Goldwater denounced the deal as "a domestic Munich"), and

Goldwater's backers—who now included Albert Fay of Texas and Dean Clarence Manion of Notre Dame Law School—told him there were 287 delegates ready to vote for him. That was nowhere near a majority; but it was a respectable minority, and Goldwater decided to allow his name to be placed in nomination as a symbolic gesture. Arizona obliged, and then, by prearrangement, Goldwater addressed the convention and asked that his name be withdrawn. Telling his protesting friends to "grow up," he reminded them that "We are conservatives. This great Republican party is our historic house. This is our home. . . . I am going to devote all my time from now until November to electing Republicans from the top of the ticket to the bottom of the ticket, and I call upon my fellow conservatives to do the same." It was an example that many of his liberal Republican rivals failed to follow when their turn came just four years later.

Thus ended the conservative movement's first attempt—premature, amateurish, and futile—to bend the Republican party to its purposes. But major political efforts are seldom without their sequelae, and the Goldwater drive at the 1960 Republican convention had at least one important and lasting consequence. Its spear carriers—the rank and file, so far below Goldwater and his advisers as to be virtually out of sight—included a number of young conservative activists, still in or just out of college, who were now furious at the GOP and unwilling any longer to confine their politicking to the Young Republican National Federation (which, naturally enough, was now gearing up to campaign more or less enthusiastically for Nixon).

Meeting early in September 1960 on the spacious green lawn of Great Elm, the Buckley family estate in Sharon, Connecticut, about ninety of these young activists formed a new national conservative youth organization, independent of any political party. They decided to call it Young Americans for Freedom.

As it happens, I was sitting twenty or thirty yards away, having a drink or two with Brent Bozell and Marvin Liebman, while YAF was formed. I remember not liking the acronym much—and liking it even less when Liebman, possessor of one of the world's most mordant wits, became the first to point out that this made the rest of us Old Americans for Freedom, or OAFs.

But such was the choice of the young founding fathers and mothers, and that evening, invited to say a few words to them, I quoted some lines from Goethe that had long inspired me:

> Heard are the voices,
> Heard are the sages—
> The worlds and the ages:
> Choose well; your choice is
> Brief, and yet endless.
> Here eyes do regard you
> In eternity's stillness.
> Here is all fullness,
> Ye brave, to reward you.
> *Work, and despair not.*

YAF's founding meeting at Sharon accompanied its announcement of the launching of the new organization with a statement of beliefs that summarized, pithily and well, the conservative principles that had been hammered out in the preceding ten years by the movement's theorists. Called "The Sharon Statement," it is worth quoting here in full because nowhere else, for many years, did anyone attempt so succinctly and comprehensively, let alone so successfully, to describe what modern American conservatism was all about. YAF's founders had done their homework well:

> In this time of moral and political crisis, it is the responsibility of the youth of America to affirm certain eternal truths.
> We, as young conservatives, believe:
> That foremost among the transcendent values is the individual's use of his God-given free will, whence derives his right to be free from the restrictions of arbitrary force;
> That liberty is indivisible, and that political freedom cannot long exist without economic freedom;
> That the purposes of government are to protect these freedoms through the preservation of internal order, the provision of national defense, and the administration of justice;
> That when government ventures beyond these rightful functions, it accumulates power which tends to diminish order and liberty;
> That the Constitution of the United States is the best arrange-

ment yet devised for empowering government to fulfill its proper role, while restraining it from the concentration and abuse of power;

That the genius of the Constitution—the division of powers—is summed up in the clause which reserves primacy to the several states, or to the people, in those spheres not specifically delegated to the Federal Government;

That the market economy, allocating resources by the free play of supply and demand, is the single economic system compatible with the requirements of personal freedom and constitutional government, and that it is at the same time the most productive supplier of human needs;

That when government interferes with the work of the market economy, it tends to reduce the moral and physical strength of the nation; that when it takes from one man to bestow on another, it diminishes the incentive of the first, the integrity of the second, and the moral autonomy of both;

That we will be free only so long as the national sovereignty of the United States is secure; that history shows periods of freedom are rare, and can exist only when free citizens concertedly defend their rights against all enemies;

That the forces of international Communism are, at present, the greatest single threat to these liberties;

That the United States should stress victory over, rather than coexistence with, this menace; and

That American foreign policy must be judged by this criterion: does it serve the just interests of the United States?"

Robert Schuchman, a student at Yale Law School, was elected as the first chairman of YAF, and Douglas Caddy, a recent graduate of Georgetown, as its full-time national director. Marvin Liebman made office space available in his own PR office suite at 79 Madison Avenue, and YAF was under way.

One other event of the year 1960 deserves at least passing mention, and that is the dinner in honor of *National Review*'s fifth birthday held at the Plaza Hotel in New York City on October 27.

Bill Buckley has a remarkably keen public-relations sense and has always believed that, in the immortal words of John L. Lewis, "He who tooteth his own horn thereby insures that it shall be tooted." Buckley was determined, and rightly, that *National Re-*

view's achievement in surviving for five years should not go unnoticed merely because the media were so grimly determined not to notice it. The surest attention-getting device, he decided, would be a glittering black-tie dinner in the Plaza's ornate Grand Ballroom. The occasion would take the form of a party in honor of *National Review* tendered by a committee of the biggest names we could persuade to participate.

Ultimately a most impressive dinner committee was rounded up. Admiral Lewis Strauss, the former chairman of the U.S. Atomic Energy Commission, served as its chairman, and other members (not all of whom could attend the dinner) included Herbert Hoover, Douglas MacArthur, five U.S. senators, and most of the leading figures of the American conservative movement—92 in all.

Nearly 1,000 people squeezed into the Grand Ballroom that night—and we took care to reserve a table for the press. After dinner there were brief speeches of praise and encouragement by Admiral Strauss, Howard Phillips (a youthful conservative who had somehow become president of the Harvard Student Council), M. Stanton Evans, editor of the *Indianapolis News*, and James Jackson Kilpatrick.

Then Ambassador Strauss turned the gavel, so to speak, over to me, and after a few words of my own, I introduced *National Review*'s senior editors, each of whom (save Willmoore Kendall, who was out of the country) spoke briefly. The concluding speech, somewhat longer, was by Buckley, of course, and Bill seemed genuinely moved—so much that for a moment he was unable to speak—by my introduction and the standing ovation he received from those attending.

After appropriate expressions of thanks, he spoke of the towering collective prominence of the committee of sponsors and then added a characteristic Buckley touch. "I am proud beyond my powers to describe to be associated with so distinguished a list of sponsors," he declared "—and they should be proud to be associated with *National Review*."

He went on to mention the two most prominent members of the sponsoring committee (neither of whom, however, was present that evening), Herbert Hoover and Douglas MacArthur—both, of course, almost holy names to the conservatives assembled in the

Plaza. Buckley noted that both had remained steadfast "when the tidal wave roared up before them." So, he suggested, must we. It was unlikely, he said, that conservatives would in our time enjoy "those topical gratifications" associated with political victory. "We are, all of us," he ventured, "in one sense out of spirit with history." But one assurance he did leave with his friends: "So long as it is mechanically possible, you have a journal—a continuing witness to those truths which animated the birth of our country and continue to animate our lives."

Such occasions are seldom intrinsically important, but Buckley had correctly perceived the function that rewards perform and had noted the skill with which the dominant liberals manipulated them. For a loyal liberal journalist, for example, there might be a Nieman Fellowship at Harvard, then (if he really made his mark in the profession) a Pulitzer Prize, and finally even, to crown his career, honorary degrees from various colleges and universities. Similarly, for entire publications that signally advanced the liberal line, there would be still other Pulitzer Prizes. Awards and recognition of all sorts rained down on politicians, clergymen, even businessmen in favor with the reigning orthodoxy.

Conservatives and conservative institutions, though, could expect no such recognition or encouragement in the 1950s and early 1960s, and Buckley accordingly decided that we would provide our own.

It is always tantalizing to speculate *what might have happened* if events had taken a different course from that which they in fact did. Nixon's loss of the election to Kennedy in November 1960 was by the smallest imaginable margin: 114,673 votes out of 68,328,015 cast for one or the other of the two. It is believed by many professional politicians to this day that Mayor Richard Daley simply stole Illinois—and with it the margin of victory—for Kennedy. And interestingly enough, even if Kennedy won Illinois legitimately, he still did not have a popular majority over Nixon unless all of the 318,303 "Democratic" votes in the state of Alabama are counted for him—despite the fact that the Democratic votes in that state were actually cast for a slate of eleven electors, six of whom were pledged to, and did, vote for Harry F. Byrd, an independent and highly conservative Democrat. Nixon, however, refused to shake the foundations of our electoral system, as a prolonged battle over such esoterica would necessarily have done, and Kennedy was duly inaugurated.

What, though, if Nixon had won? What would have become of the conservative movement, poised as it was on the verge of a plunge into active politics? We know what Nixon did when he was in fact elected eight years later (see Chapter IX, infra), and it was little enough: appoint to his staff a few loyalists with close conservative ties, with instructions to keep Nixon on as friendly terms with the movement as circumstances permitted, but give conservatives precious little of the real action. We know, too, what Nixon in his memoirs, written another seven or eight years farther along in the mid-1970s, tells us he *intended* to do after his 1972 reelection, if only the Watergate controversy had not derailed the plan: reorganize the Republican party along "New Majority" lines, specifically including blue-collar and ethnic components of the old Democratic coalition. But these are the self-serving acts and assertions of Nixon from 1968 to 1971 and 1975 and 1976 respectively, when conservatism was far more visible and politically more impressive than it had been in 1960 or would have been thereafter if Nixon had won in that year.

It is impossible, of course, to be sure (would there, for example, have been some equivalent of Watergate in a Nixon administration of the early or mid-1960s?), but my guess is that Nixon would have pacified the conservative Republicans like Goldwater more or less and thereby successfully narrowed and weakened the potential political base of the conservative movement. In all likelihood some major fraction of the movement would ultimately have broken with the GOP altogether and attempted to field a third ticket—perhaps even a third party—committed squarely to conservatism. But we shall never know.

What did happen was that Nixon lost, with incalculable consequences for the future of both the Republican party and conservatism. His defeat seemed to tell the world that the GOP, without some charismatic national hero like Eisenhower at its head, was still a born loser. Almost worse yet was the leadership vacuum: The old Taft organization was gone, and so, for all practical purposes, was its vanquisher, the Dewey machine that had nominated Eisenhower. Eisenhower himself had no political organization, and now Nixon's lay in ruins almost before it could take concrete form. Goldwater's friends believed they could have mustered nearly 300 delegates for their tiger at Chicago against Nixon, but it was a trick untried and in any case far short of a majority. Secure in his New York bailiwick, of course, Nelson Rockefeller no doubt felt, after Nixon's defeat in November, that things were going his way; but he scarcely guessed, and never really understood, the depth and bitterness of the opposition he generated among more conservative Republicans.

And yet "You can't beat somebody with nobody." I have always counted as one of the conservative movement's darkest days the occasion, early in 1961, not long before Carroll Reece's death, when I walked into the lobby of Washington's Metropolitan Club and ran into the old gentleman sitting at a large round table near the center of the room. We exchanged greetings, then began instinctively to talk of politics.

"Bill," Reece asked hesitantly, "can anything be done with Nelson Rockefeller?" I saw all too clearly where he was heading.

So it had come to this—that one of Robert Taft's last surviving allies had been reduced, in February 1961, to wondering hopelessly "if anything could be done with Nelson Rockefeller"! I assured him nothing could and hurried on to my luncheon appointment.

As a matter of fact, in my own state of New York a group of conservatives were at that very moment getting ready to "do something with"—or at any rate to—Nelson Rockefeller, though it was scarcely what poor old Carroll Reece had in mind.

Rockefeller's nomination and election as governor of New York in 1958 had made the Republican party in the state his personal fiefdom and committed it to his brand of liberal Republicanism. Since the only other major Republican officeholder in the state was Senator Jacob Javits, who was to the left of Rockefeller, there was clearly not much consolation for conservatives in the New York GOP of the early 1960s. Worse yet, there seemed little hope that matters would improve in the foreseeable future: Rockefeller's limitless wealth would finance his reelection as governor while he pursued the presidency. (He was already widely regarded as the front-runner for the 1964 nomination.) And Javits's hammerlock on the large ethnic Jewish vote in the state (delivered through the small but crucial Liberal party, which regularly gave him its nomination), combined with the votes he could expect to garner on the Republican line, made him almost equally invulnerable.

To be entirely fair, Rockefeller, though indisputably liberal in many of his policies, was no left-winger. On matters involving defense and foreign affairs—subjects which, however, rarely came within the purview of a governor of New York—he was relatively hard-line. But his attitude on the general subject of welfare was "compassionate" enough to satisfy the most demanding liberal, and his fiscal policies, which he professed to regard as conservative, got faster and looser as he went along. His special invention, the Urban Development Corporation bonds, for which the state allegedly had a "moral obligation" but not a legal one, and which as a result led the way when New York City sagged toward bankruptcy in 1974, was simply the gaudiest and most irresponsible of Rockefeller's successive plans for raising and spending more money on state projects. Nevertheless, Rockefeller was exasperated at conservative intransigence toward him. "I'm hard on defense and fiscal policy and soft on welfare. You've got two-thirds of me—what more do you want?" was the plaintive way he put it to one group of conservatives he was wooing. His exasperation was returned by conservatives, with interest.

It was the existence of the little Liberal party in New York that set one group of conservatives to thinking, after Nixon's defeat in November 1960. The Liberal party was the spin-off and surviving component of the old American Labor party, which had been founded to enable miscellaneous leftists to vote for Roosevelt in the 1936 election without sullying themselves by associating even briefly with Tammany Hall. The ALP had acquired an explicitly pro-Communist tilt, however, and when this became intolerable after World War II, David Dubinsky and his International Ladies Garment Workers Union split off and formed the Liberal party. Thereafter this little "party" resided almost entirely in Dubinsky's hip pocket, seldom getting more than 100,000 or 200,000 votes in a statewide election. But that margin was often decisive, or at least potentially so. A candidate who could get the Liberals' blessing was halfway home, as far as the state's cautious Democratic bosses were concerned; and a Republican who was liberal enough to receive it—e.g., Javits—had an edge over every other Republican on the ticket. Year after year the Liberal party pushed both major parties in New York perceptibly to the left of the positions they would have taken in its absence.

Why not, certain young Wall Street conservatives reasoned, form a Conservative party in the state, to endorse some Republicans and run candidates in the general election against others? Under the leadership of a remarkable pair of brothers-in-law— Kieran O'Doherty and J. Daniel Mahoney, both attorneys—the effort was organized and pointed squarely at the gubernatorial election of 1962.

One important point: Neither in 1960 nor thereafter was the New York Conservative party regarded by its sponsors as the precursor of a national third-party effort. It was solely and simply the response of New York conservatives—most former Republicans, but including a surprising number of former Democrats—to a state of affairs in New York politics which they regarded as unbalanced and intolerable.

The story of the New York Conservative party's birth throes and its subsequent struggle to survive has been well told by the party's longtime chairman, J. Daniel Mahoney, in his book *Actions Speak Louder* (Arlington House, 1968). In 1970 the party scored its most dazzling triumph, electing James Buckley to the U.S. Senate on the Conservative line alone, defeating both the Democratic and Republican candidates. Today, still under Mahoney's shrewd and farsighted leadership, it is an accepted part of New York's unique quadripartite political scene and since 1966 has regularly outpolled the Liberal party.

For our present purposes it is sufficient to note that the impetus which resulted in the successful launching of New York's Conservative party manifested itself late in 1960, in the wake of Nixon's defeat by Kennedy, and that the founding members were busy right through 1961, laying the organizational and financial groundwork for their effort. Like the foundation of Young Americans for Freedom, the formation of the New York Conservative party was an instinctive move, by a significant category of conservatives, to translate their principles into effective action in the political sphere. (Like YAF, too, they hung their hats for a time in Marvin Liebman's hospitable PR office.)

There were roughly similar conservative parties formed in

the early 1960s in half a dozen states, sometimes with the explicit intention of participating in a national third-party effort, but they lacked the local inspiration that Rockefeller and Javits provided to conservative New Yorkers. Besides, the biggest conservative political drive of all was hovering in the wings, and it had nothing to do with the idea of a national third party. Instead, in less than four years it would actually capture the Republican party itself.

One major factor influencing the conservative movement to seek control of the Republican party in the early 1960s, rather than found a new party of its own, was the sheer disarray of the GOP after Nixon's defeat by Kennedy. The party had not a single leader of truly national dimensions. Eisenhower had retired; Nixon had been discredited by his defeat; Goldwater was the spokesman of what seemed a very narrow segment of opinion; and Rockefeller was the victim of the animosities his liberalism had created. The analogy that insistently forced itself upon my mind, as winter turned into spring, was that of a football in play, lying there on the field. Which player would get to it first and take control of the ball?

As so often, the precipitating impulse to action grew out of a victory for the other side. In the YR national convention in June 1961, the long reign of the increasingly conservative coalition built by Clif White and his allies in the 1950s was ended by the election of Leonard Nadasdy, a Minnesota "moderate," as chairman. Early in July I flew down to Washington to repair a few fences after the storm—talk to some of our old friends in the capital and lay plans for the survival and perhaps ultimately the comeback of our conservative faction in the Young Republican National Federation. One of my calls was on Ohio Congressman John Ashbrook, the former YR chairman, who took me to lunch in the members' dining room of the House of Representatives.

Ashbrook and I discussed the void in the GOP at some length, and I found myself thinking nostalgically of that splendid national network of Young Republican allies we had built up, and with which we had won so many conventions, in the 1950s.

"You know, John," I mused, "if we held a meeting of our old YR crowd today, I'll bet it would be about the third largest faction in the Republican party." (Actually I was being cautious; probably only Rockefeller could, at that point, have fielded a larger personal organization than ours.)

Ashbrook agreed, and when lunch was over, he took me back to his office, pulled out the drawer of a metal filing cabinet, and showed me—arranged alphabetically within states—the neat files of the correspondence he had maintained, ever since his retirement as YR chairman two years before, with our friends all over the country.

This was a remarkable group of individuals—perhaps forty or fifty people in all. In 1961 their average age was thirty-five or forty, and like White, Ashbrook, and myself, they had retired from YR politics. But they had been, in almost every case, longtime leaders of the Young Republican organizations in their states, and now they had simply transferred their influence and activity to the senior party. Already they were, in many cases, political leaders in the Republican party in their states.

More important still, all of them had had long and uniformly successful experience working with Clif White and each other in the YR national conventions of the 1950s and looked back on those years as the Good Old Days. They had developed, to a high degree, a sense of team spirit and mutual loyalty as well as a formidable expertise in the black art of winning conventions. Finally, with few exceptions (Charlie McWhorter, the YR chairman who became Nixon's administrative assistant, was perhaps the most important), they had, like White and myself, grown steadily more conservative during the preceding ten years.

I had no doubt whatever that if invited to a reunion and confronted with a proposal to help draft Barry Goldwater for the 1964 Republican nomination, these old friends of ours would be overjoyed at the chance to work together again. With my mind abuzz with such speculations, I returned to New York and phoned Clif White.

White, whose name has already featured in this narrative as the real leader of Young Republicans during almost the entire decade of the 1950s, was and is a remarkable man, and we must now pause to regard him more carefully.

He was born in 1918 in upstate New York, took his degree (in social science) at Colgate, and served as a navigator on a B-17 in the Eighth Air Force in Britain in World War II. Home again, married, and with children coming along, he found work as an instructor in political science at both Cornell University and Ithaca College, and became active in his local Young Republican organization. His lanky form and innately modest personality were soon familiar in YR circles all over the state, and in 1950 he was elected president of the Young Republican State Association. (I became, in that same year, the chairman of its board of directors—a lesser post.) In 1951 White led the successful battle of the Dewey-Eisenhower forces for control of the YR national convention and was thereafter the undisputed leader of the national YR movement until our joint retirement from YR politics after Ashbrook's election as chairman in 1957.

During Dewey's last term as governor (1951–55), White accepted a post in the state administration as deputy commissioner of motor vehicles. After the Republicans' defeat in the gubernatorial election of 1954 he managed to earn an adequate living as a political consultant for various businesses, instructing their middle management in effective participation in local politics. In 1958 White was associated with the brief and unsuccessful effort of Walter Mahoney, majority leader of the State Senate, to challenge Rockefeller for the Republican gubernatorial nomination, and in 1960 he had a leading role in the national campaign committee called Volunteers for Nixon.

Along with everybody else in our national YR faction, White had learned from his experiences during the 1950s, and by the opening of the new decade he was undoubtedly one of the ablest politicians of the managerial variety then active in the Republican party. Unfortunately his modesty had its disadvantages, and as a result, he was widely underappreciated by many professional politicos whose skills were far inferior to his own. But I had known and worked with him closely since 1949, and I was positive that he was the man to head the drive for conservative control of the GOP.

We discussed the idea over lunch one day in mid-July in the Tudor Room of the Commodore Hotel (now the Grand Hyatt). I was still unsure, in pure theory, that the Republican party would ever consent to serve as the vehicle for the conservative movement; but it was where all our political contacts were, and it struck me as inexcusably wasteful not to put them to work. More-

over, the GOP sccmcd ripe for a takeover, if not by us then by
someone else. White grasped my point at once; in fact, it is hard to
believe that some such idea was not already hovering just below
the conscious level in his creative mind. We agreed to think it over
and meet again.

After several more talks over the phone and face-to-face, we
invited John Ashbrook to fly up to New York early in September to
help lay concrete plans for a reunion of our old YR crowd. The
three of us drew up an invitation list, regretfully excluding those
few old friends who we knew would be uncomfortable in a caucus
as conservative as the one we were engaged in putting together.
All in all, there were about twenty-six names on the list we finally
assembled, and we divided up more or less equally the job of getting in touch with them by phone and inviting them to our little
get-together. One of our Illinois contacts reserved the nccessary
number of rooms in a motel on South Michigan Boulevard in Chicago. (Chicago was a favorite city for national political caucuses of
all sorts because of its excellent transportation facilities and its
proximity to the geographic center of the nation's population,
which at that time was in a cornfield in south-central Illinois.) A
date was set: Sunday, October 8, 1961.

It is impressive testimony to the loyalties engendered during
our years in the Young Republican movement that of the twenty-
six people from all over the United States who were invited to join
us at their own expense in Chicago on the appointed day, nineteen
actually did so—making twenty-two present in all. Since this was
the meeting and these were the people who launched the draft of
Barry Goldwater for the Republican presidential nomination—a
drive that not only succeeded but placed the Republican party
under new and more conservative management that has continued
ever since and thus led by demonstrable steps to Ronald Reagan's
election as president in 1980—it is worthwhile to examine the individuals involved in some detail. In addition to White, Ashbrook,
and me, they were:

Charles Barr, of Illinois, an extremely knowledgeable lobbyist for
Standard Oil of Indiana among the legislatures of the Midwest.

James Boyer, of Louisiana, a close friend of White's and a nominal
Democrat (the only even nominal Democrat at the meeting), whom
White had come to know and respect as a Volunteer for Nixon in 1960.

Donald C. Bruce, a Republican congressman from Indiana.

Robert F. Chapman, of South Carolina, a businessman and soon to be Greg Shorey's successor as chairman of the Republican State Committee.

Ned Cushing, of Kansas, the young banker and Republican state finance chairman whose election as national YR chairman in 1959 had first demonstrated that New York and its allies could be beaten, in a convention representative of the national GOP, by a coalition of the South and West.

Sam Hay, of Wisconsin, a businessman and chairman of the Milwaukee County Republican Committee.

Robert E. Hughes, treasurer of the state of Indiana.

Robert Matthews, also of Indiana, a former chairman of its Republican State Committee.

Gerrish Milliken, of Connecticut, one of the owners and officers of the textile firm of Deering Milliken, Inc.

Roger Milliken, of South Carolina, Gerrish's brother and board chairman of Deering Milliken, Inc.

Roger Allan Moore, of Massachusetts, an attorney, counsel to the Republican State Committee, and chairman of the board of National Review, Inc.

Robert Morris, of Texas, president of the Unversity of Dallas.

David Nichols, of Maine, chairman of the Republican State Committee.

Len Pasek, of Wisconsin, a businessman and friend of White's.

Speed Reavis, Jr., of Arkansas, another Volunteer for Nixon recruited by White.

John Keith Rehmann, of Iowa, businessman and Republican politico.

Greg Shorey, of South Carolina, chairman of the Republican State Committee.

Charles Thone, of Nebraska, Republican national committeeman from that state.

Frank Whetstone, of Montana, a small-town newspaper publisher and general *éminence grise* in the Republican politics of Montana.

This was the group that gathered at the Avenue Motel in Chicago on the morning of October 8, 1961, to spend the afternoon conferring and the evening dining together and reminiscing about the inevitable Good Old Days.

Clif White presided, by common consent, at the formal meeting. Those present knew in a general way what was up for discussion—concerted action of some sort in the senior GOP, looking toward a conservative outcome for the Republican national convention of 1964. They also were well aware that this very probably meant a drive for the nomination of Barry Goldwater. Most of the twenty-two, in fact, were (like myself) already enthusiastic advocates of precisely that course. But all twenty-two were politicians and shared a healthy instinct against premature commitments. In addition, several were in delicate political situations in their home states which could be seriously compromised if it became known that they had signed up for a particular nomination drive almost three years ahead of the convention. So the conferees stayed deliberately short of making a firm decision to back Goldwater specifically and instead circled cautiously around the idea, assessing conservative strength in the party in more general terms.*

White opened the conference by presenting an overview of the situation in the Republican party and stressing its tempting vulnerability to a well-organized drive to capture it and turn it in a more conservative direction. He discussed Nixon's plans (which now clearly included a 1962 bid for the governorship of California) and where they might lead; Rockefeller's obvious ambition and the chances of thwarting it; Goldwater's strengths and also his weaknesses (lack of a large-state base, etc.). He also touched on the condition of the Republican National Committee and its finances. Nor did he overlook President Kennedy and ways in which he might be beaten for reelection in 1964.

Even at this early stage, White's analysis followed the basic lines already at least dimly familiar to everyone in the room: The road to victory over liberalism, both in the 1964 Republican convention and thereafter in the general election in November, had been blazed by Cushing's victory over New York and its pro-Rockefeller allies in the YR national convention of 1959. It lay through a coalition of the East-Central states (Taft's old stamping grounds—Ohio, Indiana, Wisconsin, and Illinois), the South, and the West. Never in modern memory had this combination defeated New York and its relatively more liberal allies (Pennsylvania and Massachusetts, plus a bevy of smaller states in the East, the Midwest, and the Northwest) in a Republican National Conven-

---

* On top of everything else, of course, Goldwater himself knew absolutely nothing about our meeting and had not authorized anybody at all—let alone us—to start working for his nomination.

tion. But the demography of the nation was changing. The old Democratic "Solid South" had been cracked here and there by conservative Republican candidates, who would now be making their voices heard in the national GOP. And the population shift to the West was already under way, making many states in that vast region both larger in population and more conservative in their politics than they had been in the days of FDR.

Beyond such considerations, almost everyone present shared White's and my own instinctive conviction that there was "a tide in the affairs of men" which, for a change, was running in our direction: the conservative direction. America had had a long romance with liberalism, and the Democratic coalition that had sustained that affair was now all too clearly in trouble. John Kennedy was popular, but more so in Washington itself and in his native Northeast than in the country at large. He and the liberalism he represented were deeply vulnerable in the South and the West. To the men around the table in the Avenue Motel, it seemed very probable that a major swing to the right was impending in American politics.

Accordingly, the group asked White to take the lead in drawing up a plan of action and a budget and decided to meet in Chicago again in just two months' time: on Sunday, December 10. Meanwhile White was also to call on Senator Goldwater and advise him of the existence of the group, whose defined purpose at this stage remained simply to turn the Republican party in a more conservative direction. White accepted his assignment provisionally, with a decision on his longer-range role to await developments.

Once back in New York, I concentrated on helping Clif set up the proposed appointment with Goldwater. White knew the senator casually, but as publisher of *National Review* I was on slightly closer terms with him, so on November 9 I sent a letter to his Arizona home, requesting a meeting. It was Goldwater's first notice of the existence of what was to become the National Draft Goldwater Committee:

Dear Senator Goldwater:
    I am sending this letter to you Special Delivery at your home in Phoenix, because a development is taking place which I think is

potentially of the utmost importance, and which rather directly concerns you.

Briefly, a number of us who started out together in Young Republican politics, and who are now all active in major ways in the senior Republican Party in various states around the country, realized two or three months ago that collectively we represent a by no means negligible fraction of the national GOP. Drawing up a list, and including contacts we have made more recently but with whom we are now extremely close, we found that the list included a number of Congressmen, several Republican state chairmen, some influential county chairmen and some of the important finance people, to name only four categories.

Weeding out the list to exclude wide divergences in age (a process which resulted in a group with an average of about 40), we proceeded to invite 26 people to meet in Chicago on Sunday, October 8th. No less than 22 came, from 15 states all over the country; and it is a tribute to their seriousness that nobody even inquired, until the meeting adjourned about 5:30 P.M., who had won the World Series game that afternoon.

The group that met in Chicago on October 8th has set some serious goals for itself, and for the Republican Party. It constituted itself a permanent (though informal) committee for these purposes, and elected my old friend and political ally Clif White (about whom I have spoken to you previously) as chairman and, hopefully, full-time coordinator of the whole project. Given his experience and ability, this insures that the whole thing will not just fade away, as such projects sometimes have a tendency to do.

The whole committee meets again in Chicago on Sunday, December 10th. Meanwhile it wants a small delegation of its members to meet with you, to outline to you the plans of the group. The composition of the delegation will of course depend, to some extent, on where and when it can arrange to meet with you; but a likely combination is White, Roger Milliken, state chairman Charles Thone of Nebraska, Congressman John Ashbrook of Ohio and myself.

Your office in Washington has told me how crowded your schedule is between now and Christmas, but I do most earnestly hope that you can carve an hour or two out of it for a serious talk with our delegation. I would not bother you about this, as I think you know, unless I were convinced that it represents the beginning of the most serious professional effort in almost a decade to turn the Republican Party into a more conservative channel.

Would you, therefore, please let us know where and when you might be able to meet with us? The eastern United States is naturally a little easier for us, but I have no hesitation in saying that all of us would be happy to travel to Phoenix, if you feel that would be preferable. Since I will be away from my office during most of the next two weeks, allow me to suggest that you reply directly to Clif White, who knows that I am writing to you and who will be awaiting your response. His office address is: F. Clifton White, Suite 523, 122 East 42nd Street, New York 17, New York. The telephone number is: Murray Hill 2-4767.

I hope you enjoyed your vacation, and that you are ready for the exciting year ahead—and the perhaps still more exciting ones that lie beyond it. With all good wishes to you and to Mrs. Goldwater, I remain

> Yours cordially,
> /S/   Bill

Senator Goldwater promptly instructed his Washington office to arrange an appointment. Ultimately it was set for November 17, on which date, as luck would have it, neither Roger Milliken, John Ashbrook, nor I could be in Washington, so Clif White and Charlie Thone were the Chicago group's sole representatives.

They described the October 8 meeting to the senator in detail, identifying it as an effort to turn the GOP into more conservative paths. There was no hint that it might metamorphose into a Goldwater campaign organization, and indeed, White got the impression that Goldwater was pretty much resigned to Rockefeller's nomination in 1964. But the alignment of forces in the party being what it was, everyone in the room, including the Arizona senator, must have understood his very special relationship to the group that had come together in Chicago.

Goldwater expressed his pleasure that somebody beside himself was at last ready to lend a hand at trying to conservatize the GOP. He agreed to White's request that the members of our group be given the names of Goldwater's own contacts in their areas, so that their efforts could be coordinated. White and Thone, in turn, promised to keep Goldwater informed of our progress.

Encouraged by the success of this first contact with Goldwater, White flew to Chicago on December 9 to greet and chat with the assembliing troops. The weather over the Midwest closed in during the night, and five of our friends who had attended the October meeting were unable to fly into Chicago at all: Ashbrook, Bruce, Cushing, Hughes, and Matthews. Eleven additional invitees, however, had made it in time and joined us on the morning of the tenth around the conference table in the Avenue Motel. They were:

Samuel Barnes, of California, a friend of White's and former chairman of the Orange County Republican Committee.

Sullivan Barnes, a South Dakota attorney who had been our (successful) candidate for the chairmanship of the Young Republican National Federation in 1953.

Edward O. Ethell, administrative assistant to Senator Gordon Allott of Colorado.

Richard Herman, of Nebraska, an Omaha businessman we had first met through our Young Republican activities in the 1950s.

Albert E. Fay, the Republican national committeeman from Texas who, along with Roger Milliken and others, had insisted on putting Barry Goldwater's name before the 1960 convention.

John Mather Lupton, a Connecticut advertising executive and member of the State Senate.

William G. MacFadzean, of Minnesota, a Minneapolis businessman and lobbyist with a solid grasp of the politics of every state in the northern Great Plains.

Governor Donald Nutter, of Montana, who was to lose his life tragically just a few weeks later, in the crash of a National Guard plane en route to visit his friend Frank Whetstone in Cut Bank.

John Rousselot, a former YR chairman of California who had just been elected to Congress from suburban Los Angeles the preceding November.

Elton E. ("Tad") Smith, Republican state chairman of Texas.

John Tope, an executive of Republic Steel with extensive contacts in both business and politics, whom White and I had helped elect YR national chairman back in 1949.

A casual glance at this set of names, and those listed earlier as present at our first meeting on October 8, may leave the impression that there was something oddly miscellaneous about this group. Nothing could be further from the truth. On the contrary, their friendships had been forged, in many cases over a dozen years, in the heat of many political battles. They shared, more-

over, a common conviction that a turn toward conservative principles was essential for the nation and also the road to victory both
in and for the Republican party. Rarely has a political grouping of
comparable size been able to boast a similar combination of dedication, cohesion, and ability.

As in October, White presided, and he opened with a report
on the visit he and Charlie Thone had paid to Goldwater. The
senator was clearly still a long way from declaring his candidacy
for the 1964 presidential nomination, but that did not particularly
disturb us. The group itself, as I have already indicated, considered it far too early to settle irretrievably on a Goldwater candidacy anyway, though everyone was well aware that that was what
the future seemed to hold in store. Meanwhile it was enough that
we were preparing to organize Republican conservatives for action.

White next submitted the budget and plan of organization for
a full-time effort that he had been asked at the October meeting
to draw up. For 1962, he calculated, he would need $65,000: a
salary of $24,000 for himself, plus one for his indispensable
secretary, Rita Bree, and the rental cost of a small office in New
York. The rest of the money would cover White's phone and travel
expenses.

Then, turning to a map of the United States, White divided
the country into nine regions (New England, the Middle Atlantic
states, etc.) and proposed, mostly from the group around the table,
a part-time director for each. These people would be responsible
for finding state directors for the states in their regions, who in
turn would organize their states down to at least the congressional
district level and, if possible, the precinct level. No state would be
overlooked or "written off"; the organization would be national
and comprehensive, for we knew that there were conservatives,
and therefore potential allies, in the Republican organizations of
even the most liberal states. Recruits would also be sought, and
were sure to be found in large numbers, in the party's auxiliary organizations: the Republican Women and the Young Republicans.
Civic leaders, too, who were not personally active in politics but
were known to be broadly conservative would be approached.

Contrast White's vision of the national effort to conservatize
the GOP with the well-financed effort of Governor Nelson Rockefeller, then already under way, to nail down the 1964 presidential

nomination for himself. Rockefeller was following "by the book" the traditional means of rounding up convention support. Approaches were being made to the leading Republican officials in every state where Rockefeller was believed to have a chance. If a prospect nibbled, he would then be flown to New York in one of the Rockefeller family's private planes and ushered into the smiling presence of the Candidate himself. There he would be subjected to whatever blandishments a staff of diligent researchers had suggested might have the best chance of working. Quite a few leading Republicans, seduced by this treatment, signed up and came aboard the Rockefeller Express.

Years later, in the summer of 1964, after Barry Goldwater had been nominated on the first ballot by the Republican convention in San Francisco, a shocked political commentator for a liberal Iowa newspaper expressed in a column his astonishment and dismay at the sheer cheekiness of the Goldwater backers. They hadn't, he complained, even consulted the established national leaders of the party—men like Dewey, Rockefeller, and Nixon— before setting out to draft and nominate Goldwater!

It was quite true. White knew that if the contest was confined to a battle for the support of the existing leaders of the Republican party (such as they were, in its debilitated condition), conservatism was bound to lose. The leap from the careful "moderation" of Eisenhower and Nixon to the exuberant and unapologetic conservatism that was then welling up all over the country was simply too great for the average politician to make. Rockefeller might be a bit too liberal for many such people; but he was going through all the right motions, and in any case, his liberal bark was no doubt worse than his bite. Besides, hadn't the liberal John Kennedy defeated the moderate-to-conservative Richard Nixon for the presidency in 1960?

White, therefore, proposed to waste no time on campaign techniques that were as routinized and predictable as the mating dance of the whooping crane. As he saw it, and was to put it in 1967 in his own book-length account of the Goldwater draft, "the situation was ripe for revolt."* Say, rather, "for revolution," for it was nothing less than a revolution that White and his colleagues were planning—the seizure of control of the Republican party by

---

* F. Clifton White, *Suite 3505* (Arlington House, 1967), p. 50.

brand-new forces, based in the Midwest, the South, and the West rather than in the East and dedicated to the fast-growing cause of conservatism rather than to either liberalism or that pusillanimous cop-out called moderation.

White's budget and organization plan were discussed, with a short lunch break, right through the day, and in the end they were approved with few changes. Considerable thought was given to what to call our little group, and the final decision was as shrewd as it was surprising: nothing. Any such title as the Committee to Draft Goldwater would be repudiated instantly by the senator, and names along the lines of the Committee to Conservatize the Republican Party sounded ridiculously pretentious. Besides, we were not eager for publicity at this stage. By not giving our effort a name, we succeeded brilliantly in avoiding it.

As the meeting was ending, I remember Governor Nutter of Montana asking permission to say a few words. He spoke with intense earnestness of the importance of what we were setting out to do and pledged his utmost help. And then he requested us to join him in a simple prayer, to ask divine blessing on our efforts. It suggests something of the mood in that room that what amounted to a political caucus ended in such a way.

The bad weather had now moved eastward, and my flight to New York was canceled owing to fog at the airports there, so I extended my stay at the Avenue Motel for another night and joined nearly a dozen other becalmed members of the group for dinner at a Chicago restaurant. It was a convivial affair; politicians are rarely so happy as when they have embarked on a course they believe in and which they are convinced has a real chance of succeeding. Although we could not know it that evening in Chicago, our cause was to prosper indeed.

It was at this point that I decided to take the editors of *National Review* into my confidence with respect to the activities of Clif White's group. Buckley and various of the others had been aware in a general way, of course, that I was flying off from time to time for political caucuses in Chicago and elsewhere with my old Young Republican cronies; but the precise focus of our activities had not been explained to them, and I was eager to let them know what an important project was in the works.

Accordingly, after the senior editors had had one of their regular fortnightly dinners, in this case in a private dining room at
New York's Westbury Hotel on Tuesday, January 2, 1962, I asked
them to stay a few minutes longer so I could tell my tale. Buckley
himself, as I recall, had to catch a late train to Connecticut and
begged off, as did his sister Priscilla, who had become our managing editor; but Burnham and William Rickenbacker (Captain
Eddie's son, who had recently become a senior editor), were staying overnight and agreed to linger for a nightcap while I described
the anonymous group that was quietly organizing the GOP for
conservatism and (implicitly) for Goldwater.

I am not sure precisely what reaction I expected from these
two old friends—perhaps I was naïve enough to suppose they
would be as excited by the prospects as I was, though it was unreasonable to assume that, on the basis of one brief account, they
could grasp the idea as clearly or take it as seriously as I did. But I
was certainly not prepared for the reception I did encounter,
especially from Burnham, which rather reminded me of the pleasure expressed by a parent when a retarded child does exceptionally well in school. He and Rickenbacker heard me out, expressed
their gratification, and praised the initiative of my political colleagues, but it was clear that they didn't take my report seriously.
It was rather as if the whole series of events I was describing
hadn't actually occurred. Brooding over the discussion afterward, I
hit on an explanation which I later formulated mordantly as one of
Rusher's Laws: *No* National Review *editor ever believes anything
until he has read it in the* New York Times.

We are all much more dependent than we realize on certain
sources for our information. An extreme example would be those
cynics of old who "never believed anything until it was officially
denied by the British Foreign Office." More typically, we tend to
credit what we read in some favorite newsmagazine or some supposedly authoritative newspaper. I don't go so far as to say that
National Review's editors believe everything that appears in the
Times. Far from it! But particularly where domestic news is concerned, the fact that a report has appeared in the *Times* tends to
have a sanctifying or, more precisely, a *reifying* effect. If the
story hasn't been in the *Times,* it is, at the very least, suspect.

In the case of my little scoop (which, of course, was not for immediate publication in any case, but for what journalists would call background), no whisper of these events had yet reached the *Times,* so it was extremely hard for my colleagues to take them seriously. Rusher was, of course, telling the truth, but the whole thing was no doubt wildly exaggerated.

So as the months went by, I duly reported, in our regular editorial conferences, on the spectacular progress in the organization of the Goldwater forces for the 1964 Republican convention, and my colleagues nodded amiably and took care to understate the story in their editorials in the magazine and the Bulletin. It was only early in 1964, when Lyndon Johnson himself told a press conference that by Johnson's own count, Goldwater was well ahead in the race for the Republican nomination, that I had my revenge. Up until that point the media had snoozed happily on, in the wholly unjustified belief that Nelson Rockefeller was the front-runner. (The *Times'* James Reston had gone so far as to declare that "Nelson Rockefeller is in no more danger of losing the Republican nomination than he is of going broke.") Those on the Draft Goldwater Committee knew better, of course; but the media would not listen, and it eventually began to seem fairly pointless to keep on telling them. Johnson's statement, therefore—coming as it did from a certified authority with no visible ax to grind—shook the Washington press corps wide-awake, and within days the *New York Times* and just about every other newspaper and television station in the country were echoing Johnson's astonishing discovery and publishing detailed descriptions of the key Goldwater organizers. The next time I walked into a *National Review* editorial conference I was greeted with smiles that might have been appropriate for a brand-new and highly distinguished senior staff member whom nobody had ever met before. The *Times,* you see, had spoken.

One probably inevitable by-product of the growing size and importance of the conservative movement was a number of major personnel changes, and a few sharp struggles for power, in various of its components at about this time. *National Review,* as we have seen, was spared power struggles—as distinguished from internal disputes over issues and personalities—by the saving grace of Buckley's monopoly of the voting stock. But Willi Schlamm had broken with Buckley and left the magazine in 1957. In the spring of 1959 Suzanne LaFollette had retired, seizing the occasion of some now-forgotten difference of opinion to account for her departure. And now in the early 1960s Willmoore Kendall's long friendship with Buckley began to curdle as Buckley, in his late thirties and growing into his role as conservatism's chief non-officeholding spokesman, inevitably came to depend less heavily on his old mentor. Kendall, a formidably brilliant but distinctly prickly man, reacted by interpreting every difference of opinion or failure to consult him as a rebuff. For a time Frank Meyer and Brent Bozell mediated the constant quarrels, but at first slowly, then decisively, Kendall moved away from the magazine. A bit later Bozell, too—a proud personality, who must have found it difficult to live comfortably in Bill Buckley's shadow—began to occupy himself independently with Catholic affairs, taking a distinctly ultramontane position.

These important places were quickly filled with new people more easily reconciled to working under Buckley. One key appointment, however, went to someone scarcely "new." Priscilla Buckley succeeded Suzanne LaFollette as *National Review*'s managing editor, a position she has held ever since. Priscilla, the only one of the ten Buckleys in her generation who did not marry, had worked as a reporter for the United Press in Paris and could legitimately claim to have more authentic journalistic experience than anybody else on the magazine, including her famous brother. Certainly as managing editor she brought to the daily management of the magazine's editorial operations a professional touch, plus diplomatic skills, that have been absolutely indispensable to its success and possibly even to its survival. Priscilla defers to Bill as the editor in chief; to this day, he makes all major decisions. But when Priscilla chooses to insist, it is Bill who defers. As Secretary of State Richard Olney said to the British during the Venezuela boundary dispute (except that he was speaking of the United States in relation to the Western Hemisphere), "[her] fiat is law upon the subjects to which [she] confines [her] interposition."

Over at *Human Events,* the early 1960s also brought changes, and these, too, were relatively peaceful. James Wick had become its publisher in 1955, taking the burden of the business's management off the hands of editor Frank Hanighen, who detested such details. Gradually Wick acquired ownership of the publication, and when Hanighen died suddenly of a heart attack early in 1964, Wick was left in sole control. He himself, however, was ill with cancer and died in November of that same year.

Fortunately a younger generation of conservatives—Tom Winter, Allan Ryskind, and Robert Kephart—had begun working for *Human Events* in the early 1960s and they were able to purchase the publication from Wick's estate and carry on in his spirit and Hanighen's. Kephart eventually sold his interest to Winter and Ryskind to concentrate on other business affairs, and the latter two remain its dominant figures today: Winter as editor and Ryskind as Capitol Hill editor.

As for the John Birch Society, it remained peaceably, and apparently permanently, in the control of its founder, Robert Welch, until his retirement in 1983. No doubt the society's bylaws or other corporate documents made his control unmistakably clear. Welch did have the guidance of a national council of some twenty-eight members, but if dissension ever arose in this body, it stayed there, without rippling the placid surface of the society. The organization remained remarkably free, too, of the sort of kiss-and-tell defectors ("I Was Robert Welch's Chef," or whatever) whom the liberal media have often cultivated to damage individuals and organizations they dislike.

One conservative organization, however, was less fortunate in the matter of quarrels. Control of Young Americans for Freedom, founded in September 1960, was vested under its constitution in a national board of directors of twenty-five members elected at its biennial conventions. Since this board chose all the full-time staff members of the organization and actively dominated its policies, the temptation to form factions and acquire majority control of the board was overpowering from the start to a number of healthy young conservative politicos. It remains to this day YAF's worst and most intractable problem.

The form the power struggle in YAF took in 1961 was extraordinarily curious. The organization's staff had been housed from the outset in the PR office of Marvin Liebman on lower Madison Avenue. Liebman, who had innocently fallen into the role of a sort of rich and adoring uncle who could deny these youngsters nothing, unwittingly spoiled a number of them badly. They were allowed, even encouraged, to spend the organization's funds lavishly—by which I do not mean to imply anything improper. I remember, though, Liebman's complaining helplessly to me that one board member had charged, and been reimbursed for, expenses on a weekend round trip between Boston and Philadelphia that were in the neighborhood of a thousand 1961 dollars. It was simply a case of some young men's inexperience in handling money being matched by an older man's inexperience in handling young people.

Far worse, however, was the growing evidence in 1961 that certain highly dubious forces were maneuvering to take over YAF. As the site of its founding meeting—the Buckley estate in Sharon, Connecticut—implied, the organization's general ideological position was more or less congruent with that of *National Review:* stoutly conservative, but not at all Birchite. Now it transpired that one board member who was personally close to Robert Welch was interested in acquiring control of the board. So was another, who had indirect ties to Nelson Rockefeller. What made the situation especially piquant was that both of these directors, and their factions (for they each had allies), correctly perceived the relatively centrist bloc of pro-*National Review* directors as the chief obstacle to their triumph—and they joined hands to overpower it.

Welch and Rockefeller, in league, through their youthful agents, to wrest control of the national board of YAF from the friends of *National Review!* When Liebman, now confronting ugly rebellions almost daily, appealed to me for help in midsummer 1961 and I had analyzed the distribution of forces on the board, I hardly knew whether to laugh or cry. It was apparent, though, that action would have to be taken, and swiftly, if YAF was to be saved from the clutches of this zany coalition.

So, at the age of thirty-eight, and for the first time since I retired from Young Republicanism after Ashbrook's election as YR national chairman four years before, I waded back into the murky waters of youth politics: phoning, conferring, pleading, politicking, *ad nauseam.* The climax came at a meeting of the national board in Liebman's office on September 2—the Saturday of a mercilessly hot Labor Day weekend. To make matters worse, the office air conditioner wasn't working, so we almost literally steamed all afternoon. The battle entailed elaborate parliamentary arabesques plus repeated votes on key issues. Again and again the outcome hung by a thread. When it was all over, the *National Review* faction had won, but I cannot recall many occasions on which I have felt so exhausted.

That critical victory put an end to the hopes of Rockefeller and Welch that forces loyal to them would ever control Young Americans for Freedom. YAF's national board remained loyal to the conservative mainstream as represented by *National Review* and forgot (for a time) its bitter internal rivalries in the growing excitement of the drive to nominate Barry Goldwater for president in 1964.

Thus 1961 drew toward its close. Almost any way you wanted to count it, the conservative movement was now at least six years old and could boast some solid achievements. It had, for one thing, several respectable, though not large, publications to sound its themes and keep informed conservatives in communication with one another. It had two or three grass-roots membership organizations serving the same important purposes. It had made its presence heard and felt, albeit not altogether effectively, in the Republican National Convention of 1960. Although the general public was not yet aware of this, separate efforts were under way to create a new Conservative party in New York State to do battle with liberal Republicanism on its home grounds, and to organize at the national level a massive effort to take control of the Republican party and make it the political vehicle of the conservative movement. Last but by no means least, conservatism had in Barry Goldwater and Bill Buckley two spokesmen—one in the political arena, the other in the field of journalism—who had already dented the public consciousness and imprinted thereon the basic theses of their cause. Conservatism was not yet a success—far from it—but it was fast becoming a recognized "presence in the room."

That, no doubt, is why the leaders of the dominant liberal segment of opinion decided about this time that it was necessary to address this disagreeable phenomenon squarely. Ignoring it— the basic strategy adopted by the liberals in the mid-1950s and pursued with religious devotion ever since—hadn't worked. Accepting it as a legitimate presence on the cultural and political scene was, it went without saying, simply out of the question from the standpoint of the ruling dogma. There remained only one alternative: It must be denounced. The denunciation would take various forms, depending on which particular liberal enterprise was being heard from: The humorists would poke fun at it; the theologians would anathematize it; the social scientists in all their variety would analyze and "expose" it; the journalists would throw mud at it; the politicians would turn their backs on it; the editorialists would probe and underscore its weak spots; etc., etc.

To Bill Buckley, who had undergone his own personal baptism of fire after the publication of *God and Man at Yale,* and later watched the ritual condemnations of *National Review* when it first appeared, the process was unpleasantly familiar: He called it the echo-chamber effect. First one liberal opinion source would take up the cudgel, and then another, followed by yet another, and then still others, until the very rafters in the arena of political commentary were ringing with variations on the same central theme. There was no conscious conspiracy involved in this process (though it was not altogether unknown for a given theme first to appear in channels susceptible to Communist suggestion and then to widen out into the liberal community like ripples in a pond). The organs of liberal propaganda began discussing the conservative movement about 1961 because they no longer really had any choice in the matter. They denounced it because, in strategic terms, that was much their wisest course. If their denunciations sounded strangely alike, it was for the same reason that the noises made by a flock of geese sound strangely alike. Conspiracy had nothing to do with it.

Since the liberal opinion molders knew their job well, it took them no time at all to zero in on the young movement's weakest link: its more extreme elements and, above all, the John Birch Society. The bizarre conviction of Robert Welch, the society's founder and president, that Dwight Eisenhower had been "a conscious, articulate instrument of the Soviet conspiracy for all of his adult life" was a positive godsend. Not surprisingly, it had proved beyond Welch's powers to keep his startling conviction a secret once he committed it to paper in his privately circulated book *The Politician* (also called, in honor of its cover's color, *The Black Book*). Attempts to separate membership in the John Birch Society from any necessary affirmation of this particular article of faith were only partially successful—not least because some members were willing to accept Welch's leadership even in this particular revelation.

But after Eisenhower's retirement from the presidency in 1961 not even blind fanaticism on the subject of his supposed services to communism could keep Welch from looking a little ridiculous. If a "conscious, articulate instrument of the Soviet conspiracy" had stepped down from the presidency and handed it over to John F. Kennedy, that was surely a major step in the right direction, wasn't it? The situation at the top of the U.S. government had thereby gotten spectacularly better, hadn't it? Or—horror piling upon horror—was Kennedy himself still *another* secret Communist, installed by Eisenhower's masters in the Kremlin and ordered to continue his predecessor's dirty work? And if so, what about all the other presidents who would file through the Oval Office in the years ahead?

It should be stressed that most members of the John Birch Society wasted little time dwelling upon such absurdities. They agreed profoundly, though, with Welch's broader contention that secret Communist machinations were at the bottom of most, if not all, of the troubles of the American society. Grimly, quietly, without ostentation, they set to work to rectify this situation: staffing the society's bookstores (for Welch and his colleagues believed strongly in the power of the written word and authored a flood of literature, from the monthly *American Opinion* and the weekly *Review of the News* to the books published by his Western Islands Press); distributing leaflets, bumper stickers, and pins promoting JBS themes; holding membership meetings where their numbers justified this; and anonymously backing certain approved conservative candidates for public office.

Naturally enough, the society was stronger in some areas than others, with a large part of its membership (out of a national total of perhaps 60,000) based in relatively affluent suburbs, especially in the South and West. Here and there some conservative candidate for office in such an area incautiously joined the society. (It later transpired that John Rousselot, our California YR ally who had been elected to Congress in 1960, was one of these.)

By and large conservatives who were not in the society—and this was, of course, the vast majority—tended to scoff at its devotion to the conspiracy theory. At the same time they were unwilling to denounce its entire membership as a bunch of unsavory crackpots—the course the liberals were implicitly demanding they follow. Early in 1961 Bill Buckley, disregarding both internal and external attempts to dissuade him from addressing the subject in the magazine, had recorded *National Review*'s attitude in a carefully drawn series of answers to questions that were frequently being put to it:*

Q. Why is there so much interest in the John Birch Society?
A. Because there is so much interest in the quickening tempo of conservative activity. The Liberals, and to the extent their programs coincide, the Communists, feel threatened by the revived opposition. Accordingly they have taken hold of a vulnerable organization and labored to transform it into a national menace.
Q. What is the John Birch Society?
A. An organization of men and women devoted to militant political activity. Its principal aims are to arrest the Communist conspiracy, and resist the growth of government. It is dominated by its Founder, Mr. Robert Welch of Boston, who has plenipotentiary powers within the organization.

Q. What has been the history of the relations between Robert Welch and *National Review?*
A. I have myself known Robert Welch since 1952. I have read all his books, and most of his articles and editorials. He bought stock and debentures in *National Review* in its early years (less than one per cent of our original capital). We have exchanged over a dozen letters, and spoken from the same platform on two occasions. I have always admired his personal courage and devotion to his cause. In 1958, after reading his privately circulated book, *The Politician,* I wrote him to say I rejected totally his thesis about Eisenhower as a conscious agent of Communism, as also the supporting presumptions of endemic disloyalty elaborated in that book. I wrote that I hoped to show him his thesis was incorrect. . . .

Q. Doesn't *National Review* believe the Communist conspiracy is a deadly serious matter?
A. Most definitely we do. But we certainly do not believe it is in

---

* *National Review* (April 22, 1961), pp. 241–43.

control of the government, as Mr. Welch maintains not only in the so-called *Black Book,* but in many issues of his monthly magazine and bulletin. . . .

Q. To what extent does the membership of the John Birch Society subscribe to Mr. Welch's views?

A. It is impossible to answer that question categorically. There are, presumably, some members of the Society who subscribe to Mr. Welch's views on all matters, even incuding his views on the allegiance of Mr. Eisenhower. I myself have never met a single member who declared himself in agreement with certain of Mr. Welch's conclusions. I therefore assume that the overwhelming majority of the members of the Birch Society, never aware of Mr. Welch's *Black Book,* were caught completely by surprise at the revelation of some of its contents by the press.

Q. Is it possible to consider the *Black Book* as totally irrelevant to the John Birch Society?

A. No, for the reasons I have touched on. The *Black Book* itself rests on the conspiratorial theory of history, and other mistaken premises about the causes of America's recent defeats. Those premises and assumptions deeply influence the literature of the John Birch Society.

Q. Do you believe the charges that members of the John Birch Society are fascistic, and crackpot?

A. Such charges are as irresponsible as any of the charges attributed to Robert Welch. I do not agree with some of the corporate projects of the Society, but I cannot think of one that is so scandalous or so mischievous as, for instance, the call for nuclear disarmament, or world government, or what have you, upon which the press at large has yet to register its anxiety, or scorn.

Q. Why, then, are these charges being made so widely?

A. Certain elements of the press are opportunizing on the mistaken conclusions of Robert Welch to anathematize the entire American right wing. In professing themselves to be scandalized at the false imputation of pro-Communism to a few people, the critics do not hesitate to impute pro-fascism to a lot of people. In point of fact, the only thing many of these critics would dislike more than a conservative organization with vulnerabilities, is a conservative organization without vulnerabilities.

Q. What is the future of the John Birch Society?

A. I hope it thrives, provided, of course, it resists such false assumptions as that a man's subjective motives can automatically be deduced from the objective consequences of his acts.

Barry Goldwater, pressed again and again to repudiate the support he received from the society, repeatedly refused, insisting that the society was supporting him, not he the society. Besides, he said frankly, some of "the best people in Phoenix" were among its members. (One of these, it was learned years later, was Denison Kitchel, who was to serve as Goldwater's campaign manager in the 1964 campaign.) But Goldwater concluded, too, that the Republican party, and in particular his conservative wing of it, had to put daylight between itself and Welch's cockeyed theory about former President Eisenhower. (He was urged toward this conclusion by Republican colleagues in the Senate who, as practical politicians, simply regarded Welch as a "loose cannon" capable of doing serious harm to the GOP by propagating this particular canard about the party's most recent and most popular president.)

None of these careful efforts, however, managed to deflect the liberal attack that now began. The most important blast was delivered by President Kennedy himself, in the course of a speech to a Democratic fund-raising dinner at the Hollywood Palladium on November 18, 1961. Sensibly enough, though quite unfairly, Kennedy ignored the large and growing number of responsible conservatives and zeroed in on the movement's extremes:

In recent months I have spoken many times about how difficult and dangerous a period it is through which we now move. I would like to take this opportunity to say a word about the American spirit in this time of trial.

In the most critical periods of our nation's history, there have always been those on the fringes of our society who have sought to escape their own responsibility by finding a simple solution, an appealing slogan or a convenient scapegoat. Financial crises could be explained by the presence of too many immigrants or too few greenbacks.

War could be attributed to munitions makers or international bankers. Peace conferences failed because we were duped by the British or tricked by the French or deceived by the Russians.

It was not the presence of Soviet troops in Eastern Europe that drove it to communism, it was the sell-out at Yalta. It was not a civil war that removed China from the free world, it was treason in high places. At times these fanatics have achieved a temporary success among those who lack the will or the vision to face unpleasant facts or unsolved problems.

But in time the basic good sense and stability of the great American consensus has [sic] always prevailed.

Now we are face to face once again with a period of heightened peril. The risks are great, the burdens heavy, the problems incapable of swift or lasting solution. And under the strains and frustrations imposed by constant tension and harassment, the discordant voices of extremism are heard once again in the land. Men who are unwilling to face up to the danger from without are convinced that the real danger comes from within.

They look suspiciously at their neighbors and their leaders. They call for "a man on horseback" because they do not trust the people. They find treason in our finest churches, in our highest court and even in the treatment of our water. They equate the Democratic party with the welfare state, the welfare state with socialism and socialism with communism. They object quite rightly to politics intruding on the military—but they are anxious for the military to engage in politics.

But you and I and most Americans take a different view of our peril. We know that it comes from without, not within. It must be met by quiet preparedness, not provocative speeches.

And the steps taken this year to bolster our defenses—to increase our missile forces, to put more planes on alert, to provide more airlift and sealift and ready divisions—to make more certain than ever before that this nation has all the power it will need to deter any attack of any kind—those steps constitute the most effective answer that can be made to those who would sow the seeds of doubt and hate.

So let us not heed these counsels of fear and suspicion. Let us concentrate more on keeping enemy bombers and missiles away from our shores, and concentrate less on keeping neighbors away from our shelters. Let us devote more energy to organizing the free and friendly nations of the world, with common trade and strategic goals, and devote less energy to organizing armed bands of civilian guerrillas that are more likely to supply local vigilantes than national vigilance.

Let our patriotism be reflected in the creation of confidence rather than crusades of suspicion. Let us prove we think our country great by striving to make it greater. And, above all, let us remember that, however harsh the task, the one great irreversible trend in world history is on the side of liberty—and so, for all time to come, are we.

Though Kennedy did not identify his targets by name, the media quickly remedied the omission. The next day's *New York Times* carried on page one a by-line story by Tom Wicker from Los Angeles that began as follows:

> President Kennedy spoke out tonight against the right-wing John Birch Society and the so-called Minutemen in a speech at a Democratic party dinner here.
> The President mentioned neither group by name but left no doubt whom he meant.

The "echo-chamber effect" now swiftly took hold in the media. *Time* magazine's issue for November 24 began its lead section, "The Nation," with an account of Kennedy's speech entitled "Thunder Against the Right." Noting that similar attacks had come, more or less simultaneously, from the Department of Social Action of the National Catholic Welfare Conference, the Union of American Hebrew Congregations, and Attorney General Robert Kennedy, it nevertheless concluded that "The most telling criticisms of the extremist group were delivered by President John Kennedy.... It was a speech, said aides, that Kennedy had long wanted to get off his chest."

In an article in the *New York Times Magazine* for November 26 entitled "Report on the 'Rampageous Right,'" Alan Barth, a noted liberal journalist and editorial writer for the *Washington Post*, broadened the attack to include a somewhat wider spectrum of conservative organizations and personalities and explained their existence, in pseudoclinical terms, as essentially a psychopathological phenomenon:

> Frustration, which produces tantrums in babies, can lead to equally irrational fits of rage in adults. Unhappily the contemporary world is, in many respects, a frustrating one. It is rotating not only on its axis but on all its axioms as well. It is involved in profound change—in its international power relationships, in its eco-

nomic organization, in its social arrangements. And so it confronts many Americans with inevitable alterations in ways of life they cherish and with insurmountable obstacles to ways in which they want their country to move. . . .

That there is a great deal of frustration in the land today is made evident by a proliferation of societies, leagues, committees, councils and crusades which propose to stop the clock—or to turn its hands back to some easier, earlier time when men could move more readily and directly to achieve what they wanted. How to classify these groups politically raises a difficult problem in semantics.

They are commonly called "Rightist"—a term which connotes conservatism. But in sober truth there is nothing conservative about them. They are much more in a rage to destroy than a fervor to conserve. . . .

Sometimes they are referred to as the "radical right." But the fact is that there is nothing radical about them. They offer no novel solutions to the problems that plague them; indeed, they offer no solutions at all. They are immensely discontented with things as they are and furiously impatient with almost everyone in public office who can in any way be held responsible for their frustrations. But it cannot be said that they hold any clearly stated objectives or have any specific program either in common or individually. They are fundamentally and temperamentally "aginners." And perhaps the commonest characteristic among them is anger. They can fairly be called, if nothing else, the Rampageous Right.

Barth then went on to identify three "lowest common denominators of philosophic outlook" that, he declared, characterized these pesky groups: (1) They "tend to see complex problems simply, and to define problems in terms of 'either-or' choices"; (2) they "subscribe wholeheartedly to the conspiratorial, or devil, theory of history and tend to attribute every frustration to betrayal by traitors"; and (3) they share "a deep distrust of democratic institutions and of the democratic process—a distrust, in short, of the people."

In addition to identifying the John Birch Society and the Minutemen as among the organizations he was describing, Barth specified one other example: the Christian Anti-Communist Crusade headed by Dr. Fred Schwarz. Then he poured his ink indiscriminately over the rest of the conservative movement, saying darkly, "A score or more of Rightist groups are now vying with one another for supremacy"—but naming none of them.

Newsweek got into the fray belatedly but enthusiastically with its issue for December 4. The cover story was entitled "Thunder on the Right: The Conservatives, the Radicals, the Fanatic Fringe" and featured a photograph of Major General Edwin A. Walker, who had allegedly "taught troops Birch dogma."

Like its title, the article made a halfhearted attempt to distinguish the extremist elements in the conservative movement from its responsible core, but its conclusion treated the entire phenomenon as a potential danger to national unity:

> Just what effect today's thunder on the right will have no one can say definitely now, of course; President Kennedy believes that the voices of extremism will be muffled in due course by "the good sense and stability of the American consensus," and he is probably correct.
>
> Even so, the frustrated fanaticism in evidence now is not to be shrugged off. The nation was not built on distrust and suspicion; it was built by men *together* pledging their lives, their fortunes, and their sacred honor.
>
> There are crises today in the cold war more hazardous and more trying than any the nation has ever known in the past—and now, as ever, only in union is there strength.

Time magazine returned to the attack in its issue dated December 8, with a long article entitled "The Ultras."* Once again the emphasis was on the more extreme rightist personalities and groups, and—like *Newsweek*—*Time* ended its analysis by stressing the need for national unity:

> Simply denouncing the policies of the far right is not likely to temper its fanaticism, for it thrives on martyrdom—and is only too happy to add its critics to its list of subversives. If the members of the far right are to be wooed back into normal channels of political expression, politicians must patiently face the task of convincing them that at the present time the real danger to the nation lies from without, and that the way to fight that danger is to encourage unity at home and unflinching policies abroad that reflect the best interests of the U.S.

---

* At *National Review*, assistant publisher Jim McFadden became so exasperated at the liberal practice of preceding the word *conservative* with the prefix *ultra* that he incorporated the magazine's commercial-art subsidiary as Ultra Arts, Inc.—the name under which it prospers to this day.

The December 10 issue of the *New York Times Magazine* carried an article by Thomas M. Storke, editor and publisher of the *Santa Barbara News-Press*, entitled "How Some Birchers Were Birched," recounting an exhilarating tale of how his publication had, over a period of months, attacked the activities of the John Birch Society so effectively that it was (allegedly) all but put out of business in Santa Barbara—a Herculean job of stable cleaning for which he had subsequently received the Lauterbach Award of the Nieman Foundation for Journalism, an annual prize for "outstanding work in defense of civil liberties."

Meanwhile, the electronic media were, of course, as eager as their brethren in the print division to join in the attack. One particularly successful stroke was delivered during a Walter Cronkite interview with former President Eisenhower on the CBS television network on November 23. Cronkite managed to lead the general into a discussion of military men who express opinions "on political matters or economic matters that are contrary to the President's"—something Eisenhower promptly condemned as "bad practice—very bad." Lest the significance of this passage be lost on the nation, the *New York Times'* two-column story on page one the next day explained that Cronkite "did not cite, but obviously referred to," *Newsweek*'s cover man, Major General Walker. Cronkite then elicited from Eisenhower a further typically vague but nonetheless useful jab at unspecified "extremists": "I don't think the United States needs super-patriots. We need patriotism, honestly practiced by all of us, and we don't need these people that are more patriotic than you or anybody else."

The important thing to note about this whole barrage (aside from the spectacular echo-chamber effect) is how deftly emphasis was placed on the John Birch Society and a handful of other relatively extreme organizations and individuals. Such responsible national spokesmen of the conservative movement as Goldwater and Buckley, far from being acknowledged as its spokesmen and leaders, were mentioned and quoted only when they themselves condemned right-wing extremism—as they were (rightly) quite willing to do. Such reputable conservative organizations as Young Americans for Freedom, the Intercollegiate Society of Individualists, the American Enterprise Institute, and Americans for Constitutional Action, as well as such publications as *National Review*,

Human Events, and *Modern Age,* were not mentioned at all. The possibility that the conservative movement might have something constructive to contribute to our national political dialogue was not so much as considered; the notion that it might someday actually become a major force in American public life was deemed too absurd to mention.

No doubt the apologists for our liberal media would argue today, in the light of hindsight, that they were talking only about the extreme right: They simply weren't *discussing* Goldwater, Buckley, and responsible conservatism. To which the response is: True; but why not?

In any case, the net effect of the liberal barrage was a dramatic upsurge in the amount of media attention thereafter devoted to the conservative movement—virtually all of it, to be sure, hostile. The biennial indexes published by the *Readers' Guide to Periodical Literature* record the upswing in conservative coverage. The *Guide* indexes by topic, in alphabetical order, all articles appearing in 125 periodical publications. The publications to be indexed are chosen by a vote of the nation's librarians every five years and in general are the most widely read and/or highly regarded periodicals in the country.

From March 1, 1957, to February 28, 1959, the *Guide*'s listing of articles on conservatism, both pro and con, consumed just 1¾ inches. In the *Guide* for the period from March 1, 1959, to February 28, 1961, it required 4 inches. In the *Guide* for the ensuing twenty-four months—from March 1, 1961, to February 28, 1963—the listings under "Conservatism" covered 18 inches, or well over a two-column page. About a fifth of this total—some 3½ inches—was attributable to listings of articles in *National Review,* which the librarians in 1960 voted to index (the first conservative publication so honored); but even with these excluded, the number of indexed articles on conservatism in those two years represented an increase of at least 350 percent over the number in the preceding two.

By the end of 1961, therefore, the conservative movement had, so to speak, been formally introduced to American society, even though its debut had been largely sponsored and orchestrated by its worst critics. From now on it might be denounced and condemned, but at least it wouldn't be totally ignored.

Chapter V

Draft Goldwater!

As far as conservative politics were concerned, one of the major early events of 1962 was the mass rally sponsored by Young Americans for Freedom in Madison Square Garden (then at Eighth Avenue and Forty-ninth Street in New York City) on Wednesday, March 7. The inspiration and organizing know-how were Marvin Liebman's, but the drive and enthusiasm that made the affair the huge success it was belonged to the youthful conservatives themselves. For the first time the media were forced to acknowledge that conservatism was developing that sine qua non of democratic politics: significant numbers.

It was no easy matter for a political movement to fill Madison Square Garden, even free of charge and in the midst of a major election campaign. YAF did it in an off year, when not even the mayor was running, and actually charged money for tickets, grossing $80,000. To be entirely accurate, there were about 18,000 people present; the auditorium could have held a few more if every seat in the topmost balconies had been occupied. But such saturation was a counsel of perfection; the point was that the Garden looked and for all practical purposes was comfortably full, and the great hall rang to the rafters with the cheers of young conservatives as their heroes came forward to address them.

The proceedings were paced by that most indispensable ingredient of any political rally: a loud and lively brass band. First, members of YAF's national board stepped up to the microphone to announce the recipients of the organization's "second Annual Awards." These, not all of whom were present in person, included former President Herbert Hoover, Senator Strom Thurmond (R., S.C.), the Honorable Charles Edison, John Dos Passos, Dr. Ludwig von Mises, Roger Milliken, Professor Richard Weaver, M. Stanton Evans, and John Wayne. There was also a "Special Award" to Moise Tshombe, president of the breakaway Congolese state of

Katanga, "for his contributions to the cause of freedom and anti-Communism."*

The two featured speakers of the evening were Senator John Tower and Senator Goldwater himself, but those who were there agree that the evening's most electric moment came when the keynote speaker, Brent Bozell, nailed to the mast conservatism's central theses in the field of foreign policy. It is some measure of the distance America has traveled since 1962, in the matter of military capacity when compared to that of the Soviet Union, that Bozell's bold proposals now sound so impossibly visionary:

> What the West needs today, above all other things, is faith in itself. . . . If we know our mission, we will then find the steel in our backs to carry it out, and the orders will go out:
>
> To the Joint Chiefs of Staff: Make the necessary preparations for a landing in Havana.
>
> To our commander in Berlin: Tear down the Wall.
>
> To our chief of mission in the Congo: Change sides.
>
> To the Chairman of the Atomic Energy Commission: Schedule testing of every nuclear weapon that could conceivably serve the military policies of the West.
>
> To the chief of CIA: You are under instructions to encourage liberation movements in every nation in the world under Communist domination, including the Soviet Union itself; and you may let it be known that when in the future men offer their lives for the ideals of the West, the West will not stand idly by.

The rally fell far behind schedule, as rallies tend to do, and Goldwater's own speech was pushed into the wee hours—a circumstance that inspired some vintage Arizona profanity backstage. But nobody was leaving, and the welcome Barry Goldwater received when he was finally introduced must have made all the waiting seem worthwhile.

The next morning an astonished nation learned over breakfast that a large number of extremely enthusiastic conservatives, at least some of them apparently quite young, had held a pro-Goldwater rally in New York City the previous night, fully twenty-eight months before the Republican National Convention was

---

* The State Department denied Tshombe a visa to come to New York to accept the award.

scheduled to open. It was one more warning to the observant that conservatism, whatever it was, was becoming a force to be reckoned with.

Meanwhile, the New York State Conservative party had been making impressive progress toward its goal of becoming an official party in the state. New York's laws were designed to render such a thing virtually impossible, requiring that a new party must obtain, for its gubernatorial candidate, nominating petitions containing the signatures of at least 50 registered voters in each of the state's sixty-two counties, and a total of at least 12,000 signatures altogether. If by any chance some new party performed this miracle, its candidate for governor would duly appear on the ballot, but the party as such would not achieve continuing "official" status unless said candidate thereafter received at least 50,000 votes in the election. If, against all the odds, he did so, the party would be recognized as an official party in the state, entitled thereafter to have its candidates for office nominated by the same statutory procedures that applied to the Democratic, Republican, and Liberal parties: certification by its state committee or other appropriate body, subject to provisions for primaries where a nomination was contested. But official status would be lost if the party's candidate for governor ever polled fewer than 50,000 votes.

It was the genially democratic custom of New York's major parties not to contest the often highly dubious nominating petitions filed by the gubernatorial candidates of such splinter parties as the Communists and the Socialist Workers, because everybody knew they had no chance whatever of polling 50,000 votes in the election and there seemed no great harm in letting them run. But it was soon apparent that Nelson Rockefeller's Republican State Committee intended to take no such amiable attitude toward the Conservatives, who began circulating their nominating petitions for the governorship in the summer of 1962. Orders were issued to every Republican county chairman in the state, instructing him to contest the Conservative petitions to the hilt.

But fate now intervened, not merely once but twice, to assist the Conservatives just when they most needed help. The first intervention initially seemed, as fate's kindest acts so often do, wholly unfortunate. The Conservatives, after approaching unsuccessfully a number of more glamorous possibilities, had succeeded in persuading David Jaquith, a prominent businessman in Syracuse and a leading Methodist layman, to become their candidate for the office of governor. But Senator Jacob Javits, a Republican even more liberal than Rockefeller, was also up for reelection in 1962 and (as usual) was handed the Republican nomination, uncontested, by the Republican State Committee, without having to fight for it in a primary.* The Conservatives, casting about for a suitable candidate against Javits, were delighted when their offer of the senatorial nomination was accepted by a member of a well-known upstate family who had retired not long before from the U.S. Foreign Service. Imagine, then, their dismay when they discovered that this gentleman had, years earlier, twice voluntarily committed himself to a mental hospital—and (of all incredible coincidences) that the attorney who had handled the paper work for him was now Senator Javits's campaign manager!

Swiftly, silently, and painfully, the Conservatives disentangled themselves from their commitment (from which the proposed nominee was bitterly unwilling to release them), and Kieran O'Doherty, the state chairman of the Conservative party, agreed to resign from that position to make the race against Javits. He was replaced as chairman by his brother-in-law, J. Daniel Mahoney, who has served in that capacity ever since.

It reflects no discredit on O'Doherty to say that in Dan Mahoney the New York State Conservative party found the perfect leader—a genial, good-humored, honorable, and highly intelligent man, a skilled attorney, and a masterly politician who quickly won the respect of the fraternity of professional New York politicians of all parties and also of the corps of political reporters who cover New York State politics. It is the simple truth that the survival and success of the Conservative party in the ensuing twenty years, despite all the inevitable disappointments and internecine conflicts, are largely owing to the able leadership of this extraordinary man.

Fate's second intervention that summer likewise involved the appearance on the scene of a key figure. James Leff was one of a small group of conservative Tammany Democrats who, unable to

---

* The first and only time Javits ever had to seek renomination in a Republican primary—eighteen years later, in 1980—he promptly lost to the unknown Alfonse D'Amato.

reconcile themselves to the defeat of Carmine De Sapio by the so-
called Reform Democrats in the struggle for control of the party in
lower Manhattan, had left the Democratic party altogether and
joined the Conservatives. Leff, an attorney whose specialty was
the election laws, was put in charge of legal aspects of the Conservatives' drive to get on the ballot by petition, and he proved brilliantly competent at his job. Taking absolutely nothing for
granted, he delivered to the office of the secretary of state in Albany, on the last day for filing, petitions containing 44,606 signatures for the Conservative nominees for statewide office, including
not less than 200 (or four times the required number) from every
county in the state. The law technically required that the petitions
be filed in a single volume, with the pages numbered serially in the
alphabetical order of the counties—a ridiculous requirement,
since in this case the petitions formed a pile three feet tall. Leff
had been assured orally by the secretary of state's office that it
would be all right to file the petitions in several convenient volumes, but he was unable to get this assurance in writing. So the
clerks in the office of the secretary of state were astonished when
the door swung open on the appointed day and Jim Leff strode
in, dragging a dolly (or wheeled platform) on which rested a
three-foot stack of petitions, properly alphabetized by counties,
serially numbered, and bound in a single huge volume as the law
required.

The attorneys for the Republican State Committee gave those
petitions one of the great legal goings-over of all time but were finally forced to concede that they were dismayingly valid. Almost
worse, various newspapers in the state began calling editorially on
the GOP to stop trying to knock out the Conservative petitions on
some technicality, inasmuch as it was obvious that large numbers
of New Yorkers wanted the party on the ballot. At last the Republican leaders threw in the sponge, and on October 1 they announced that they were dropping their challenge to the
Conservative petitions.

There was a champagne party that afternoon in the Conservative party's offices on Lexington Avenue. I remember seeing
there former Governor Charles Edison of New Jersey—son of the
inventor and a Democrat (in fact, at one time FDR's navy secretary), but a thoroughly conservative one, who had interested him-

self in the conservative movement late in life and was one of the chief "angels" of this fledgling party. Also present were some of the far younger, less famous, and less wealthy people who had worked their hearts out to put the Conservative party on the ballot. (I particularly remember Dan Mahoney's phoning me, one day that summer, to say that two girls who had clerical jobs in the office, and who knew of the party's financial problems, wanted to contribute their life savings of about $1,000 apiece to the cause. He was troubled over whether to accept gifts so overwhelmingly generous in relative terms. I discussed the matter with Bill Buckley, whom we both tended to regard as a sort of moral guru, and was ultimately able to persuade Dan that he should accept the contributions, one of the conservative movement's basic principles being that an individual should have the right to dispose of his property as he or she sees fit.)*

Then it was on to election day. By now there were at least a few movement conservatives in almost every medium-sized town in America—subscribers to *Human Events* or *National Review*, members of Young Americans for Freedom, etc., and Mahoney was able to tap such resources all over the state of New York to organize the Conservative party county by county. In addition, though funds for advertising were vanishingly scarce, it was simply not possible for the media to ignore the new party and its candidates altogether, especially when polls in such widely read newspapers as the *New York Daily News* began showing the Conservatives attracting a respectable minority of the voters.

When the returns had been counted on November 6, the Conservatives were exultant. On the absolutely crucial gubernatorial line, running against the puissant Nelson Rockefeller (who was reelected by a reduced margin), David Jaquith had racked up not merely the essential 50,000 votes but a cool 141,877, with the party's other candidates not far behind. The Conservative party was now, for at least four years, an official party in the state of New York, legally entitled to Row D (since the Liberal party had narrowly outpolled it, thereby retaining Row C) on every ballot. It

* As for James Leff, he was elected to the State Supreme Court in 1968—or in other words just as soon as the Conservative party developed enough political muscle to insist on his designation by the major parties. He has remained there ever since: outspoken, colorful, independent, controversial, but famously incorruptible—widely recognized as one of the ablest judges in the whole state system.

was not a happy augury for Nelson Rockefeller, or for liberal Republicanism in general.

During 1962 the conservative forces that had drawn together under Clif White at our two Chicago meetings in the autumn of 1961 maintained a low profile, organizing silently for the battle ahead. So low was the profile, in fact, that it very nearly disappeared altogether.

Following the meeting in Chicago on December 10, 1961, White and Rita Bree had moved into a two-room suite of offices (the later-famous Suite 3505) in the Chanin Building at Lexington Avenue and Forty-second Street in New York City. Slowly and systematically they began to build a file on the Republican party in every state in the Union: its history, peculiarities, and current leaders; its officeholders, down to and in many cases below the level of state legislators; the names of delegates and alternates to the 1960 and 1956 Republican National Conventions; the names of major contributors and leading conservatives, both in and out of party office; and so on.

In addition, White himself took to the road, to the extent that his exiguous budget for travel expenses permitted. He crisscrossed the country, visiting the part-time regional directors he had designated at Chicago and calling on potential supporters in key states. His job was difficult: to line up support, at least conditionally, for a candidate who had never authorized any such effort, who it was by no means certain would run, and whose prospects of victory in any case—either in the convention or in the general election—were, to say the least, nebulous.

But White had a case to make, and it was a good one and he knew it, and so, instinctively, did most of the people he approached. Goldwater's personal reluctance to run was recognized as genuine but was easy to dismiss. Politicians, after all, are in the business of running for office, and very few of them would actually turn down the presidential nomination of a major party if they could be shown any reasonable hope of obtaining it. Beyond that, the conservative Republicans to whom White spoke sensed that their time—and Goldwater's—was approaching. The disarray in the GOP, the slow but steady disintegration of the old Roosevelt coalition in the Democratic party, the growing strength and significance of the South and West on the national scene—all of these suggested that the time was ripe for the Republican party, under new auspices, to make a major bid for blue-collar support. Again and again White went through the roster of the states, showing his listeners how victory might be achieved.

In mid-April he summoned the group that had met in Chicago to a "working weekend" amid the still-icebound lakes and snowy landscape of northern Minnesota. Minnesota Mining had a lodge near Bemidji for relaxed conferences of one sort or another, but the regular season for its use by the corporation hadn't begun yet, and a sympathetic officer of the company arranged to make it available to us. Once again some thirty people assembled quietly from all over the country—this time at Homan Field, the St. Paul airport, whence two 3M planes transported us in comfort to the lodge.

It was a genial occasion—a reunion of a group of old friends with some very big plans for the future. In the little cabins where some of us bunked, between the main lodge and a nearby lake, or in the lodge itself by a roaring fire, we compared notes and tried to divine the future. White, assembling us for a more formal caucus, called for reports from the regional directors and gave his own estimate of the situation among Republicans in Congress, at the national committee, and in the rousingly conservative women's and youth arms of the party. He also discussed the Rockefeller campaign, which was already in high gear and confidently expected to nominate its tiger in 1964, as well as the attempt of Richard Nixon to relaunch his political career by winning the California governorship in November 1962.

It was agreed that White would spend the rest of 1962 in the quiet work of organization. Then in December, with the midterm elections and all their distractions (and possible lessons) behind us, we would meet again. If the indications were still favorable, it would be time to approach Goldwater.

As matters turned out, those midterm elections nearly spelled the end of our fragile project. Practically everyone present at Bemidji, as well as every other political contact we had, was deeply involved, in some way, in one or another of those elections: either running for office himself or campaigning furiously for someone else. The 1964 convention seemed remote. A governorship here, a seat in Congress there were on the line *now*, in 1962, and November was only a few months away. Worse yet, every one of the few sources of money accessible to us was likewise being drained to finance the campaigns of 1962. Little more than half of the ridiculously low $65,000 that White estimated he would need in 1962 was actually raised. By midsummer he had almost no funds left to cover his travel expenses, and it was a serious question whether he could pay even Rita Bree's modest weekly salary.

White has not, so far as I know, ever publicly revealed that he drew on the funds set aside for his son's college education to keep the nascent Goldwater operation alive during the year 1962. In *Suite 3505* he mentions only that by November he had put $6,000 of his "family savings" into the operation. He adds that one or two major contributors came through in the nick of time, and no doubt this support did help save the day. But the facts concerning White's own sacrifice deserve to be recorded—especially in view of the vicious rumors spread by envious critics (and later apparently even believed, for a time, by Goldwater) that White was actually profiting personally from his unauthorized drive to organize the conservative wing of the GOP.

By such hand-to-mouth means, in any case, the little office survived until the November elections. The results of these included strong Republican gains in the South and West and thereby powerfully fortified the case for a Goldwater nomination. I promptly wrote an article to that effect for *National Review*, entitled "Crossroads for the GOP," which appeared in the February 12, 1963, issue of the magazine. Reprints were offered for sale, and the piece became one of the most popular reprints ever published by *National Review*, with sales totaling tens of thousands of copies. Many conservatives bought it in quantity to distribute to their friends, and it played a not-unimportant role in putting the technical case for Goldwater before Republican politicians in the first half of 1963.*

In the article I pointed out that no Republican candidate was likely to carry either New York or California against President

* In 1965 Professor John H. Schacht of the University of Illinois, in a pamphlet entitled *The Journals of Opinion and Reportage: An Assessment*, prepared for the Magazine Publishers' Association, described this piece as one of the few established instances in which an article in a journal of opinion directly influenced the political process.

Kennedy in 1964 and that in all likelihood any Republican candidate could carry "the GOP's Midwestern heartland, and such peripheral fiefs as northern New England and certain of the Mountain states, amounting in all to perhaps 140 electoral votes (with 270 needed to win)." But "Goldwater," 4 insisted, *"and Goldwater alone* (for in this respect Scranton and Romney are in no better position than Rockefeller), can carry enough southern and border states [with 165 electoral votes] to offset the inevitable Kennedy conquests in the big industrial states of the North and still stand a serious chance of winning the election."

Comparisons of this analysis with Goldwater's actual totals, achieved against Lyndon Johnson after the trauma of the Kennedy assassination, are quite beside the point. Its basic message was that the GOP should look to the southern and border states for the conservative reinforcements it would need to win nationally, rather than try to outbid the Democrats for liberal support. It was an argument that would win many converts as 1963 progressed.

Meanwhile, 1962 drew to a close. It was clearly time for another meeting of our group, and again Chicago was chosen as the site. This time White substantially expanded the number invited, and some fifty-five actually attended—occasioning a transfer of the operation to the somewhat larger and more luxurious Essex Inn, also on lower Michigan Avenue. The date chosen was Sunday, December 2, and those invited began arriving, as usual, the previous day. They included, in addition to the veterans of previous sessions, such important recruits as Ione Harrington, Republican national committeewoman from Indiana; Mrs. Pat Hutar, co-chairman of the Young Republican National Federation; Republican State Chairman Peter O'Donnell of Texas; Congressman William Brock of Tennessee; and Jeremiah Milbank, Jr., of Connecticut, one of the GOP's best fund raisers.

It was clear by now that the conservative standard-bearer in 1964 would have to be Barry Goldwater. There was simply no other conservative with the requisite national stature. Fortunately most of those assembled in Chicago believed that Goldwater would consent to run, and it was quickly agreed that White would approach him as soon as the upcoming holidays were over. Meanwhile, there was plenty of planning to do.

White submitted a budget of $3,200,000 for the entire year

and a half remaining before the 1964 convention (most of it for primary campaigns in early 1964), and a finance committee was designated to start raising that imposing sum. Then, after the plenary session, the regional divisions of the movement were convened separately, to lay plans for a drive aimed at netting 700 delegate votes (with 655 needed to win) before the 1964 convention was even called to order.

Finally, White called the full group back into session and proposed March 1963 as the time for the public launching of the National Draft Goldwater Committee. So it was agreed.

Thus far the anonymity, small size, and instinctive discipline of our group had succeeded in preserving its secrecy. Not so much as a hint of its existence, or of the activities being conducted out of Suite 3505, had appeared in the press. But the group's necessary, though risky, expansion, plus the growing plausibility and therefore newsworthiness of its plans, made it inevitable that the story would leak out, in one way or another, sooner or later. As luck would have it—luck aided, White and I have long believed, by a disloyal young politico whom White had had the bad judgment to invite and who apparently attended wearing a tape-recorder wristwatch—the news of the meeting was leaked to the media just hours after its close, and a hostile account of what took place, containing some tantalizingly verbatim quotations, later appeared pseudonymously in *Advance*, a Ripon Society publication dedicated to the cause of Nelson Rockefeller.

The media, by and large, treated the news that fifty-five Republican politicians had gathered privately in Chicago to promote the nomination of Barry Goldwater as if it were a conspiracy to overthrow the government by force of arms. Walter Cronkite showed his CBS audience TV scenes of the empty suite in which the dastardly plot had been hatched. I particularly enjoyed the editorial denunciation that appeared in the pro-Rockefeller *New York Herald Tribune*, which clearly thought, but did not quite want to say, that political activity by conservative Republicans ought to be against the law: "Neither the plotting to promote Sen. Goldwater for the Presidential candidacy nor the conspiracy to block Gov. Rockefeller contributes to the health or harmony of the party. . . . The conservatives are guilty of bad timing, narrow motives and poor politics."

In one way, we did not greatly mind the disclosure of the existence of our group. The major media, with no justification whatever, had been treating Nelson Rockefeller as the virtually inevitable Republican nominee against Kennedy in 1964. The discovery that efforts were actually under way to deliver that nomination to Barry Goldwater had roughly the disruptive effect of somebody standing up at a wedding and actually stating, as invited, why the happy couple ought not to be joined in holy matrimony after all. It poked a substantial hole, in short, in the supposed inevitability of Rockefeller's nomination.

But the leaks were intended to hurt, not help, our little plan, and in one supremely important way they did hurt it. Barry Goldwater had, of course, known that our group existed and that its purpose was to turn the Republican party into more conservative channels. He must also have known—and known that we knew—that, in practical terms, much the best device for accomplishing this would be his own victorious candidacy for the Republican nomination. But it was also true that Goldwater had not yet decided to make that race, or authorized us to take any steps whatever, however preliminary, on his personal behalf. It can be imagined, moreover, after the leaks about our meeting in Chicago, how many of Goldwater's political associates and supporters must have rushed to him with reproaches about being left out of the secret and with pledges of support if he had indeed decided to run. Understandably Goldwater reacted angrily.

At the same time the individual who was responsible for the leaks, and no doubt other critics as well, appear to have gotten to Goldwater with lurid accounts of how White was paying himself a lavish salary, out of contributions from Goldwater's supporters, to launch a campaign Goldwater had never authorized him to undertake. And that brings us, as well as anything can, to one of the enduring minor mysteries of the history of those days: the curiously unsatisfactory chemistry of the relationship between Barry Goldwater and Clif White.

I had known White since 1949 and knew him to be a man of great tact and restraint and absolutely spotless personal honor. But I was also dimly aware that White often had difficulty—a difficulty I could discern even in his earlier and distant relationship with Thomas Dewey—in getting on relaxed and comfortable terms with a superior. It was not that White was too arrogant; on the contrary, he was if anything too deferential. A man like Dewey or Goldwater (or later Reagan or James Buckley), for whom White worked in a political capacity, seemed to become elevated in White's mind to a level at which easy interpersonal communication became difficult. White tended to conceal this deference, from himself and others, by an almost comical insistence on calling all politicians, however slight his acquaintance with them, by their first names, or even their nicknames: Barry, Nels, Dick, Jerry, and Ron. (I once quipped that he would probably call the pope Paul.) But essentially he was a shy, warm human being who found it difficult to express easily his deep affection for those for whom he worked. Instead he sought to act out his sentiments by truly selfless devotion, informed by silent but flawless expertise.

Unfortunately politicians as a class have no trouble at all expressing, or even feigning, their affection for others and have a hard time imagining that anyone else is different. To more than one of his political idols, therefore, Clif White may have seemed just a particularly nerveless operator with some undeniably useful political abilities.

Unhappily White's inhibitions were complemented almost perfectly by Barry Goldwater's. For Goldwater—half Jewish, from a small western state, projected by fate onto a national scene for which his modesty alone would have told him he was inadequate—was in his way as insecure as White. But the craggy Arizonan had almost nothing else in common with the taciturn "appleknocker" from upstate New York. Perhaps as a cover for his own political nakedness, Goldwater had developed over the years (as his conservative supporters had discovered in 1960) a profound admiration for the Republican party's pros—those professional politicians who, whether as candidates or managers, had climbed the ladder rung by rung and who now held the party's major offices or carried its flag into battle as its designated candidates against the Democrats. In terms of principle, Barry Goldwater was a staunch—in fact, a magnificent—conservative; but in the Senate he admired the pros almost regardless of the way they voted, and often deferred to their well-advertised expertise.

Whatever Clif White's little group consisted of—mostly ex-Young Republicans and nonpartisan ideologues, as nearly as Goldwater could make out—it seemed painfully short of pros. Where in its ranks, bar one or two, were the state chairmen and national committeemen, let alone the senators and governors, that could make a political organization respectable in Goldwater's eyes? Yet this was the crowd that, according to the media, was scheming, without his permission, to draft him!

As a final turn of the screw, White's postholidays appointment to report to Goldwater was coincidentally set for the late morning of the day—Monday, January 14, 1963—on which the new assignments to Senate committees were posted. As it happened, Goldwater failed to get certain assignments he badly wanted—more evidence, he must have suspected, that despite his popularity among grass-roots conservatives he simply wasn't taken seriously by the Senate's pros. Goldwater was therefore as sore as a boil when he returned to his office for his appointment with White.

The result was a foregone conclusion. The senator expressed his anger over the leaked story that the secret meeting in December had been planning to draft him. He hadn't authorized any such thing, and he flatly refused to be drafted. White was ordered to cease and desist from all further efforts on Goldwater's behalf. He came down Capitol Hill, as he glumly put it to me later that afternoon, "looking for a job."

What to do? There was, so far as we knew, no precedent whatever in American presidential politics for drafting a man who really and truly didn't want to be drafted. In desperation I decided to try my own hand at mollifying the senator, in a letter dated January 18:

Dear Senator Goldwater:

I know that Clif White spoke with you in Washington last Monday, and I know too that there are plans for a further get-to-gether in the near future. I hope to be present at the latter, but in case that proves impossible I want to set forth below a few considerations which I think are terribly important, and which I earnestly hope you will bear in mind. Recent newspaper reports—which I realize may not be trustworthy—are nevertheless somewhat disturbing.

First let me emphasize that I understand perfectly well, or think I do, the whole myriad of considerations that incline you against permitting Clif White's organization, or any organization, to solicit money and delegate votes at this stage of the game on the undertaking that, if enough of both are obtained, you will definitely be a candidate for the presidency in 1964. I agree fully with what I understand to be your position on this matter: namely, that it is strategically too early for you to make such a decision, and certainly tactically far too early to announce it. In general, I agree with your view, as quoted in the press in recent weeks, that approximately one year from now will be time enough for making and announcing such a decision, one way or the other.

On the other hand, I am extremely anxious that the time and effort which Clif and I and all the others have expended on our project over the past 15 months or more shall not go to waste—as it inexorably will if we are not allowed to launch, on our own, a national draft-Goldwater organization in the near future.

I think you may not fully realize how far advanced our organizational plans are; how large and influential a portion of the national leadership of the Republican Party, state by state across the country, is involved in them; and what a deadly blow to the morale of everyone concerned—not to mention to the organizational framework itself—a seeming repudiation of this project by you would be. The small office they have maintained would have to close down, and all that would remain would be a few files of names, in mothballs.

Please understand: it is not necessary for you to give your blessing to what we are doing, or indicate that you have authorized or in any sense initiated it. What *is* essential, however, I earnestly submit, is that we be allowed to go ahead on our own. It would be both natural and seemly for you to be able to say that you have heard, in a general way, of our activities; that you are of course flattered; and that—not having started the organization—you do not feel that you are in a position to order it to stop. All this, it seems to me, is fully consistent with your declared intention to wait about a year before making up your own mind.

I hope you won't consider that I have been presumptuous in talking so frankly and so urgently about a matter that, after all, touches you personally and very deeply indeed. But I am profoundly convinced that the organization we have built in the past year is very probably the last one that will ever seek, in a serious and systematic way, to turn the GOP into more conservative channels, and I know that you would deplore as sincerely as I would anything that might prevent that from happening.

No reply to this letter is necessary; I merely wanted you to have these thoughts in hand before you meet with Clif and the others. I trust you know that my own good wishes go with you always.

Faithfully yours,

/S/   Bill

But Goldwater could not be budged. The second meeting between White and the senator, in which White was accompanied by their mutual friend Charlie Barr, took place in Washington on February 5 but yielded no ray of hope. Gloomily we called yet another meeting of our nameless group, this one to be held on Sunday, February 17, in the O'Hare Inn near the Chicago airport.

This time both prudence and efficiency dictated a smaller gathering: Only the hard-core members were summoned to this one, and not even all of these could make it. Present for the key session on the morning of the seventeenth were White, Barr, Frank Whetstone, Robert Matthews, Robert Hughes, Peter O'Donnell, Tad Smith, Andy Carter, Congressman John Ashbrook, and I.

It was one of the strangest political caucuses I have ever attended. As usual White presided, but I cannot recall that he had much to say beyond giving us all a laconic description of his disastrous talks with Goldwater. The people in the room were sincere, even idealistic conservatives; but they were also realists, and they were well aware that without Goldwater's consent, or at least his willingness to refrain from a specific repudiation, our efforts on his behalf were bound to be futile.

And yet . . . and yet . . . the political desperadoes assembled in Chicago felt sure they were onto something. They sensed in their bones that the Republican party was ready for Goldwater and for conservatism, if only Goldwater could be made ready for the GOP. It seemed too cruel a fate to be deprived of such a historic triumph merely because the candidate was, for the moment, not willing to run. We understood, of course, that by agreeing to accept the presidential nomination, Goldwater would necessarily forfeit his rightly prized Senate seat, which would be up that year: He had teased Lyndon Johnson mercilessly, in 1960, for inducing the Texas legislature to rewrite the laws of the state so that Johnson could run for the vice presidency and the Senate simultaneously.

But what did even a senatorship matter, when the stakes in the presidential nomination contest were control of the Republican party and, very possibly, the whole future direction of the United States?

Disconsolately we picked at the problem. The argument was dismally circular. At last, somewhere over my left shoulder, a voice with a midwestern or southwestern twang cut through the gloom: "Let's draft the son of a bitch."

A muffled voice of reason posed the inevitable question: "What if he won't let us draft him?"

To which the first speaker shot back: "Then let's draft him *anyway!*"

It sounded crazy—even desperate. But it hit just the note that those present had, without realizing it, been waiting to hear: Our movement simply would not consent to being stopped by Goldwater's January fiat to White. We would let the draft-Goldwater sentiment demonstrate its breadth and depth; perhaps, in time, it would impress him to the point of changing his mind. Meanwhile, all of Clif White's and Rita Bree's efforts for the past fifteen months would not be wasted; the momentum we had developed would not be lost. Maybe there was a chance after all.

The December plans for announcing the formation of a National Draft Goldwater Committee were therefore swiftly confirmed. As its chairman we chose Peter O'Donnell, the Republican state chairman of Texas (and thus one of those pros Goldwater admired so much, but also a deeply committed conservative and an oilman of independent means—a man, in short, whom nobody could order around). Clif White, of course, would be the committee's full-time executive, with the title of national director. Our state and regional directors, most of them already in place for a year or more, moved smoothly from their anonymous posts into the corresponding public assignments. When the meeting broke up after lunch, it was with the heady conviction that Barry Goldwater would simply not be able to resist what was being put together.

But everything, of course, in fact depended on his reaction. A single denunciatory blast from him, and it would all be over. By the grace of God, however, his reaction—when it came a few weeks later, after the committee's formation was at last announced on April 8 at a press conference in Washington—was, though grumpy, at least bearable: "I am not taking any position on this draft movement. It's their time and their money. But they're going to have to get along without any help from me." Not much, but at least not an explicit repudiation.

Actually there is reason to believe that Goldwater reconsidered and slightly revised his opinion on the subject of a possible candidacy between his talks with White in January and February and the April 8 announcement of the launching of our committee. I was told, for example, that Goldwater had read and commented favorably on my article, "Crossroads for the GOP," which was now circulating widely in reprint form, spreading the gospel that a new coalition, including conservative former Democrats in the South and border states, had a serious chance of prevailing, both in the Republican convention and in the nation at large. And undoubtedly, since the December leak, Goldwater had received advice from many friendly quarters counseling him not to slam the door irrevocably on a race for the presidency.

At any rate, O'Donnell and White quickly bent every effort to get the draft-Goldwater drive off the ground as a public movement. The media responded to the first press release with a collective sneer: "Another" draft-Goldwater committee had been formed, they yawned—not bothering to notice the connection between this one and the secret meeting whose fell purpose they had "exposed" four months earlier. But the response from conservatives around the country was little short of ecstatic. This was the plunge into active politics they had been waiting for, and they responded with vibrant enthusiasm. When the committee held a rally—itself almost unprecedented, coming as it did more than a year in advance of the convention and before its candidate had even privately agreed to run—at the National Guard Armory in Washington on July 4, 1963, buses from all over the eastern states brought upwards of 9,000 Goldwater fans to the capital to cheer speeches by Governor Paul Fannin of Arizona, Senators Carl Curtis and John Tower, Congressman John Ashbrook, and a group of Hollywood personalities.

No doubt my own memories of the year 1963 have been smoothed of many a bump by the softening effects of time, but my recollection of the contrast between that gloomy final meeting of our anonymous group in February and the tremendous upsurge of pro-Goldwater sentiment all over the country during the rest of that year is certainly far from imaginary. Elsewhere I have compared the change to the famous transition between the third and fourth movements of Beethoven's Fifth Symphony. At the end of the third movement all is dark and furtive; the only sound we hear is a few flickering strings against an unrelievedly somber background. Then somehow—we are not quite sure just how—the strings flicker a little higher, and their message becomes more hopeful. Higher and higher they work their way, and suddenly we sense—before we actually hear it—the tremendous crescendo that opens the fourth movement.

That was what happened to the draft-Goldwater movement between winter and summer in that remarkable year 1963. In mid-February there had seemed no hope; even the skies over the O'Hare Inn had been uncompromisingly gray. But from the public launching of the National Draft Goldwater Committee onward, everything seemed to go almost laughably well. To take one small example: The National Guard Armory, where the committee held its mass rally on the Glorious Fourth, had no air conditioning. To fill it with 9,000 people on a July afternoon, given the probabilities of a Washington summer, risked notable discomfort, if not mass heat exhaustion. But the Fourth turned out to be a mild, though brilliantly sunny, day. Naturally (or so it seemed).

The precious files in Suite 3505 were moved to new and larger premises on Connecticut Avenue in Washington, where it had been decided that the national presidential drive should be headquartered. Clif White and Rita Bree accompanied them, and the complex and delicate work of turning the enthusiasm of our Goldwater troops into delegate votes at the 1964 Republican convention rolled forward. When it was all over, the envious author of one book about the campaign betrayed his staggering ignorance of such matters by writing that White's accomplishment was actually negligible, because Goldwater's nomination was practically inevitable—"The trick in 1964 would have been to stop the convention from nominating Goldwater."* This, of course, is utter nonsense. Republican presidential candidates are nominated, not

* Karl Hess, *In a Cause That Will Triumph* (Doubleday, 1967).

by thousands of clamoring ideologues in a National Guard armory, but by about 1,300 specific and carefully selected delegates, chosen by varying processes, not all of them highly democratic, in every state and congressional district in the country. There is, of course, a relation between "what the people want" and what these delegates do, but there is rarely, if ever, a simple equation between the two—especially when, as in 1964, bowing to the popular will entails surrendering forever a control of the GOP that had lasted for decades.

It is the historic achievement of Clif White and his colleagues in the National Draft Goldwater Committee that they brought about that surrender—on the first ballot at that—and laid thereby a solid political foundation for the ultimate victory of the conservative movement in the United States.

The surfacing of the draft-Goldwater movement in the spring of 1963 naturally did not go unnoticed in the Rockefeller camp, and on July 14 Rockefeller counterattacked. The precipitating event was the Young Republican national convention, which was held in San Francisco in late June.

By now these conventions were widely recognized as harbingers of trends in the GOP as a whole. Rockefeller did not take it at all kindly, therefore, when Goldwater's YR backers, united as the conservatives had not been when they lost control of the YRs in 1961, narrowly won the YR chairmanship, defeating a candidate preferred by Rockefeller's supporters. The new Young Republican chairman, Donald E. ("Buz") Lukens, had openly endorsed Goldwater for the presidential nomination before the balloting began.

According to Michael Kramer and Sam Roberts in their investigative biography of Rockefeller, *I Never Wanted to Be Vice-President of Anything* (Basic Books, 1976), Rockefeller's counterattack was conceived as a broad strategic response to the threat now posed by the conservative movement:

> 'Nelson needed an issue," recalls one of his closest advisers "and the extreme right was it." The YR antics served as Rockefeller's excuse to abandon his neo-conservatism, much as his own remarriage had given the party's true conservatives the excuse to abandon him. Rockefeller threw down the gauntlet in the "Bastille Day Declaration" of July 14, 1963. Party harmony had been necessary to his presidential prospects before his remarriage had crip-

pled his plans. Party discord was needed now. And that is exactly what Rockefeller created. . . .

First, Rockefeller had to explain why he had waited until now to denounce the Republican right: "Many leaders of the Republican Party, myself included, have been working to put the party in a position to face the challenge of the 1964 election as a strong and united fighting force."

Moving on, Rockefeller said: "In making this effort toward unity for principle, it was my conviction that the activities of the radical right, while deeply disturbing in many ways, would represent an inconsequential influence on the Republican Party." Rockefeller went on to list "fundamental articles of Republican faith"—preservation of freedom throughout the world, equal opportunity for all, the federal system of government, the free enterprise system, fiscal integrity, freedom of speech and information. "Many of us," said Rockefeller, "have been taking too lightly the growing danger to these principles through subversion from the radical right." . . .

It was time to wake up: ". . . the Republican Party is in real danger of subversion by a radical, well-financed, and highly disciplined minority." As evidence of the impending coup, Rockefeller offered the Young Republican gathering two weeks earlier in San Francisco. It was the only proof he had:

. . . "every objective observer at San Francisco has reported that the proceedings there were dominated by extremist groups, carefully organized, well-financed, and operated through the tactics of ruthless, roughshod intimidation. These are the tactics of totalitarianism." . . .

By refusing to target specifically those who had actually disrupted the Young Republican convention in San Francisco, Rockefeller seemed to be branding all conservative Republicans as radicals. He waited a full month before correcting that impression. In a letter to Jean McKee, head of the New York Young Republicans, Rockefeller wrote of his July 14 declaration: "This statement . . . is not an attack on responsible conservatism in our Party." . . .

But it was, in fact, precisely that, and *National Review* moved briskly to conservatism's defense in a lengthy editorial in its July 30 issue:

Up until recently, Mr. Rockefeller was Number One in the Republican Party, or so he was reported to be by the Gallup Poll. Certainly he never doubted that he was.

And then the decline began. What were its symptoms, and its causes? A diminished majority at the November election; corruption among his closest associates; an outraged reaction to his solemn contention that a rise in "fees" was not a rise in "taxes"; a growing awareness of the fiscal hocus-pocus on which he has relied in "balancing" the budget; his grating erraticism as critic of Mr. Kennedy's foreign policy . . . and then the remarriage—which capped, rather than caused, the decline in his public esteem. . . .

Mr. Rockefeller's present statement . . . can only appeal to a kind of extremist. Only an extremist can seriously believe that America's "radical Right"—however you define it—is "every bit as dangerous to American principles and American institutions as the radical Left." On that point, Dr. Fred Schwarz's response remains the classic answer, that "on the one hand is an international dictatorship disposing of thermonuclear weapons and controlling the movements of one-half the people in the world, while on the other is a candy manufacturer, with one million bonbons." To say that the radical Right "utterly rejects [the] fundamental principles of our heritage" is nothing more than genocidal political polemics, of the drastically irresponsible kind, the left-wing equivalent of the crazy-Right statement that "Washington is controlled by the Communists."

But in that vein Mr. Rockefeller, in a statement dubbed "eloquent" by the *New York Times*, continues. The Young Republicans in San Francisco were "disgracefully subverted" by the radical Right. "Subverted." Another totalist word, from the Republican Party's Great Moderate. Indeed, the Right intends to "subvert the Republican Party itself." Its program would "destroy [the Republican Party] altogether." The Republican Party threatens, under the Goldwater leadership, to become "a party of extremism," "a party of sectionalism," "a party of racism." . . .

These are the words of an overwrought man, who would rather bring down his party and his country with him, than face the fact that the people appear to have no further use for him. What we need, says Mr. Rockefeller, is "unity for principle." His idea of principle is to defame large blocs of the population, to impute racism, fascism, and un-Americanism to all who decline to fawn upon him, to betray a colleague who has scrupulously repudiated the berserk Right and endeavored to preach unity in the Republican Party. So much for principle. Let Mr. Rockefeller preach his ideas of the principled life to his various families, and spare the nation his cynical moralizing. We have, after all, higher dreams to dream than serving as Mr. Rockefeller's constituency.

Thus, as Kramer and Roberts remarked, "The Holy War began":

> The governor seemed eager for combat. He challenged Goldwater to debate (declined) and told a press conference: "The great threat is whether the radical wing, part of Senator Goldwater's following, will be able to capture its leader."
>
> "I'm not going to answer this sort of thing from Rockefeller," the senator replied. "He's using an old trick which the Democratic forces used against us for a long time, and I'm not going to fall for it."
>
> Here was the rub. Rockefeller had happily preached party unity when he seemed certain to be the nominee. Now that the tide had turned, it was no holds barred, and he was giving aid and comfort to the Democratic enemy.

The growing references (often hostile, but still references) to conservatism in the media were now beginning to generate increasing requests for conservative speakers on college campuses, at business conventions, and as a part of various local lecture series around the country. In addition, the conservative activists who existed, at least in small numbers, in virtually every state (e.g., the YAF members who were organizing chapters in many a college) were able to stimulate a certain demand for conservative speakers on fair-play principles even where enthusiasm for conservative ideals was close to nil.

Ronald Reagan had been busy making pro-free-enterprise speeches for General Electric on "the mashed-potato circuit" since the late 1950s, but those of us on the campaign trail for conservatism rarely came across his spoor because his speeches were largely given either to GE employees or to other business audiences. The spokesmen for the conservative movement who hit the road in the early 1960s differed from Reagan in several important respects: Their speeches were much more frankly political and issue-oriented (often with a substantial foreign-policy component), and they concentrated much more heavily on college audiences, partly because they were convinced that the battle had to be fought and won there. Also, whereas GE had originally financed Reagan's talks, the new spokesmen ordinarily charged their travel expenses plus whatever fee the traffic could reasonably bear.

Barry Goldwater himself was, of course, the prime conservative spokesman in those days, with Bill Buckley—thanks to the prominence he had already achieved in radio and television debates—not far behind. A few others, myself included, rounded out the list. Goldwater refused to be drawn into direct discussions of his possible presidential candidacy until early in 1964, but the rest of us talked about little else. These speaking engagements became important means of rallying the Goldwater troops in city after city as 1962 and 1963 progressed.

To be sure, having a conservative spokesman on a college campus didn't necessarily guarantee him a warm reception. Goldwater and Buckley, as certified celebrities, probably received more attention and better treatment than the rest of us, but I can remember literally dozens of occasions on which the college lecture committee, say, having reluctantly added a lone conservative to a list of half a dozen or so liberal and leftist speakers, would insist that his particular speech must, uniquely, take the form of a debate with some radical faculty member—apparently to decontaminate the audience as swiftly as possible. Or, if a local YAF chapter was the sponsor, the college administration often unaccountably delayed permission to use the requested campus auditorium until the very last moment—making it impossible for the promoters to say where, precisely, the meeting would be held. Or when: The college newspaper, through incompetence or sheer malice, frequently got the date or the hour wrong, even though permission to use the auditorium had been obtained.

Still, it would be quite wrong to depict most of these speaking experiences as unpleasant—even in the later sixties when student protests were at their height. On the contrary, we conservative speakers had all the zeal of the early Christian missionaries, and like them we could be sure of a hard core of local supporters, however small. Goldwater in particular was always personally popular with college audiences, and the rest of us were at least the beneficiaries of a growing curiosity.

Perhaps an even more important way of stating the conservative case, and increasing the awareness and responsiveness of the conservative public, was the radio and television "talk show" that now slowly began to open up to conservative spokesmen. The hosts on the late-night radio shows, for example, were always on the lookout for new and controversial "guests" who could be counted on to make the telephone switchboard light up, and about 1960 they began to discover conservatives. Few of the hosts in those early days were (at least openly) sympathetic,* but that scarcely mattered; the point was that such programs afforded a matchless opportunity to counter the barrage of liberal propaganda that dominated the major newspapers, newsmagazines, and television news programs.

The same was true, *mutatis mutandis,* of other sorts of talk shows: radio and TV panel discussions, for example, in which a conservative was now often invited to participate, albeit in a ratio of one to two or three liberals and leftists of varying hues. Even "Meet the Press" and comparable programs would interview suitably prominent conservatives now and then.

The print media were slower to make room for a fair proportion—or even an unfairly small proportion—of conservative columnists, perhaps because the ingredient of *controversy,* which conservatives undeniably possessed and which alone could almost guarantee an invitation to appear on a late-night radio talk show, was not as important in the case of a columnist as *celebrity,* a quality the liberal media still tightly controlled and which, naturally, they tended to confer only on their favorites. Bill Buckley became, in 1962, the first of the new conservative spokesmen to launch a syndicated newspaper column, and even he did not really make a splash in that medium until 1966, well after Goldwater's nomination and defeat and after Buckley's own candidacy for mayor of New York and all the publicity that involved (as will be recounted in due course).

The work of the National Draft Goldwater Committee and the spectacular successes it began to rack up during the year 1963

---

* One exception who deserves mention (and there were others, to whom I apologize for not naming them, too) was Barry Farber, a New York night-radio host who as early as 1960 was frequently inviting conservative spokesmen to appear on his program and making his sympathy for their views unmistakably clear. In 1977 Farber ran for mayor on the Conservative party ticket against the popular Democrat-Liberal Ed Koch and nearly edged Republican Roy Goodman out of second place.

have been fully described by Clif White, with the help of William Gill, in his own account of the Goldwater Revolution: *Suite 3505,* published by Arlington House in 1967. Essentially it was the hard, slogging work that any preconvention nominating campaign in those days entailed: selecting and running candidates for delegates in the states that chose their delegates in primaries, and bargaining with local leaders in the "convention states," where the party machinery still largely controlled the process of choice. But the Goldwater drive early displayed some markedly new characteristics, both ideological and technological, and some of its pioneering procedures are now standard in the convention operations of both major parties.

In the matter of ideology White's basic thesis, of course, was that Goldwater could bring into the Republican camp large numbers of former Democrats and independents—enough to tip the balance in many formerly Democratic strongholds in the South and West and, together with the usual sources of Republican strength, carry the country. As we conceived the coalition in the early years of the decade, the states constituting the potential Goldwater majority would include what until then had long been regarded as the Republican party's Alpine redoubt—the big industrial East Central states of Ohio, Indiana, Illinois, and Wisconsin and the smaller agricultural states of the Great Plains (the Dakotas, Nebraska, Iowa, and Kansas)—plus most of the previously Democratic bastions of the Deep and Border South (Maryland, Virginia, the Carolinas, Georgia, Florida, Kentucky, Tennessee, Arkansas, Alabama, Mississippi, Louisiana, Oklahoma, and Texas), and finally an unpredictable but important share of the states of the Southwest, beginning with Goldwater's own Arizona, and the Rocky Mountain region.

The bonding ingredient of the new coalition would be its common exasperation with the economic and, above all, the social consequences of liberalism. Hard hats, blue-collar workers, and small farmers, all of whom had learned to call the Democratic party home in the long decades when the basic political struggle was against employers and creditors, had watched the growth on their left of a brand-new constituency, accustomed to receiving welfare payments and other forms of subsidies from the federal government. In addition, by 1963 most of the trends that were to typify the decade—the upswing in drugs and pornography, the loosening of sexual restraints, and much else—were already having a powerful impact on voters in many of the states already mentioned. On such people the populistic conservatism of Barry Goldwater and his supporters—as different as anything could be from the eastern Republicanism of Nelson Rockefeller—exerted a powerful attraction.

Not until 1969, with the publication of Kevin Phillips's *The Emerging Republican Majority* (Arlington House), would these political realignments be publicly identified, scientifically established, and properly evaluated. But they had been sensed by many people as early as 1961 and played a vital part in the Goldwater drive and its successful capture of the Republican party.

In assessing the intentions and strategy of the draft-Goldwater leaders, historians of the future will find especially valuable a short documentary film entitled *Choice*, whose production White authorized after Goldwater's nomination (in his reduced capacity as executive director of Citizens for Goldwater-Miller) for use wherever Goldwater's support was large enough to warrant a showing—and by late 1964 that was just about everywhere. When the film is seen today, its grainy black-and-white photography seems painfully dated, but what it was pointing at was crystal clear. Five years before Phillips published his brilliant book, analyzing the trends that had disaffected the "social conservatives" from the old Democratic coalition, White's film—a pastiche of clips—put its finger squarely on the key issues: riots in the streets, school prayer, pornography, etc.

Significantly, Goldwater himself vetoed distribution of the film anywhere at all. Here again, as in his earlier impatience with the conservative ideologues who weren't pros and his later inveterate preference for Nixon (the organization's man) over Reagan (the ideological conservative), we see Goldwater shying away from the very insight that made his candidacy different from any other. At heart Goldwater was, and remains, a perfectly orthodox, budget-balancing, main-line Republican, whose heart beats in near-perfect accord with Jerry Ford's. Tapping entire new veins of political strength, including millions of former Democrats and independents profoundly disturbed over decay in the moral and even religious underpinnings of the American society, simply didn't appeal to Goldwater at all.

The liberals, noting these developments without fully understanding them, promptly dubbed them, for polemical purposes, the Southern strategy. As far as they could see, this strategy consisted simply of recruiting to conservative Republican ranks bigoted Southern red-necks outraged at the wholehearted conversion of the Democratic party to the cause of civil rights for blacks.

Nothing could have misconceived more completely—or underestimated more dangerously—what was actually happening. No doubt the South's white racists swelled both the Wallace vote in 1968 and Nixon's huge margin over McGovern in 1972, as their century-long identification with the Democratic party at last came to an end. But they represented a relatively insignificant proportion of the great body of opinion that pivoted away from the Democratic party toward an independent but unmistakably conservative stance in the decade of the 1960s. Even more important than the South, as the decade rolled on and the states of the North lost population steadily to those of the Southwest and West, were the growing clout and outspoken conservatism of these latter, formerly Democratic bastions.

To me personally—given my midwestern cultural background, my boyhood hostility to things eastern, and my political record (in the Young Republicans) of alliances with upstate New York against the city, and national coalitions against Rockefeller— the concept of a southern- and western-based coalition against the East was both familiar and thoroughly congenial. It was to prove less so to some of my colleagues at *National Review* when they finally became aware of it toward the end of the decade.

Congenial or not, the attraction of the draft-Goldwater movement for former Democrats and independents was powerful. In Texas and other southern and southwestern states during 1963, White had the unprecedented experience of seeing entire Democratic county committees stage "resignation rallies" and join the Republican party en masse to work for Goldwater.

But it was in the GOP itself that the really decisive strides toward a convention victory were being made. In silent fascination, while the media continued to yawp about the inevitability of Nelson Rockefeller, the Goldwater forces watched the senator's strength, in terms of delegates pledged and probable, plus those likely to be elected early in 1964 in the primary states, edge upward toward the point of unstoppability. Barry Goldwater was watching, too, and he now decided it was high time to impose his own control on the movement that was not far short of handing him the Republican presidential nomination on a platter.

There had never been any doubt in the minds of the leaders of the National Draft Goldwater Committee that a time would come when Goldwater himself would have to sanction their efforts, take over control of his own nomination drive, and designate whatever individuals he chose to lead it. Many observers—I among them—assumed that he would simply ratify the then-current assignments of the team that had served his cause so superbly: O'Donnell, White, and their regional and state directors. But everyone recognized that the choice was Goldwater's.

The choice, when it came, took the form of putting the campaign in the hands of what quickly became known as the Arizona Mafia. In the summer of 1963 there came to Washington, quite obviously at Goldwater's behest, a man named Denison Kitchel, a Phoenix attorney who had served as general counsel to the Republican State Committee of Arizona and was currently billed as manager of Goldwater's 1964 campaign for reelection to the Senate. Washington seemed an odd place for the manager of an Arizona campaign to hang his hat, however, and his real purpose became still more apparent when he was joined that autumn by a young Tucson lawyer named Dean Burch who had served as Senator Goldwater's administrative assistant in the late 1950s. Ensconcing themselves in offices in the Carroll Arms Hotel (significantly closer to the Senate Office Building, and therefore to Goldwater, than the headquarters of the National Draft Goldwater Committee on Connecticut Avenue near the Mayflower), Kitchel and Burch, together with a pair of veteran Washingtonians named William Baroody (director of the American Enterprise Institute) and Edward McCabe, became the nerve center of Goldwater's personal political operation. White and the other officials of the committee, recognizing that Kitchel and his colleagues were, for better or worse, Goldwater's chosen instruments, did their best to cooperate with the inevitable, despite a dismaying tendency on the part of the little group at the Carroll Arms to wall off Goldwater from all influences but their own.

No sooner had the Draft Goldwater Committee begun meshing its machinery with that of the Arizona Mafia, however, than the whole political fabric of the nation was rudely shaken by the assassination of President Kennedy on November 22, 1963, and the entry of Lyndon Johnson into the Oval Office. How would this dark and dramatic development affect Goldwater's chances, both for the Republican nomination and in the general election?

In retrospect, it probably damaged Goldwater's chances in the general election considerably, but it was simply too late to keep him from winning the Republican nomination.

It is fashionable nowadays, in view of Johnson's landslide victory over Goldwater in November 1964, to assume that Goldwater was a loser from the start and that Kennedy would, if anything, have trounced him even worse than Johnson did. But this is by no means certain, and it is noteworthy that some disinterested observers didn't think so at the time. *Time* magazine, discussing the Goldwater phenomenon in its issue of October 4, 1963, expressed the opinion that the Arizona senator represented a serious threat to Kennedy: "Until recently most political observers figured that Democrat John Kennedy was a sure 1964 winner, and that it did not make much difference who the GOP candidate would be. Now, many are changing their minds. To be sure, a President is historically at low ebb at the tag end of a pre-election year and between now and November 1964 a lot of things can happen—and probably will. But a state-by-state survey by TIME correspondents indicates that at least Republican Barry Goldwater could give Kennedy a breathlessly close contest."

Bear in mind that Goldwater's popularity as a conservative candidate stemmed in very substantial part from the sharp contrast between his personal and political qualities and those of John Kennedy. Time, and the poignant fact of Kennedy's subsequent assassination, have softened and sanctified our memories of the man; but two decades ago he was a living, breathing politician, not an icon, and a great many people were prepared to consider an alternative in 1964. Kennedy was from the oldest part of the country, the Northeast, and connoted many qualities associated with it: Harvard, great wealth, sophistication, and political liberalism. Goldwater hailed from precisely the opposite and newest corner of the nation, the Southwest, and personified most of the human characteristics associated with its people: a sort of rugged, earthy, manly innocence. If he did not personally hold some of the social-conservative views that were then coming to the fore among large segments of the population, including many lifelong Democrats, most of his political organizers certainly did, and the movement they were coordinating projected its own inchoate fears and longings onto the tall Arizonan.

Kennedy's sudden replacement by Johnson, therefore, was little short of a disaster for Goldwater's hopes of election as president. Instead of confronting a northeasterner, with whom he could contrast spectacularly and perhaps to advantage, Goldwater would now be pitted against a fellow southwesterner, and one bigger in almost every dimension at that: from mighty Texas, not little Arizona; not just a senator, but a former majority leader of the Senate and then, as vice president, its presiding officer; from a background not merely less opulent than Kennedy's, but dirt poor. Worst of all, Johnson, despite his political origins in FDR's New Deal, was identified, and rightly, with the relatively conservative southern wing of the Democratic party. That was why Kennedy, in 1960, had chosen him, rather than Adlai Stevenson or Hubert Humphrey, as his running mate. Goldwater and his managers would never be able to persuade most American voters that Lyndon Johnson represented any of the new tendencies in the country which so many of them feared and opposed.

I confess that this line of reasoning was lost on me in the days immediately following Kennedy's assassination. I was still gripped by the vision of social conservatives joining the Republican party by the millions under Goldwater's banner and was confident that the combination would sweep the country. So, if Kennedy had been our opponent, it might have; so, years later, it did. But 1964 was not to be the time.

Clif White, looking at the scene with the weary but acute vision of a political realist, understood what a blow our cause had suffered. He did not waste much time contradicting my chirping optimism, but he knew already what would happen in November 1964. Meanwhile, there was the Republican nomination to pursue and nail down—no small objective, for with it would go control of the Republican party and its machinery. And for the nomination the prospects still looked bright. The conservative movement's powerful head of steam would carry it that far at least.

Chapter VI

The Watershed Year: 1964

It is a commonplace to say that 1964 was a year of disaster for American conservatism, and of course, in one sense it was: Lyndon Johnson defeated Barry Goldwater that November by 43,126,506 votes to 27,176,799, or 61 percent to 39 percent. Goldwater carried only six states (Alabama, Arizona, Georgia, Louisiana, Mississippi, and South Carolina) with a total of fifty-two electoral votes. It was indeed, as the media proclaimed, "a landslide."

But to say that, and stop there, is to overlook almost entirely the real political significance of 1964. On any serious accounting, 1964 was the most important and truly seminal year for American conservatism since the founding of *National Review* in 1955. It laid the foundations for everything that followed. Before 1964, conservatism was at best a political theory in the process of becoming a political movement; after 1964, and directly as a result of it, conservatism increasingly became the acknowledged political alternative to the regnant liberalism—almost fated, in fact, to replace it sooner or later.

Lyndon Johnson's huge victory had, in restrospect, little significance as a measure of public sentiment. It didn't even nail down Johnson's control of the Democratic party: Less than four years later he did not dare seek renomination as president. Nor (as we shall see) did it have, on the Republican party, the effect of shaking the GOP permanently free from the grip of conservatism and delivering it, as logic might have been supposed to dictate, to Nelson Rockefeller.

The year 1964 actually had three major political consequences, and all of them were favorable to the longer-range prospects of the conservative movement:

1. It handed the Republican party over—permanently, as matters turned out—to a new and basically conservative coalition based on the

South, the Southwest, and the West, ending the long hegemony of the relatively liberal East in the GOP's affairs. Republican conventions were not through making mistakes, but henceforth these would require the participation of substantial numbers of conservatives.

2. It sensitized large numbers of previously dormant conservatives, turned them into political activists, and introduced them to each other through direct-mail techniques.

3. It launched the political career of Ronald Reagan and thereby provided the conservative movement with its most important political leader.

That is quite a lot for any one year to accomplish, and it is why thoughtful conservatives are, in retrospect, profoundly grateful for that much-misunderstood 1964.

When the new year dawned, the Goldwater Express was firmly on the track and bearing down hard on San Francisco. Goldwater formally declared his candidacy on January 3, just as the rising sun trigged a photoelectric cell and raised the American flag—as it did every day—over his Phoenix home. Then he was off on a grueling series of campaign trips through the primary states.

Here again the basic text is Clif White's *Suite 3505*. To those of us close to the campaign and therefore aware of what was happening, it seemed almost inevitable, even on the day Goldwater first declared his candidacy, that he would be nominated in July. And yet the media, with rare exceptions, continued to treat Goldwater as some sort of painful but self-limiting disease. As previously mentioned, it was only President Johnson's candid assessment that Goldwater was well ahead, given in a press conference early in 1964, that finally shook the media awake.*

For conservatives, therefore, it was a joyous spring—though, of course, not having the gift of clairvoyance, we could not be absolutely sure that the GOP's tottering eastern hegemonists wouldn't find some way to deprive us of our victory, even at that late hour. And there were, in addition, disappointments along the way. Goldwater lost the New Hampshire primary to Henry Cabot Lodge, our urbane ambassador in faraway Saigon, whose name was thrown into the hopper at the last minute by the desperate

* Cf. p. 112, supra.

liberal Republicans and who appears to have struck New Hampshire's Republican voters as an irresistible chance to demonstrate their disproportionate clout as participants in the nation's first primary. Lodge's appeal, however, did not carry far beyond New Hampshire: He and Goldwater both lost to Rockefeller in Oregon, which thereby acquired the dubious distinction of being the only state in which Nelson Rockefeller ever won a seriously contested Republican primary.

But meanwhile, Goldwater was rolling up impressive victories in such major Republican bastions as Illinois and Indiana, not to mention the passionately conservative southern and mountain states, and by the time of the California primary on June 2, which was attracting a lot of attention and in which the polls indicated that Rockefeller and Goldwater were neck and neck, it was in fact all over: Clif White had a list of pro-Goldwater delegates, already selected or elected and nailed down, who would give Barry Goldwater the nomination no matter *who* won in California.

Just at this point occurred one of those small hitches that can spoil, at least in the beholder's eye, even the rosiest prospect. Bill Buckley somehow became convinced (1) that Goldwater might well lose the California primary (which was true), (2) that in that case he was bound to lose the nomination (which was, at that point, flatly and mathematically impossible), and (3) that accordingly, if Goldwater did lose in California, *National Review* ought to call upon him to pull out of the race altogether, to avoid a humiliating defeat.

I don't know what led Bill to this bizarre conclusion; like most of us, he has weaknesses as well as strengths, and a sort of coarse political horse sense has never been one of his stronger suits. (He even spent a fair amount of time during the first half of 1964 on a scheme to make Dwight Eisenhower Goldwater's vice presidential running mate.)

In any case I was far too deeply committed to the Goldwater candidacy—had urged too many of my friends to support it—to call for its abandonment even if it did indeed become futile, let alone when it was trembling on the edge of triumph. Sorrowfully I prepared to submit my resignation as publisher of *National Review* if Goldwater lost in California and the editorial appeared. Luckily Goldwater won by a whisker—1,089,133 to 1,030,180—so the problem resolved itself. (When he learned that I had planned to resign, Bill urged me to tell him in advance next time: "I am medium-good at finding compromises on these things.")

With the primaries behind us, the convention itself—held at the Cow Palace in San Francisco July 13–17—was almost anticlimactic, although various last-minute maneuvers by the opposition (including a disappointingly ill-tempered blast at Goldwater and the supposed kookiness of his conservative views by William Scranton, who had replaced Rockefeller as the liberals' last hope) kept us on our toes.

It was at this convention that White introduced various technological innovations that have dominated the management of convention politics in both parties ever since.* Previously campaign managers had operated from the convention floor itself, with leg power supplied by aides carrying messages to delegates in distant parts of the hall. At San Francisco, however, White and his regional directors were installed in a spacious air-conditioned trailer, parked just outside the rear entrance of the Cow Palace and protected against intruders by uniformed guards. From this trailer a bewildering array of multicolored wires led to telephones at seventeen strategic locations on the convention floor itself, where state leaders of the Goldwater delegates could pass the word to their troops. In addition, the rival candidates were authorized to have a number of roving representatives, equipped with walkie-talkie radios, on the floor itself. To and from these went messages for key individuals, etc.

In the trailer White sat with his deputy, former YR chairman Tom van Sickle, at right angles to a row of six cubbyholes, each containing one regional director. These six men had phones connected to delegates on the floor, in touch with every state in their respective regions. White had a larger phone unit that could, at the push of a button, connect him with all seventeen floor locations simultaneously. (He had, of course, one other line as well—a direct line to Senator Goldwater's suite in the Mark Hopkins, atop

* To give credit where credit is due, I believe the first methodical and extensive use of walkie-talkies at a Republican convention occurred in 1963, at the Young Republican national convention in Omaha. I remember Bill Timmons, one of the managers for our side at that convention, describing the plan to me, in advance, with great relish. I thought the idea was childish—another spectacular example of how blind I can sometimes be.

Nob Hill in downtown San Francisco.) Each regional director also had in front of him a television set on which he could monitor the regular network broadcasts of the convention sessions. White and Van Sickle shared three—one for each network, to be certain that nothing would be missed.

Fairly early in the convention the Scranton forces—which had, of course, received equal treatment from the presiding authorities and duplicated White's arrangements as far as they were aware of them—became puzzled because the Goldwater walkie-talkies enjoyed so much clearer reception than their own. They were projecting their radio beams inward from various unsatisfactory antennas around the edges of the hall and did not discover until years later that the foxy White had hired as his electronics expert a wizard who, several days before the convention began, had climbed the rafters and catwalks in the ceiling of the Cow Palace and installed there, at dead center, invisible from the floor but powerfully audible to the bearers of Goldwater walkie-talkies below, a master antenna connected to the trailer nerve center outside.

Close as I was to White personally and to the whole Goldwater movement, I found it no easy matter to get into that fascinating trailer once the convention was under way. Finally White relaxed his professionalism enough to admit me, and I shrank against a wall to watch my old YR cronies win a Republican national convention at last.

One thing puzzled me: Every so often a door would open at the far end of the trailer (i.e., behind White) and a young man would come out of a small room there, bearing a slip of paper which he would hand to White. White would look at the note but, as far as I could tell, never took any action as a result of it. It was only after the convention that I discovered the function of that room: It contained equipment whereby the Scranton walkie-talkies could be monitored. (But couldn't they also monitor ours? Yes, I was told—our VHF walkie-talkies could theoretically be monitored just like theirs. But White's fearsome electronic wizard had anticipated and forestalled this possibility by equipping the Goldwater forces with a complete parallel set of UHF walkie-talkie equipment, which was much less vulnerable to eavesdropping. This was always used for highly classified messages.)

The convention sessions rolled forward to their predestined

end, with Roger Moore, a Boston attorney and longtime protégé of mine (he served in the early 1950s as president of the Harvard Young Republican Club, which I had founded in 1947), monitoring the parliamentary aspects of the situation for the Goldwater forces. Under their bylaws Republican National Conventions are governed by the rules of procedure of the U.S. House of Representatives, and these in turn are based on Jefferson's *Manual.* Moore had very nearly the only copy of Jefferson's *Manual* at the Cow Palace and had mastered its intricacies thoroughly.

At one point Governor Rockefeller found occasion to address the gathering—and received a resounding chorus of boos. His steadfastness in bearing up under this negative reaction was much commented on at the time by his admirers (notably in the media) and unquestionably cast the Goldwater forces—as he knew it would, and probably intended it should—in a poor light: as ungracious and vindictive winners, etc. White, of course, realized this and promptly pushed the button to all seventeen floor locations, barking at his floor managers to silence the Goldwater delegates. But they quickly assured him their delegates were decently silent: The boos were coming strictly from the galleries—a fact that White and other television viewers hadn't realized because the networks neglected to mention it.

At last, on Wednesday evening, the fifteenth, came the roll call of the states for the party's presidential nomination. Slowly, mesmerized by all the noise and color, I walked completely around the third ring above the huge, floodlit arena, looking down on the scene. I thought of my lunch with Ashbrook in Washington, just over three years earlier; I recalled my subsequent talk with White and Ashbrook's September visit to New York; I mentally saluted that little band of twenty-two friends who met in Chicago in October 1961 and again that December. I remembered Governor Don Nutter's prayer at the latter meeting and his death in a plane crash only a few weeks later. Did he somehow know, I wondered, what was happening, on this night two and a half years later? I was sure he did.

Barry Goldwater was nominated on the first ballot, with 883 votes out of 1,308—"more votes," he was to write proudly years later, "than any candidate in either party had ever achieved on the first ballot of a contested convention where the roll call was permitted to continue." Clif White's final preconvention prediction—884 votes—overshot by exactly 1 vote.

There was an interval of several hours between the traditional Goldwater demonstration (when his name was formally put before the delegates) and his nomination by the convention that night. During it, about 5:00 P.M., I was summoned to a phone to receive a call from New York. It was Bill Rickenbacker, and he had very bad news: Bill Buckley's younger sister Maureen, whom I had dated occasionally when I first got to know the family in the 1950s, had suffered a brain hemorrhage and was unconscious; she was not expected to live out the night. Would I please notify Bill?

Grimly I edged my way toward the press gallery (*National Review*'s only pass to it had gone to Buckley) and sought him out. Spotting him chatting amiably with someone, I called to him across the barrier, and he came over. When he heard my news, his face seemed to freeze into an expressionless mask. "Get me to a telephone," he said quietly.

From a pay phone in the Cow Palace he reached his sister Priscilla, who confirmed my report and added details. Maureen, now thirty-one, happily married to Gerry O'Reilly and the mother of five children, had been struck down in her home without warning. There was no hope of survival. Bill said he would be on the next plane to New York.

As it happened, that was the 10:00 P.M. "red-eye," so Bill Buckley, who had done so much to lay the intellectual foundations of the movement that was triumphing that evening at the Cow Palace, was winging eastward out of San Francisco, his thoughts altogether elsewhere, when the convention nominated Barry Goldwater as its candidate for President of the United States.*

Of Goldwater's speech the next evening, much has been written. The conventional wisdom, at any rate at the time, was that Goldwater had revealed the essential fanaticism underlying the conservative movement by the following sentences, plucked from their context: "I would remind you that extremism in the defense of liberty is no vice! And let me remind you also that moderation in the pursuit of justice is no virtue!"

The media professed to understand these sentences as a de-

---

* Maureen Buckley O'Reilly survived, unconscious, for two more days.

fense of the John Birch Society and other "extremist" conservative enterprises. No matter what is done (misrepresentation, McCarthyism, or whatever), they interpreted Goldwater as saying, it is permissible as long as one's purpose is the salvation of the country. The end, in other words, justifies the means.

Harry Jaffa, the Claremont College political science professor who had provided the controversial sentence, can hardly be accused of intending thereby to defend the John Birch Society, and he was probably equally innocent of any purpose to justify evil means on the basis of good ends. But nobody who has ever watched the media in full career—zealously aided, in this case, by both the Democrats and the liberal Republicans—can doubt the impact of the job they proceeded to do on Barry Goldwater's acceptance speech.

Clif White tells me he knew at once what a mistake that controversial passage was. If so, he once again established his superior prescience, at least as far as I am concerned. I saw nothing in the offending utterance except a rather prettily put contention that there's nothing wrong with zealousness when it comes to patriotism and the related virtues. But as the event proved, I was wrong: Within days millions of people who couldn't have quoted Goldwater's statement correctly if their lives depended on it were sure that it revealed his essential kookiness.

But let's not get ahead of ourselves. As matters stood in San Francisco that summer evening, a tremendous transition had indisputably taken place. The Republican party, after long domination by its relatively liberal eastern wing—the wing that had successfully nominated Willkie in 1940, Dewey in 1944 and 1948, Eisenhower in 1952 and 1956, and Nixon in 1960—had passed into the hands of a new management. And that management wasn't just the Arizona Mafia, by a long shot: It was the larger movement represented by the membership of the National Draft Goldwater Committee— the new young leaders of the party in the fast-growing (and therefore newly powerful) states of the South, the Southwest, and the West. What moved these people, to an extent not common in American party politics, was idealism: a deep and sincere belief in the moral, political, and economic principles of conservatism.

Before long, the new party management would develop its own important internal disagreements—such is the law of nature, or, at any rate, human nature. But strangely enough, despite Goldwater's drubbing by Lyndon Johnson that November, the Republican party did *not* rebound into the waiting arms of Nelson Rockefeller, or George Romney, or any other clearly liberal Republican. Nor has it ever done so since. Very probably the conservative movement coincided with, and benefited by, a transfer of power within the GOP that was ordained by population shifts in the nation at large. But if so, it is also true that the populations that were shifting geographically were as well shifting psychologically and politically—to the right. "The eye was placed where one ray should fall, that it might testify of that particular ray."

One of a presidential nominee's first tasks is to assume control of the party machinery and designate the individuals who will manage his campaign. Once again, as when Goldwater decided to take over the draft movement, I assumed that he would more or less ratify the status quo so far as the campaign staff was concerned. After all, it had succeeded brilliantly to date. And I hoped, not very secretly, that he might designate Clif White as chairman of the Republican National Committee—a job for which White was superbly fitted and which I was sure he privately wanted.

But Goldwater had other ideas, and in the circumstances there was no doubt whose ideas were going to prevail. White and his crew of ex-Young Republicans and conservative ideologues had run a fine convention, but by Goldwater's definition they still weren't pros. Worse yet, they weren't even, in the strict sense, Goldwater's men. In his eyes they were simply a roving band of samurai who had attached themselves to him, drafted him into a presidential election he was now probably going to lose, compelled him to give up a safe seat in the Senate he revered, and were obviously quite prepared to offer him up as a living sacrifice on the altar of their beloved conservatism.

So Goldwater acted swiftly—many would later say, brutally—to assert personal control of the party and the campaign. In as Republican national chairman (replacing William Miller of New York, whom Goldwater tapped for vice president) went Goldwater's former administrative assistant, Dean Burch of Arizona. Reconfirmed as campaign manager was Denison Kitchel, also of Arizona. Off to the far sidelines went Clif White, to head up a new and predictably meaningless letterhead called Citizens for Goldwater-Miller. Out too, as far as anyone could tell, went the whole expert staff of state and regional directors White had so laboriously assembled over a space of three years. They would have to scramble, now, to find posts for themselves in whatever campaign hierarchy Kitchel decided to sanction, and several managed to do so. A number of others, heartsick and angry, didn't bother to try.

For a day or so my mind simply refused to accept the significance of what had occurred. Nonsense, I told worried friends; everything would work out all right. Goldwater naturally wanted his Arizona pals around him, but he wouldn't, he couldn't totally overlook what White and his team had accomplished ... could he?

At a "celebratory" party of Clif's group on Thursday evening, the sixteenth, in the Crystal Room of the famous old Fairmont Hotel on Nob Hill, after Burch's appointment as Republican national chairman had been announced, I still resisted the wakelike atmosphere. Okay, I argued, Goldwater was an ungrateful SOB, but look at the victory for conservatism! Most of my friends smiled wanly; they were happy for conservatism, but somehow it wasn't enough.

The next afternoon Bunny White, Clif's wife, tracked me down by phone at a local Polynesian restaurant where I was lunching with some friends. She and Clif and their two children had been scheduled to leave that day for a rest in Hawaii, but Clif had been unable even to pack. A sort of agonizing lethargy had settled over him. She wanted me, as Clif's oldest friend in San Francisco, to talk to him, to try to pep him up. I did my best.

I thought I understood what was really bugging Clif, and I told him so. It wasn't losing the Republican national chairmanship or anything like that; it was—after nearly three years of constant, unremitting, high-pressure effort—the awful sensation of *having nothing to do*. A man's psyche can no more stand such a sudden release of pressure than his body can stand explosive decompression after a long, deep dive. I told him that Winston Churchill, explaining how he happened to take up painting as a pastime in 1916, described almost exactly the same symptoms:

When I left the Admiralty at the end of May, 1915, I still remained a member of the Cabinet and of the War Council. In this position I knew everything and could do nothing. The change from the intense executive activities of each day's work at the Admiralty to the narrowly measured duties of a counsellor left me gasping. Like a sea-beast fished up from the depths, or a diver too suddenly hoisted, my veins threatened to burst from the fall in pressure. I had great anxiety and no means of relieving it; I had vehement convictions and small power to give effect to them. I had to watch the unhappy casting-away of great opportunities, and the feeble execution of plans which I had launched and in which I heartily believed. I had long hours of utterly unwonted leisure in which to contemplate the frightful unfolding of the War. At a moment when every fibre of my being was inflamed to action, I was forced to remain a spectator of the tragedy, placed cruelly in a front seat.

I assured White that he would bounce back and that meanwhile, a rest was exactly what he needed. He agreed, and thanked me, and he and his family finally flew off to Hawaii as planned.

Thus it happened that I, along with most of the other members and outriders of the old draft-Goldwater crowd, was able, and indeed obliged, to watch the postconvention campaign of 1964 from the sidelines. There was plenty of nominal campaigning for us to do, of course—in my case, radio and television debates and the like—and we did it cheerfully enough, for after all, we were still very emphatically conservatives and wanted Goldwater to do as well as possible.

We all realized by now, though, that he would lose. Victory just wasn't in the cards. There was, first of all, the devastating fact that his opponent was Lyndon Johnson, not John Kennedy.* Then, too, the very shock of the assassination, and the abrupt shift from Kennedy to Johnson, made many people reluctant to vote for a second change of horses in less than a year. Finally, there was the vindictiveness of the defeated liberal Republicans, which was deep and would obviously take the form of sitting out this election, if not actively voting for Johnson. We had realized, of course, that a certain amount of bitterness was inevitable because Goldwater's victory was so clearly not just an ordinary one but a true

* A point already discussed—see p. 159, supra.

and lasting shift in party control. But the convention had left even deeper scars than we anticipated. Rockefeller and Javits, while signaling just enough nominal support for Goldwater to keep their own party loyalty from being challenged, made it very plain that their followers would be wise to refrain from voting for him. Liberal Republican newspapers like the *New York Herald Tribune* and newsmagazines like *Time* spelled out the message for the slow-witted. There would be no amnesty for Barry Goldwater.

To be sure, Goldwater complicated his problems by a series of speeches that played right into the hands of his enemies, making it easy to depict him as a fire-breathing monster who would repeal Social Security and plunge the world into nuclear war. It would be a cheap shot, however, to suggest that any appreciable portion of the blame for Goldwater's defeat should be assigned to the team that wrote those speeches and in general ran his campaign after White and his group were sidelined. Nothing in that autumn of 1964—certainly not a change in campaign themes—could have saved Barry Goldwater.

As for me, on October 19, when I had appeared on all the radio and TV panels that had invited me and had cast my absentee ballot for Barry Goldwater (and for the nominees of the New York Conservative party for lesser offices), I departed on a long-planned, six-week circumnavigation of the globe: Amsterdam, Frankfurt, Athens, Istanbul, Beirut, Teheran, Calcutta, Bangkok, Manila, Hong Kong, Taipei, and Tokyo. I was in Istanbul on November 4, in a tour bus on the Galata Bridge crossing the Golden Horn, when somebody with a radio remarked in my hearing that Johnson was winning heavily. The next day, from Beirut, I phoned my office in New York to get more precise figures as well as the results in other races.

From my standpoint, and that of other movement conservatives, it seemed reasonably clear, even in immediate retrospect, that the whole draft-Goldwater effort had been worthwhile despite his resounding defeat in November. There was a substratum of truth to Goldwater's resentful feeling that he had, in a way, been *used* by the conservative movement. There was nothing invidious in this: Movements and individuals come together, and serve each other's purposes, all the time. The Goldwater candidacy had given the conservative cause its political baptism of fire.

It had blooded enormous numbers of conservative troops. It had certainly "put conservatism on the map." Finally, it had given the conservative movement control of the Republican party and—through Goldwater—of its machinery, at least for a time. These were not negligible achievements.

But though we could not know it then, they were the merest tip of the iceberg, as far as the solid accomplishments of 1964 were concerned. Only slowly, in the deep fullness of time, would the others be revealed. Even the one visible and indisputable political change that occurred during the year—the shift in control of the GOP—looked dangerously temporary and would not be perceived clearly for a decade as the solid and permenant thing it was.

But progress, great progress, had nonetheless been made. The charm, now, was wound up. Conservatism in 1960 was basically just a set of ideas. By 1965 it was a full-fledged political movement, ready to do battle for the leadership of America.

Although its implications were almost totally invisible at the time, one of 1964's major developments was the appearance on the national political scene of the man who would ultimately lead the conservative movement to national victory: Ronald Reagan.

Reagan in 1964 was no stranger to the conservative cause. After a long and steady, though not spectacular, career as a screen actor, he had become associated with General Electric in the 1950s as the host of "General Electric Theater," a highly successful television program sponsored by the corporation. General Electric was one of those rare companies that believed in actively spreading the free-enterprise gospel and had long put its money where its mouth was, sponsoring college activities of various sorts, etc. Accordingly, it decided to put Ronald Reagan not only on the air but on the road, to take the message of free enterprise to business groups, factory workers, and schools. Reagan—handsome, good-natured, and articulate—was the ideal salesman for the free-enterprise cause, and like most good salesmen, he believed in his product. For the rest of the decade he traveled what he jokingly called the mashed-potato circuit, giving audiences his friendly homilies on the virtues of free enterprise. Naturally he laced his talks with amusing anecdotes and telling statistics, and there appears no doubt that he was an effective spokesman for the conservative cause, in particular its economic aspects. (He also became, in or about 1960, a subscriber to *National Review* and has remained a faithful one ever since.)

Now, in the autumn of 1964, Reagan was California co-chairman of Citizens for Goldwater and Miller and had taped for local use a speech on behalf of Goldwater that many people were eager to see broadcast nationally. Clif White and others in the national campaign were enthusiastic, but—almost predictably—Kitchel, Baroody, and Dean Burch's Republican National Committee were not. The issue was pressed, however, and ultimately Goldwater himself authorized the expenditure. It proved to be the best investment of the whole campaign, because Reagan's speech (broadcast nationwide on October 27) was, by almost universal agreement, a tremendous success.

It was not, to be sure, enough to elect Goldwater. But fate has a curious way of hiding its pearls in the most unlikely places, and it outdid itself on this occasion. In the last weeks of Barry Goldwater's doomed campaign—out of its very ashes, like a phoenix— arose his successor as leader of the conservative movement.

I myself missed the big event, being in West Germany on my round-the-world trip at the time, but when I returned to New York on November 29, I promptly heard about Reagan's wonderful speech. Plenty of knowledgeable conservatives were already saying that he was our future spokesman. But that, of course, remained to be seen. When at last it became clear just how important Reagan was to the present and future of the conservative movement, we had one more big reason to be grateful for 1964.

Shortly after the election somebody broke open a locked desk in the offices of the Republican National Committee. If it was ever established who the guilty party was, the news failed to reach me. But the thief's objective was clear and illustrates better than anything I could say the importance of the third great conservative achievement of 1964: the mobilization and listing of the movement's members.

There were two separate aspects to this matter. Prior to 1964 those who might legitimately be called conservative activists were few in number and widely scattered. It would probably not be far off the mark to say that they consisted largely of the combined and to some extent overlapping subscription lists of *National Review* and *Human Events*—perhaps 100,000 individuals nationwide.

The Goldwater campaign, however, was much more than merely a conservative event: It was an American presidential campaign, and Goldwater eventually received 27 million votes— not a negligible number. Moreover, his campaign—aimed, at least in White's original strategy, straight at whole new categories of social conservatives who typically had never voted Republican— brought into play, in impressive numbers, entirely new forces. Young couples who had never been involved in politics before but who were moved by Goldwater's transparently sincere idealism; elderly widows and widowers, seizing what seemed a chance to be effective at last against the better-organized forces in American society; high school students, ready (as the young always are) to enlist in a rebellion against the prevailing and in this case liberal orthodoxy: All these groups, and many more, were represented in the wave of new recruits that swamped Goldwater campaign offices all over the country (thereby frequently deceiving campaign workers about the actual distribution of opinion).

For many years after 1964 Clif White would be approached at Republican and conservative gatherings by people, often then nearing middle age, who would tell him that they "got their start in the Goldwater campaign." The importance of the 1964 campaign as a recruiting device, therefore, must not be overlooked. Most presidential campaigns are mechanical affairs, their demonstrations of popular support staged and phony. Goldwater's campaign, in terms of human beings recruited and despite his subsequent heavy defeat, was a political tsunami. More individual contributions—most of them small—were made to the Goldwater campaign than to any other American presidential campaign in history, up to that time.

And that brings us to the second aspect of the matter. Recruiting activists is one thing; getting on paper the names and addresses of one's often relatively inactive supporters is another and much larger one. But campaign contributions must, by law, be listed and filed with various public authorities. Thus it came to pass that the names and addresses of Barry Goldwater's supporters were carefully compiled into lists.

Just how important this was did not strike everyone simultaneously, and is still not always understood. In recent years, when direct-mail fund raising and propagandizing for political campaigns have become a big business, the liberals have belatedly imitated the conservative initiative in this respect with some success. But in the nature of things direct-mail activities will never be as critically important to the liberals as they have been and still are to conservatives, for a reason that is obvious when one stops to think about it.

Prior to 1964 there were only three avenues of national communication in extensive use for political purposes: the major television networks, the major newsmagazines, and (arguably) one or two newspapers that commanded national attention. With exceptions that do nothing to modify the essential point, all of these avenues were under liberal control. As a result, a new and more or less conventionally liberal candidate for the presidency, or for an important Senate seat or governorship, in either major party could pretty well count on sympathetic treatment in all of these media. Depending on his importance, he might receive anything from a favorable reference in the *New York Times* (which could then be quoted extensively in his local media) to a cover story in *Time* or *Newsweek* or both, plus special attention on the television networks' evening news.

With that sort of treatment the lucky man's career was well under way. Perhaps even more to the point, fund raising inevitably became much easier; after all, those approached for contributions had just read or heard all sorts of nice things about the candidate, and he was surrounded by a nimbus that hinted strongly at success.*

For conservatives, on the other hand, there was simply no avenue of national communication on which they could count for favorable mention—quite the contrary! A conservative candidate for a major governorship or a senatorship, or a conservative possibility for a presidential nomination, could expect relatively little coverage, and most of that unfavorable. The media's treatment of

---

* Students of this phenomenon could do worse than study the buildup that former Congressman Clifford Case received in 1954 when, after a brief stint as president of the Ford Foundation (itself almost the ultimate liberal accolade), he was launched by a *Time* cover story on a quarter century career as one of the liberal Republican halfbacks in the U.S. Senate.

Barry Goldwater's presidential candidacy is remembered even today as a spectacular example of the genre. As soon as the media became convinced that Goldwater was no longer in any danger of becoming president—which is to say, by the late 1960s—they promptly discovered his many good qualities and in fact adopted him as a sort of favorite, appreciated especially for his candor. But the Goldwater of 1964, as depicted by the media, was quite a different thing: a fanatical ideologue, willing to sanction any excess in the name of his impossible ideals and eager to plunge us into war with Russia. The most memorable (and inexcusable) instance of this was probably the famous Democratic TV commercial showing a little girl plucking the petals from a daisy until the scene fades through her eyes to a countdown at an atomic testing site and the whole screen is then filled with the familiar mushroom cloud of an atomic bomb. This, of course, was a partisan commercial, but the groundwork for it had been laid by the media over a period of many months.

The tremendous significance of the long lists of Goldwater contributors to conservatives, therefore, was nothing less than this: Necessity had mothered the invention of a brand-new avenue of national communication for political purposes. Henceforth conservative candidates for office all over the country could turn to those lists for political and financial support. A wealthy businessman in, say, Oregon, where there often was no conservative worthy of the name running for office on the ticket of either major party, would receive in the mail a letter describing the promising candidacy of some forthright conservative for the Senate in, perhaps, Florida or California. A contribution to such a candidate would help to put in the Senate a dependable foe of Oregon's liberal Mark Hatfield. And the contributor lists of *that* conservative candidate, in turn, would be husbanded and added to the growing collection of conservative names. In less than a decade these lists, fed into computers and coded to provide an elaborate array of information, were to become in effect the central nervous system of the conservative movement—a medium of swift, powerfully packaged information that could summon aid from all over the national political battlefield to precisely those points where it was most needed.

The liberals, as noted, ultimately tried to duplicate the conservatives' success in this regard, when at last they became aware of it in the mid-1970s. But in doing so they were, and remain today, to some degree the muscle-bound victims of their own strength. For the communication function of a direct-mail operation is largely redundant from the liberal standpoint. Of what use is an expensive letter describing a candidate in glowing terms if one has already read about him in those same rapturous terms in the *New York Times, Time,* and *Newsweek* and has seen a special segment, also praising him, on some network's evening news program?

And while liberal candidates can and often do use direct mail nowadays to solicit campaign contributions, the curious fact is that the chief sources of liberal campaign funds are not, as in the case of conservatives, ordinarily the small donations of large numbers of individuals, but the war chests of the labor unions and the large contributions of a relatively small number of extremely wealthy people. The result is that direct mail plays, and will probably continue to play, a far larger part in the political activities of America's conservatives than in those of its liberals.

We will return to this whole fascinating subject, and describe some of its more artistic and deadlier ramifications, in connection with our analysis of the continued growth of the conservative movement during the 1970s. Meanwhile, it is sufficient to note here that for all practical purposes, the extensive interstate use of the U.S. mails as a principal avenue of political communication was founded squarely on the Goldwater contributor lists of 1964. For conservatives, this was a breakthrough of immense importance, which alone would have made 1964 a red-letter year. They had, in effect, discovered a brand-new pass through the hitherto-impregnable liberal-controlled barrier of the Alps.

Chapter VII

A New Majority Stirs

It may seem perverse, and perhaps it is, to speak of a "new majority" stirring in the immediate wake of a defeat as disastrous as Goldwater's was in 1964. And yet there seems no other way to describe what was happening on the American right in the years 1965–68. It was a long process, replete with false starts and wrong turns; but when it was over, the new majority was there for all to see, and all that remained was for one major party or the other to recognize what had happened and move briskly to take advantage of it.

Let me begin by reiterating what is, at any rate, my own contention—namely, that Goldwater's landslide defeat was not in any sense the product of some powerful upwelling of leftist or liberal political sentiment in the country but, on the contrary, the result of three separate factors: the replacement of the relatively liberal Kennedy by a Johnson perceived to be pronouncedly more conservative, especially on what would later come to be known as the social issues; the reluctance of the voters to change horses yet again, so soon after the shock of the Kennedy assassination; and the decision of many eastern Republicans, bitter at their loss of party control, to sit out the election or actually to vote for Johnson.

There was a perceptible swing in public opinion during the 1960s, however, and it was toward the right—exemplified in the Republican party by Goldwater's nomination (which came, be it remembered, after a series of impressive triumphs in major primaries) and in the Democratic party by the swift improvement in its prospects that followed Kennedy's replacement by Johnson. What was happening, of course, was that the old Democratic coalition, after a brief reunion to elect the Catholic Kennedy in 1960 and another to elect the Texan Johnson in 1964, resumed its slow disintegration under the impact of the issues that were now arising to dominate the sixties.

From 1965 onward it was clear what those issues were: in domestic affairs the struggle of blacks for their civil rights, and in foreign affairs America's participation in the Vietnam War. Underlying and interpenetrating these, however, were other trends that did not always even take the form of political issues but challenged far more fundamentally the basic assumptions of most Americans. These were the assumptions summed up in the words *life-style* and *family*. Most Americans believed in marriage and heterosexuality; they disapproved of drugs, opposed forced busing, and condemned abortion.* Yet now, in the mid-1960s, the evidence was pouring in through the media that substantial numbers of Americans *disagreed* with these traditional views. What's more, the people who disagreed tended to be among the most vocal in supporting militant black demands for "equal rights" (and, later on, the parallel demands of other minorities—homosexuals, American Indians, etc.—as well as the female majority) and also in opposing our participation in the Vietnam War. As the sixties thundered toward their end amid bursts of gunfire and the assassinations of Robert Kennedy and Martin Luther King, Jr., these attitudes and controversies seemed to implode in America's colleges and universities. To all the other unsightly gaps was added the Generation Gap: Parents and children simply could not understand one another. We were a profoundly unhappy country.

What was the macrocosmic political consequence of all these developments? If one looked at a newspaper in the latter half of the sixties, the dominant personalities (aside from Lyndon Johnson, *ex officio*) seemed to be Martin Luther King, Jr., and a few zanies claiming to speak for what had come to be known as the New Left: Abbie Hoffman perhaps, and some of his fellow defendants among the Chicago Seven—Jerry Rubin, Tom Hayden, and Dave Dellinger. Yet aside from King, whose political following was predominantly among his fellow blacks and therefore inevita-

* Those who would challenge the last assertion, so far as concerns the 1960s, are referred to a 1969 Gallup Poll which put the question in a particularly favorable way: "Would you favor or oppose a law that would permit a woman to go to a doctor to end pregnancy at any time during the first three months?" As late as the end of the decade, the response was: Oppose, 50 percent; favor, 40 percent; no opinion, 10 percent.

bly limited, not one of these people had any public following worthy of the name. The great mass of American voters were altogether elsewhere, responding to very different leaders. In 1968 31,785,480 voted for Richard Nixon, and another 9,906,473 voted for George Wallace. Only 31,275,166 voted for that quintessential liberal Hubert Humphrey—and even he had (reluctantly) endorsed Johnson's Vietnam War.

That is the simplest statistical basis (there are others, which will be discussed in due course*) for the proposition that by 1965 or thereabouts there was a conservative majority in the United States. It was not, of course, a majority for the views of the conservative movement's dogmatic ideologues; it was a circumspect, even a "moderate" sort of conservatism. Moreover, it was not united—as Wallace's 1968 independent race for the presidency, against both Nixon and Humphrey, amply demonstrated. Least of all was it the possession of any one party; indeed, it may be doubted whether either major party ever made, prior to 1980, a firm decision to court it.

But it was there, nonetheless. And that majority was what the conservative activists, after 1964 with all its triumphs and disasters, set out to organize and express.

Regardless of Goldwater's defeat, it was obvious that an effort would be made to create some sort of political organization to carry on his battle—the struggle for conservative principles in the political arena. In a sense, of course, this would be done within the major parties themselves—in the primaries, conventions, and general elections of the years ahead. But there was also a widespread desire for some nonpartisan political entity—something along the lines of YAF, perhaps, with local chapters, but not confined to the young—that could speak out boldly for the conservative movement as a whole.

Control of such an organization would obviously be worth having, and Senator Goldwater and William Baroody, Sr., promptly made a bid for it, creating a rather scholarly little group called the Free Society Association. Denison Kitchel, who had been Goldwater's national campaign manager, was designated as

* See p. 222, infra, concerning Kevin Phillips's *The Emerging Republican Majority*.

president. This organization, which concentrated on publishing conservative pamphlets and other materials, had control of some (though not all) of the mailing lists generated by the campaign, so it could not be ignored as a factor in whatever the final outcome might be. But the Arizona Mafia had lost a good deal of its influence on November 3, and even Goldwater personally, though as beloved by conservatives as ever, could no longer give orders to the troops and expect them to be obeyed unhesitatingly.

The creation of a rival and more broadly based organization, to be called the American Conservative Union, was discussed among leading conservatives during November, and it was officially launched at a meeting in the Mayflower Hotel in Washington on December 19. I had missed the preliminary discussions because of my trip abroad but was at the Mayflower on the nineteenth and took an active part in structuring and staffing the organization. Congressman Donald Bruce (R., Ind.) was elected chairman, with my old crony Congressman John Ashbrook as vice-chairman. I accepted the chairmanship of the ACU's Political Action Committee. Less than a year later Bruce stepped down, Ashbrook succeeded him as chairman, and I became the organization's vice-chairman. Also in 1966, David Jones, who had long been active in both the Young Republican National Federation and Young Americans for Freedom, became the ACU's first full-time executive director. Under Ashbrook's leadership and Jones's astute day-to-day management, the ACU pulled slowly ahead of the Free Society Association.

There were yet other attempts to provide a central rallying point for conservative sentiment after Goldwater's defeat. Most of them fairly quickly came to naught, and slowly it became apparent that the ACU was the organization that had the staying power and, equally important, the acceptance among conservatives generally to give promise of lasting the course. Eventually, as funds grew short, Goldwater and Kitchel closed down their Free Society Association.

During the latter 1960s the ACU sought to organize local chapters around the country, not always successfully. A local live wire would typically be succeeded, in the chairmanship of his or her chapter, by a wire that was anything but live. Long spells of political inactivity were frequently enlivened in such chapters by factional disputes of inversely proportional intensity. There was always the temptation to drift away into other more immediately rewarding forms of political activity: local campaigns, other worthy causes, etc. Eventually the ACU settled into a more comfortable role as a membership organization, whose members paid their dues to Washington and received in return the organization's publication, *Battle Line,* and various other benefits. In 1969 the ACU created a Conservative Victory Fund, which makes money contributions to candidates it deems worthy of conservative support—a very useful device for conservatives who may not have the time or facilities to research such matters themselves but who don't want to make contributions through party channels that may siphon to liberal candidates a portion of all funds received. In addition, the ACU sponsors a number of other projects, including the (tax-exempt) ACU Education and Research Foundation. The foundation in turn finances the National Journalism Center, a training program for young journalists under the direction of M. Stanton Evans. The American Legislative Exchange Council, specializing in activities of the state legislatures, was also launched by the ACU.

While the ACU was getting under way in the years following the 1964 election, Young Americans for Freedom was undergoing another of its perennial crises—this one better justified, and even harder to resolve, than most of the others.

Whether or not there was a conservative majority in the country at large in the 1960s, there certainly was no such thing on America's college campuses. There the New Left was on its long rampage, and orthodox liberalism represented the (relative) right wing of student and faculty opinion. It was in this singularly inhospitable environment that YAF, right through the 1960s, sought to plant the battle flag of conservatism.

Of course, there are genetic sports in any generation, and YAF could count on its fair share of these where they appeared: strong-minded young men and women who disagreed profoundly with the direction their generation was taking and didn't mind saying so at the top of their lungs. But these were rarities, seldom more than one or two (if that) to a campus. For the rest, YAF had to prospect among those who formed what might be called the silent majority at many a college—students attracted by many of the things the New Left was doing and saying, but also repelled by some of its antics and its penchant for violence.

To these "moderates," YAF proselytizers early found one broad, paved avenue, emerging straight out of pristine conservative doctrine: libertarianism. The dogma of libertarianism—the proposition that government should be severely limited—has a highly respectable place in the intellectual ancestry of modern conservatism, even though in its extreme forms it has been (and ought to be) condemned as a heresy. From the standpoint of YAF, confronting the onslaught of the New Left on American campuses in the 1960s, the beauty of libertarianism was that it seemed congruent with many of the things that students of that generation were beginning to say and feel: Big Is Bad. Do Not Fold, Spindle, or Mutilate Me. Let Me Do My Own Thing. Stop the World—I Want to Get Off. It's My Life—Let Me Live It. Big Brother Will Get You. And so on.

The smarter New Leftists had known about libertarianism all along and had not hesitated to endorse its more extreme forms—to the vast irritation of orthodox modern liberals on the faculties. The YAF spokesmen did not go so far, but they were able to cite quite accurately, as libertarian tenets of the conservative faith laid down by their national board of directors in Washington, two propositions that were extremely popular with most of their peers:

1. There should be no military draft, and
2. Government has no business interfering with people who want to smoke marijuana.

Actually there are plenty of conservatives who would disagree with both of the above propositions. Conservatives have always been divided about the desirability of the draft, and a laissez-faire attitude toward marijuana depends heavily on the assumption (which more recent medical evidence contradicts) that it is essentially harmless to the smoker and those close to him. Also, YAF's sacred tablets of course contain many more propositions than these—many of them anathema to the campus mentality of the 1960s.

But one is entitled to stress the arguments that work, and through the worst of the sixties it is fair to say that YAF survived on many a campus by frequent references to its views on those two issues—much as Winston Churchill said he survived Irish-American audiences during his American lecture tour after the Boer War by adding, as the boos mounted to a crescendo, ". . . and then the Dublin Fusiliers arrived and saved the day!"

The exertion produced some odd compromises. I know of at least one YAF leader of the period who walked around his campus in a western state smoking pot and wearing a suit *with a vest.*

In Washington, however, YAF's national board remained firmly, though sometimes narrowly, in the grip of young conservatives who knew that the draft and pot issues were essentially expedients and who were determined that YAF would not be taken over by extreme libertarians who would push the organization too far in their direction. For several years YAF conventions featured bitter struggles between the "lib" and "trad" (="traditional") factions, but fortunately—or so it seems to me—the "trads" always won.

Like many a family at the time, YAF did not escape one or two tragic episodes involving drugs. The YAF state chairman of one large state eventually wandered away, not only from YAF but from most of the rest of his life and activities, in a sort of stoned haze. And one member of the national board had to be asked to resign when his involvement in heavy drugs became apparent and crippling.

But by and large YAF came through the trauma of the sixties in remarkably good shape. Fate dealt it, in that decade, a singularly poor hand, but it survived with its principles intact, to stand proudly beside all the other (and mostly newer) organizations when victory came at last to American conservatism.

One other episode of the mid-1960s deserves chronicling in this history of the right, and that is Bill Buckley's 1965 race for mayor of New York City.

Following Goldwater's defeat, the official liberal line was that conservatism was as dead as a doornail. It was simply a bad dream that had somehow managed to occur during America's waking hours. Goldwater's 27 million votes represented nothing and pointed nowhere. If there was one lesson to be drawn from it all—for the country, for the Republican party, for the conservatives themselves (if any remained)—it was: "NEVER AGAIN!"

At the same time conservatism really was getting much too

big to be ignored, as it had been up to about 1961, or even merely damned, which had been its fate ever since. It was time to start drawing some useful distinctions, perhaps even to play, discreetly, the old political game of Divide and Conquer.

Of all the personalities on the American right, the only one that liberals frequently got hooked on was Buckley. His blend of sophistication, geniality, and wit struck many of them as irresistible and (as already noted) hinted dangerously that liberals might not, after all, have that total monopoly of sheer fun that had been one of liberalism's greatest attractions in the first place.*

In addition, Buckley had incontestably been one of the founders of modern American conservatism and for ten years one of its leading spokesmen. If any representative of this pestiferous breed had to be accepted as a fixture in American life, therefore, let it be Buckley. Some such, presumably, were the considerations that led *Time* magazine, in the autumn of 1964, to conclude that Bill Buckley at last deserved a cover story.

Buckley, meanwhile, had not lost his considerable gift for attracting public attention. One does not know when his fertile and inventive mind first turned to the possibilities of political candidacy, but certainly there was no lack of stimuli.

In the first place, a public figure of Buckley's stature is forever being told by effusive admirers that he ought to run for president or some other office. Secondly, conservatism had now completed its transition from a pure theory to a political movement and was actively in search of candidates—as Ronald Reagan, among others, was about to discover.

In the third place, the success of Dan Mahoney and his colleagues in putting the Conservative party on the New York State ballot in 1962 had made a Buckley candidacy for just about any office in the state as easy as peeling a banana. He had only to ask Mahoney, and nomination by acclamation would follow—no heavy lifting in a primary, for example.

Finally, the Conservative party was currently (i.e., in the spring of 1965) looking for a suitable candidate to nominate for mayor of New York in the election to be held that November. The Democratic candidate would probably be Abe Beame, a diminu-

---

* See p. 81, supra.

tive and lackluster politician from Brooklyn who was then the city's comptroller and intended to vault into the mayoralty with the fetching slogan "He knows where the money is!"

Actually Beame was simply being thrown to the wolves, or rather the wolf, by the Democratic bosses. The wolf, whom everyone expected to win the election as the next stop on his foreordained road to the White House, was handsome Congressman John V. Lindsay of Manhattan. A liberal Republican of purest hue and deepest dye, Lindsay would be the mayoralty nominee of both the Republican party and the Liberal party—a bit of political crossbreeding that neatly symbolized Lindsay's own views.

And the Conservatives? They would of course fight Lindsay to their dying breath, and they shared the universal lack of interest in Beame. Nervously they canvassed their short list of former candidates; none seemed to fill the bill. It will convey some notion of their desperation to learn that they even asked Buckley to assist them in approaching me on the subject. But I had decided firmly, a decade earlier, that political candidacies were not for me, and over dinner with Bill in a midtown restaurant I firmly closed the door on the possibility of my running for mayor.

But Buckley himself had now felt the wings of temptation rustling by. He knew very well, of course, that he would lose; but it seemed entirely possible that he might, by luring enough conservative Republican voters away from Lindsay, tip the election to Beame—which we would, of course, consider a moral victory because it would stall Lindsay's White House Express in its tracks. In addition, there was a mountain of useful publicity to be gained (publicity, for a person in Bill's business or mine, is almost always later convertible into cash, in the form of speaking fees, etc.) and of course, at the end, a book to be written about it all.

So Buckley began to "show a little ankle," as the old political expression goes. A dreamy column he had written, entitled "Mayor, Anyone?," ran in *National Review*, accompanied by a cover streamer inquiring, "Buckley for Mayor? (p. 498)." New York's conservative community quickly got the points—and the rest is history.*

---

* The book about it all is, of course, Buckley's own *The Unmaking of a Mayor*, published by Viking in 1966 and brought out in paperback by Arlington House with a streamer labeled "Vindication Edition," in 1977.

Buckley did not succeed in stopping John Lindsay at the City Hall door. There are, in fact, bitter Democrats who will tell you that Buckley actually elected Lindsay, by luring more conservative Democrats (Irish, and Catholics generally) away from Beame than he lured Republicans away from Lindsay. There is no way the controversy can be resolved since analyses of the votes actually cast can only show us *approximately* how various ethnic blocs voted.[*]

But in one respect Buckley surely did major damage to Lindsay—damage more serious, conceivably, than denying him the mayoralty would have done, for it cast early into doubt Lindsay's own fundamental qualifications for high office. It is hard to realize today, when John Lindsay is just a smiling wraith on an occasional TV talk show, that he was once many an American liberal's *beau idéal.* "The District's Pride—The Nation's Hope" was the slogan on his congressional campaign posters in the early 1960s, and the implication seemed to many people not all that unreasonable. He was tall, blond, and good-looking, with a stunning smile and a handsome family. It was widely assumed that he was also witty and quick on the uptake, rhetorically speaking. In fact, I had known since our days together in the New York Republican Club from 1949 to 1953 that, as formulated in one popular wisecrack, "John got the looks and Dave"—his nonidentical twin brother— "got the brains." John Lindsay was no fool, but he was no speed demon on the uptake either, and wit was simply way out there beyond him.

Unfortunately for Lindsay the pesky little Conservative party had nominated for mayor a truly lethal combination of speed and wit who was in most other respects Lindsay's peer. Both were in the *Social Register;* both had graduated from Yale after the war (Buckley was actually four years to the day younger than Lindsay); both were men of substantial wealth; both were nationally famous in their forties.

And thus it happened that in the inevitable tripartite television debates in which Lindsay tried desperately to slaughter Beame, he succeeded only in being slaughtered by Buckley. Whereas in a two-way debate with Beame alone, Lindsay could

---

[*] For a persuasive analysis of the case against the Democratic charge, see pp. 302–6 of J. Daniel Mahoney's *Actions Speak Louder* (Arlington House, 1968).

hardly have avoided looking positively incandescent by comparison, in the three-way debates with Buckley and Beame, Lindsay
was lucky if he came away being remembered as second best. In
comparison with Buckley, Lindsay was simply drab—there was no
other word for it.

As a candidate for high office John Lindsay was ultimately
brought down by his own dismal record as mayor: He is one of the
three successive mayors (Wagner, Lindsay, and Beame) who must
share the blame for running New York City straight downhill into
bankruptcy—a technical condition (inability to pay one's debts as
they come due) from which it was rescued by some very fast work
on the part of better men who entered the picture later. But a
substantial part of the glamour that was such an essential part of
the Lindsay Legend was irrevocably tarnished by Bill Buckley before John Lindsay ever reached City Hall. Lindsay's shining hel-
met wasn't silver; it was tin—and Buckley demonstrated it.

It was in that same autumn of 1965 that *National Review* re-
newed and broadened its attack on the John Birch Society. The
society had not grown ominously since 1962, but neither had it
withered away. Buckley clearly felt that the time had come for a
complete break between the John Birch Society and what we
would continue to call the responsible right.

The attack took the form of a special section in *National Review*'s October 19 issue: a preliminary editorial; reprints of three
syndicated Buckley columns on the subject; a special two-page
"Principles and Heresies" column by Frank Meyer; a slightly
longer column by James Burnham; a section called "Questions and
Answers"; and a series of supporting statements by such unchal-
lengeable conservatives as Admiral Arthur W. Radford and Barry
Goldwater.

The concluding paragraph of Meyer's column will sufficiently indicate the flavor of the whole special section:

> The false analysis and conspiratorial mania of the John Birch
> Society has moved beyond diversion and waste of the devotion of
> its members to the mobilization of that devotion in ways directly
> anti-conservative and dangerous to the interests of the United
> States. It is no longer possible to consider the Society merely as
> moving towards legitimate objectives in a misguided way. How-

ever worthy the original motivations of those who have joined it
and who apologize for it, it is time for them to recognize that the
John Birch Society is rapidly losing whatever it had in common
with patriotism or conservatism—and to do so before their own
minds become warped by adherence to its unrolling psychosis of
conspiracy.

Despite *National Review*'s heavy attack, the society did not
oblige it by going out of business. It continued to command the allegiance of several-score thousand members, and does so to this
day. Its most visible manifestations these days are its publications,
especially the monthly *American Opinion* and the weekly *Review
of the News,* both of which hew to the general conspiratorial analysis of events without, however, dwelling unduly on their founder's notions about Dwight Eisenhower. At various points during
the 1960s and '70s the society engaged in a fair amount of overt
political activity, especially promoting the slogans "Impeach Earl
Warren" and "Get US Out of the UN" (or just "Get US Out"). But
more recently the society's profile has been lower, and in the
lengthening perspective of a quarter of a century it has gradually
become a familiar, albeit rather irascible, "presence in the room":
the accepted home of those conservatives for whom an all-encom-
passing Communist conspiracy is the only satisfactory explanation
for a most unsatisfactory world.

The various conservative efforts thus far described, from the
foundation of the American Conservative Union to Buckley's candidacy for mayor, were essentially secondary operations. For the
conservative movement, by backing and nominating Barry Goldwater, had signaled its decision to work for its goals through the
medium of the Republican party, and now in the wake of Goldwater's overwhelming defeat by Lyndon Johnson the question was
whether it could continue to do so.

Certainly the GOP's liberal wing showed every intention of
resuming control of the party if it could. The first potential test of
strength was the choice of a Republican national chairman, and
Barry Goldwater seemed to make a clash inevitable when he insisted that his former AA, Dean Burch, whom he had installed in
the job after his own nomination, must remain in that post. A little
discreet nose counting scotched that idea, however, and ultimately the chairmanship went with Goldwater's consent to a vet-

eran Ohio politician named Ray Bliss, who was known to be an able nuts-and-bolts operator and was also refreshingly free of any ideological predilections.

In the last analysis, of course, the party's direction would be determined by its choice of a nominee in 1968; but meanwhile, the Young Republican and Women's Republican organizations, both of which were still in conservative hands, would choose new leaders, and the GOP liberals decided that these contests were eminently worth winning. At the YR national convention in Miami Beach in 1965 a liberal candidate for the chairmanship of the organization, backed financially by Governor Robert Smylie of Idaho and Republican State Chairman Craig Truax of Pennsylvania, was defeated by Tom Van Sickle, who had been Clif White's chief of staff in the Goldwater trailer at San Francisco's Cow Palace the year before. Nothing daunted, the liberals simply stepped up their attack. Hugh Scott, the liberal Republican senator from Pennsylvania, denounced the conservative Young Republicans as "bigoted and immature young hellions," and in an interview with the *Washington Star*'s Paul Hope in mid-1966 made his intentions amply clear:

> Scott believes control of the auxiliary organizations to the national committee—such as the Young Republican Federation, the Republican Women's Federation and the College Republican Organization—are [sic] of major significance in the nominating process. He contends these groups, through their publications, speakers and convention activities, can get the bandwagon rolling for a Presidential candidate. . . .
>
> The next move of the moderates is to oust conservatives from the leadership of the YRs. Scott claims this will be done at the YR convention next year.
>
> But removal of Goldwater conservatives from YR leadership is only one step in the moderates' objective to take control of the party.

In point of fact, Scott's hopes were not to be realized: Both the Young Republican National Federation and the Federation of Republican Women remained in conservative hands straight through the 1960s. The battle for control of the GOP, however, naturally didn't end there: It simply shifted to the main arena— the contest for the Republican presidential nomination in 1968.

Here the logical liberal choice in the eyes of many people, including himself, was Governor Nelson Rockefeller. Despite earlier hints that his second term would be his last, he ran for reelection in 1966 and was duly returned to Albany, albeit with a margin of less than 400,000 votes—not all that impressive, given New York's size and Rockefeller's resources. But Rockefeller knew very well, by now, how much he was detested by his party's conservatives. From every standpoint, therefore, it was desirable that the liberal banner in the 1968 competition should be carried, at least at first, by someone else. Shortly after Rockefeller was reelected in November 1966, he declared himself through with seeking the presidency and endorsed Governor George Romney of Michigan for the 1968 Republican nomination.

Romney, a handsome, silver-haired businessman, had himself just been reelected governor by more than half a million votes—an impressive margin in Michigan. Romney was a devout Mormon, and his religiosity was so pronounced that critics were fond of saying that he "regards the White House as a stepping-stone." He was broadly liberal in his views, as Republicans went, but had managed not to offend nearly so many people as Rockefeller. With the boost of Rockefeller's endorsement, generously supplemented by financial support and the use of Rockefeller's matchless research staff, the Michigan governor's boom was quickly under way. In no time at all the liberal media were happily hailing George Romney as "the odds-on front-runner" for the 1968 GOP nomination.

Whether Rockefeller's endorsement was entirely sincere, and his own reemergence as a candidate in June 1968 simply a response to Romney's unanticipated collapse, or whether Rockefeller intended from the start to use Romney simply as a stalking-horse, is impossible to say. No doubt Rockefeller by 1966 had a very realistic appreciation of the obstacles to the realization of his own ambitions, and he may have decided, like Thomas Dewey before him, that the best he could do was nominate and elect someone else. But whatever he thought in 1966, Nelson Rockefeller was simply too elemental a force to remain sidelined in such a manner for long.

Meanwhile, his old adversaries, the conservatives, had found a new and formidable champion—a fact that raised some delicate questions about 1968.

❀   ❀   ❀

By early 1966, as Bill Buckley began work on *The Unmaking of a Mayor,* another conservative spokesman and hero was musing about running for office—and not merely for the satisfaction of writing a book about it afterward. The job was governor of California, and Ronald Reagan intended to win.

Reagan's speeches on free enterprise during the early 1960s, plus his readings in *National Review* and no doubt other conservative publications, had made him an able and articulate spokesman for the economic aspects of conservatism and given him a broad familiarity with, and sympathy for, the entire spectrum of conservative thought. Whether he had become, or ever became thereafter, what we have called a movement conservative, however, is a nice question.

Reagan's life and experiences in Hollywood, as president of the Screen Actors Guild, and with General Electric, had made him a results-oriented man of action. Not for him—or for many—the scholar's lamp, the twenty-five-year wait, the slow pivot of the intellectual world on the fulcrum of history. He was good—nay, superb—at working with people. He genuinely liked them, and they responded in kind and were usually willing to do what Reagan wanted done.

Such a personality would simply have been wasted among the diehard ideologues of the conservative movement. Ronald Reagan was born for politics, and he rightly sensed that it was in politics that he could best serve the cause of conservatism and therefore, as he saw it, his country. His October 1964 television speech for Goldwater had made this equally apparent to a great many other people, and by early 1965 the Californians among them were urging him to run against the incumbent Democratic governor, Pat Brown, who would be seeking reelection in November 1966.

Thus far I have avoided going needlessly over old ground already well covered by others, and I will stick to that rule and avoid inserting here a résumé of the life of Ronald Reagan. There are already several excellent biographies of him in print, and interested readers are referred to one or more of these.*

For our purposes, suffice it to say that sometime in 1965—probably a good bit earlier than the artfully phased and carefully timed public statements would lead one to suspect—Reagan made

* Cf. Lee Edwards, *Ronald Reagan: A Political Biography* (Nordland, 1980), and Lou Cannon, *Reagan* (Putnam, 1982).

up his mind to run for governor of California. Naturally enough, he did so only after wealthy friends and supporters assured him that the necessary campaign funds would be forthcoming and after he had convinced himself that he could make an overwhelming case against Brown.

The California Republican establishment did not exactly welcome Reagan with open arms. San Francisco Mayor George Christopher ran against him in the primary, arguing that Reagan was too far to the right and too closely identified with the Goldwater disaster to win. But Goldwater or no Goldwater, the conservative tide was running fast in California in 1966, as in so much of the West and South, and Reagan was right where it was converging with the tide of history itself. He walked over Christopher in the primary, and on November 8, 1966, defeated Pat Brown for the governship of America's most populous state by a margin of 965,898 votes: 57.8 percent to 42.2 percent. Just two years after Barry Goldwater's defeat by Lyndon Johnson, American conservatives had found a new, dynamic, and articulate leader.

Politics, however, is a zero-sum game, and good news for somebody is usually bad news for somebody else. Reagan's 1966 triumph did not sit at all well with at least one highly interested observer.

Richard Nixon had been watching the political scene from the sidelines with the fascination of an addict ever since his own defeat for the governorship of California in 1962 at the hands of that same Pat Brown. The 1962 bid had been Nixon's desperate attempt to rehabilitate himself after his 1960 loss to Kennedy, and when Brown beat him by 297,000 votes (aided heavily by the animosities that had been roused against Nixon in the Republican primary campaign of conservative Assemblyman Joseph Shell), Nixon hit bottom. Seeing no future for himself in politics, he told the media at his "last press conference" that "You won't have Nixon to kick around anymore." Then he shook the dust of California from his feet, moved to New York, and joined a Wall Street law firm. Strolling up Park Avenue one day, he confided to a friend that "This is where the action is—not with those peasants back in California."*

---

* I later heard this directly from the friend in question.

But politics is a difficult habit to break, and Nixon was soon watching developments in the GOP as carefully as ever. When Barry Goldwater won the Republican presidential nomination in 1964, Nixon, who knew perfectly well that Goldwater was in for a resounding defeat, was on hand in the Cow Palace to introduce the Arizonan to the convention, on the night of his acceptance speech. He even hailed him, in the traditional phrase, as "the next President of the United States." Then he hit the campaign trail and worked hard for Goldwater that autumn.

These were shrewd moves, and they were to pay dividends that must have surprised even Nixon. On January 22, 1965, Goldwater—out of the Senate and back in Arizona—told interviewers publicly that he would support Nixon for the Republican presidential nomination in 1968. Such a declaration, by a man in Goldwater's position, was wildly premature, but events were to prove, and quickly, that Goldwater meant every word of it. He spent a good part of his time urging his pro-Nixon views on leading conservatives who paid courtesy calls on him in Phoenix, and he spread the same word zealously, on trips to Washington, among his conservative cronies still in the U.S. Senate.

Goldwater's open conversion to the Nixon cause was of priceless value to Nixon, who had by now recovered his political appetite and set his sights on the presidency in 1968. "A Republican can't win without the conservatives—1962 taught me that," he told a friend in the mid-1960s (alluding to his defeat for governor after his bruising primary battle with conservative challenger Joe Shell), "but he also can't win with the conservatives alone—1964 showed that." Accordingly, Nixon's strategy for 1968 was clear: Nail down the conservatives, but then go beyond them—toward the center. Thanks to Barry Goldwater, he was well on his way to nailing down the conservatives. If Nixon was conservative enough to suit Goldwater, surely he was acceptable, was he not, to the conservative movement as a whole? Can one be more royalist than the king?

And then along came Ronald Reagan, winning by nearly a million votes the very governorship that had been denied to Nixon just four years earlier and gaining, in addition, the allegiance of millions of conservatives whom Nixon had expected to pick up easily, thanks to the blessing of his grateful friend Barry. In a by-line dispatch to the *New York Times* from YAF's convention in

Pittsburgh on September 1, 1967, Homer Bigart reported the new mood of the young conservatives:

> Gov. Ronald Reagan of California appeared today to have supplanted Barry Goldwater as the national hero of the Young Americans for Freedom, a conservative, 30,000-member organization that played an important role in the successful Goldwater nomination drive of 1964.
>
> Reagan posters and pins dominated the organization's convention here and a group calling itself Students for Reagan began a national campaign to drum up campus support for the Governor's expected bid for the Republican nomination next year.
>
> The 500 convention delegates roared their adulation for Mr. Goldwater, the main speaker at the dinner meeting tonight at the Pittsburgh Hilton Hotel. But their allegiance, despite Mr. Goldwater's continued preference for former Vice President Richard M. Nixon, seemed to have shifted solidly to Governor Reagan as the Republican hopeful in 1968.

Since it had to be assumed that Reagan, as the incumbent governor of California, might well decide to seek the GOP presidential nomination in 1968 (and close observers noted that Reagan was careful not to rule out this possibility altogether—e.g., by endorsing Nixon), Nixon was now faced with the difficult task of waging a two-front war for the nomination: against Nelson Rockefeller or some substitute such as George Romney on his left, competing with him for centrist and liberal support, and—at least possibly—against Reagan on his right, dividing the allegiance of the conservatives.

Of course, there was another way of looking at it. In a contest with Rockefeller and Reagan, Nixon was, in ideological terms, the centrist—a highly strategic position since it tended to look inherently reasonable, attracted anyone who felt disposed to compromise, and made any stop-Nixon coalition between Rockefeller and Reagan extremely difficult to engineer because the supporters of both were ideologically closer to Nixon than they were to each other.*

---

* Governor Thomas Dewey of New York had skillfully exploited a basically similar situation in 1948, to defeat Robert Taft and Harold Stassen for the nomination.

From the standpoint of conservatives, who naturally had no use for either Rockefeller or Romney, the advent of Ronald Reagan as a possible 1968 presidential contender raised important questions. Barry Goldwater was, of course, almost as inconvenienced by the whole thing as Nixon himself, having committed himself publicly to Nixon in 1965, and this may explain, all by itself, one of the more baffling mysteries in the modern history of American conservatism: Goldwater's steadfast and strenuous opposition to Reagan's presidential bids in both 1968 and 1976. Reagan himself is known to have been puzzled by it, and his friends have speculated that Goldwater might have been a bit jealous of the highly favorable response to Reagan's October 1964 TV speech on his behalf. Whatever the reason, Goldwater hewed tenaciously to his pro Nixon line right through 1967 and down to the Miami Beach convention in August 1968.

Other conservatives were less certain and to some extent divided. Many—of whom I was very definitely one—had never believed that Nixon was dependably conservative, had welcomed Reagan as the obvious new leader of the conservative movement, and now favored his nomination in 1968 even though his own experience in public office, at that point, would be limited to two years as governor of California. A good many others, however, while admitting that Reagan was more to their personal taste, felt that Nixon was conservative "enough" and more electable in what they assumed would be the political atmosphere of 1968. A relative few actually preferred Nixon to Reagan—mostly on the basis of their personal closeness to Nixon. One prominent conservative resolved the sticky problem for himself by advising friends in 1967, as an immutable proposition in the natural law, that "No actor can possibly be qualified for the presidency."*

In any case, Nixon promptly stepped up his hitherto halfhearted attempts to woo the conservatives. As one important step, in January 1966 he had hired Patrick Buchanan as a member of his personal staff, to serve as a speechwriter and also more or less as chief of what might be called the conservative desk. At the time Buchanan was a young editorial writer for the *St. Louis*

---

* In 1968, when a Reagan nomination seemed more possible, this man began to speak favorably of the idea. On being asked what had become of his dictum about actors, he replied calmly, "I've changed my mind."

Globe-Democrat, where his feisty conservatism had already attracted local notice. (Just a year later Nixon—being Nixon—also hired Ray Price, a Jock Whitney protégé who had formerly been chief editorial writer for the *New York Herald Tribune,* as a speechwriter and chief of his "liberal desk.") Another conservative recruit added to Nixon's personal staff at this time was Tom Huston, an Indianan who had served as national chairman of Young Americans for Freedom. Between Buchanan and Huston, Nixon managed to stay in touch with just about all the major personalities and institutions on the American right.

One of Buchanan's earliest assignments was to get Nixon out of a contretemps with *National Review* into which he had carelessly wandered. On October 14, 1965, during the last month of Bill Buckley's race for the New York mayoralty, columnists Evans and Novak reported that "in a recent conversation with newspaper reporters, Nixon described the Buckleyites as a threat to the Republican party even more menacing than the Birchers." A few days later Scripps-Howard by-liner Bruce Biossat reported much the same thing, telling his readers that Nixon had been "emphatic . . . in chats with newsmen" in asserting that Buckleyites were "the worst threat to the Party's difficult rebuilding efforts."

As *National Review*'s leading house skeptic on the general subject of Richard Nixon, I claimed the privilege of inviting him to deny or retract the statement attributed to him by Evans and Novak. Phone calls to friends of mine close to Nixon yielded only equivocal results. In a letter to Nixon dated October 14, therefore, I explained that "as a fairly well-known Buckleyite, I would deeply appreciate knowing whether the above remark was correctly attributed to you."

No answer.

On November 2, I tried again: "Quite frankly, I cannot believe that you uttered those words. But it is critically important to many conservative Republicans to know whether, in fact, you did or not—and only you can tell us that."

Silence.

A further inquiry, dated January 10, was likewise ignored.

At that point *National Review* itself harrumphed and got into the act. An editorial in the March 8 issue squeezed Mr. Nixon pretty hard:

Now, we do not want to complicate Mr. Nixon's life unnecessarily. On the other hand, the question he is avoiding is one of a certain importance—not only to "the Buckleyites," but to conservative Republicans in general, and for that matter to Liberals too, both in and out of the GOP.

We take "the Buckleyites" to mean those conservative Republicans who, like Wm. F. Buckley and this journal, have explicitly condemned the well-known absurdities of Robert Welch and his followers in the John Birch Society, but who also refuse to cheer mock-Republicans like John Lindsay when in capturing local outposts of the Republican Party they betray the very principles that make Republicanism worth supporting.

If Richard Nixon in fact believes this viewpoint represents "a threat to the Republican party even more menacing than the Birchers," there are a lot of people who would like to know about it. If he doesn't, then he has been seriously misrepresented and he should say so.

That finally produced the following masterpiece of broken-field running by the newly hired Pat Buchanan. It was in the form of a letter to *National Review:*

Because there seems to be some misunderstanding as to the facts in the *National Review* editorial of March 8 (p. 196), Mr. Nixon asked me to investigate the background of the matter, to check press reports, and to reply.

Last fall, while campaigning for Republican candidates in California, Virginia and elsewhere, Mr. Nixon was on several occasions asked in press conferences for comment on Mr. Buckley's candidacy, and the John Birch Society.

Mr. Nixon invariably replied that Mr. Buckley, by his repudiation of the Birch Society in his magazine and syndicated column, had thereby made himself a much stronger candidate and a greater threat to the Republican candidate, Representative Lindsay.

Upon reading contradictory press reports of that statement, Mr. Rusher telephoned Charles McWhorter, a former legislative aide of Mr. Nixon. In a return call, Mr. McWhorter related to Mr. Rusher the substance of Mr. Nixon's statement.

Certainly, as a rule, a conservative who repudiates the Birch Society becomes a much stronger candidate than one who refuses to do so.

However, Mr. Nixon is firmly convinced that the best interests of conservatives are served by their joining and working within the framework of the Republican Party.

As he has often emphasized, it would be a tragedy for this nation if conservatives should abandon the GOP to form splinter parties. The result of such divisions would mean permanent minority status for both conservative ideas and the Republican Party.

Patrick J. Buchanan

New York, N.Y.   Aide to Mr. Nixon

To which *National Review* replied editorially (April 5):

The first and most important point to make is that the Nixon statement squarely disavows the report of columnists Evans and Novak last October 14. . . . Not so at all, says Mr. Nixon's aide, Patrick Buchanan. What Nixon said—and said "invariably"—was that William Buckley, by his criticisms of the John Birch Society, had "made himself a much stronger candidate [for Mayor] and a greater threat to the Republican candidate, Representative Lindsay." Quite a difference.

One does wonder, though, assuming that this simple explanation of Mr. Nixon's controversial remark is correct (and we believe it is), why he should have refused to answer our publisher's brief and courteous letter of inquiry dated October 14. And if the reason was that he preferred not to comment during the closing days of the hardfought [sic] mayoralty campaign, why did he also leave unanswered Mr. Rusher's second appeal for a clarification, dated November 2, when the election campaign was over. Why, in short, did it take three letters, a nationwide television program, a further Evans and Novak column, and an editorial in *National Review* to wrest a written statement from "Patrick J. Buchanan, Aide to Mr. Nixon"? It is just this sort of calculating caution that has too often characterized Richard Nixon's public style, leaving even those who agreed with his stated views a little uneasy about the man himself.

But we repeat: we gladly accept the proffered explanation at its face value. . . . So all's well that ends well. And if Richard Nixon is willing to give personal leadership to the Republican conservatives, he will find them ready to follow him.

Under Buchanan's careful tutelage, Nixon made no more such blunders in dealing with "the Buckleyites."

A typical means of "stroking" conservative contacts was for

Buchanan or Huston to ask the person in question to write a memorandum for Nixon on some policy question of special interest to the writer. Flattered to have Nixon (who at this point was simply a Wall Street lawyer but was also quite possibly the next president) asking for his opinion, the targeted individual would spend long hours preparing the memorandum and then submit it to the aide who had requested it. Two or three tense weeks would pass, and then the writer would be told, "The boss liked your memo." This news usually elated the victim beyond words—he was, after all, in direct and fruitful communication with the next president of the United States! (He would also, of course, be a loyal Nixon supporter thenceforth.)

I have no idea whether Nixon ever actually saw all those memos or not, let alone whether he actually liked them. But I saw the technique used on several close friends of mine (and I am sure Ray Price was using it on vulnerable liberals), and I can testify to its efficacy.

In addition, Nixon began to arrange private meetings with leading conservatives to exchange views and quietly encourage their support for his presidential candidacy. I received two such invitations—one extended to fifteen or twenty conservative journalists, who were invited to meet Nixon one afternoon in August 1966 at the Sheraton Park in Washington, for an off-the-record chat; and the other a more exclusive invitation, to Buckley and me, to visit Nixon privately on January 14, 1967, at his apartment at Fifth Avenue and Seventy-second Street. We brought along Neal Freeman, a recent Yale graduate who had served as Buckley's personal aide during the 1965 New York mayoralty race, and Nixon had invited Buchanan and Victor Lasky, a conservative writer who was his close friend and adviser. The discussion lasted an astonishing three hours and ended then only because both Buckley and I had other appointments. I remember being particularly struck by the way in which almost every imaginable subject had, in Nixon's estimation, two sides. "On the one hand," he would begin, outlining the case for one view. "On the *other* hand," he would then continue, pressing his palms together and flipping them over like pancakes—and go on to state the other side of the question. He seemed fascinated by this dual nature of the universe.

By the latter part of 1967 such careful and persistent efforts as these had harvested an impressive share of support for Nixon's candidacy among conservatives who had fought for Goldwater in 1964. Nixon could scarcely feel comfortable about this, however, as long as he didn't know what Reagan might do. Out in California, that question was very much on the minds of the new governor and his friends.

The governor of California is, *ex officio,* a major figure in national politics. As chief executive of the country's largest state—a state so imposing in economic terms that its gross product exceeds the gross national product of all but seven countries on earth—he deals with governmental affairs on a scale smaller only than that of the president himself. Like the governors of New York when New York was America's largest state, he is automatically on everybody's list of possible presidential candidates.

Certainly this was true of Ronald Reagan when he assumed office in Sacramento in January 1967, and he knew it as well as anybody else. But there were important inhibitions on any early declaration of his presidential candidacy, and Reagan was acutely aware of these, too.

In the first place, the California governorship, though an extremely high post, was the first political office Reagan had ever held, and there were plenty of people still around in January 1967—including many conservatives—who were not sure that a lifelong professional actor could fill this important post successfully. Only time would tell—and only a year and a half would elapse before the Republicans assembled, in the summer of 1968, to nominate their presidential candidate. Could Reagan possibly qualify as *presidentabile* in such a short time?

Secondly, Californians had not, in 1967, become so accustomed to being the nation's largest state that the idea of their governor's being *automatically* a possible presidential candidate was acceptable to them. Parochially they tended to think that being governor of California ought to be enough for anybody. No doubt, too, since familiarity is a famous breeder of contempt, they may have had a tendency to withhold from their governors the honor these prophets were accorded elsewhere. Reagan sensed that the voters of California would not forgive an apparent neglect of state business in pursuit of the presidency as readily as New Yorkers forgave Nelson Rockefeller. Every time Reagan left California, from his inauguration through the summer of 1968, the Democratic majority leader of the State Assembly would loudly deplore the governor's absence. Pretty clearly, Reagan was vulnerable to such needling.

Nevertheless, Reagan's overwhelming election to the governorship of California, coupled with the high regard in which he had been held by American conservatives ever since his dramatic television speech for Goldwater in October 1964, made him a possible conservative candidate for the 1968 presidential nomination whether he liked it or not. Reagan and his inner circle recognized this, and even before he was sworn in as governor, they had given it their serious attention. According to Theodore White in his book *The Making of the President—1968* (Atheneum, 1969), "Within ten days of his election, Reagan had gathered his inner circle together, on Thursday, November 17th, 1966, at his home in Pacific Palisades for a first discussion of the Presidency. There, too, was named a captain for the adventure—young Tom Reed, a distinguished physicist turned successful industrialist. . . ."

If so, it must have been a busy day for Reed, for that very evening he flew up to San Francisco and had a drink with me as I ate a late supper in the Garden Court of the Palace Hotel. I had just arrived, on a western trip keyed to various speaking engagements, and had no doubt in my own mind that Reagan ought to be the conservative choice for the 1968 presidential nomination. I was already in personal touch with Reagan—my position as publisher of *National Review* had opened that door without the slightest difficulty—and I knew that Reed (who held the post of Republican national committeeman from California) was in charge of assessing the 1968 situation for the governor-elect. That evening in San Francisco I wasted no time on formalities: I urged him, in the strongest possible terms, to approach my old friend Clif White about joining the Reagan team and heading the 1968 effort.

White already knew Reagan casually. And White's original draft-Goldwater team, substantially modified and augmented since 1961–62 but still appropriately nicknamed the Hard Core, had kept in mutual touch after Goldwater's defeat and was not at all averse to choosing and backing a suitably conservative candidate in 1968. Most of them had even met for a reunion at the

O'Hare Inn near the Chicago airport on January 31, 1965 (a meeting I was unable to attend), and agreed to maintain a watching brief with exactly that in mind. It seemed clear even then that the great majority of Republicans still considered themselves conservatives despite Goldwater's defeat by Johnson and that events in the nation at large such as the civil rights disorders, the Berkeley free speech movement, etc. were likely to reinforce this tendency.

But Reagan in January 1965 had been only a gleam in the eye of certain farsighted conservatives. Now in November 1966 he was governor-elect of California—a spectacular illustration of the old aphorism about the superior virtue of a bird in the hand.

Reed must have been favorably impressed with my recommendation because within a week he had phoned White and arranged for the governor to confer with him. Contact and negotiations between White and the Reagan forces continued throughout most of 1967 with all indications favorable, despite a certain reluctance on both parts to seem too eager. Retaining White as a consultant, let alone as a campaign manager, would be a signal to the world that Reagan intended to run for the nomination in 1968—an intention by no means yet firm in Reagan's own mind.

As for White, he was at this time in the happy position of being "stroked" by all of the likely 1968 contenders—Nixon, Romney, and (at a later stage) Rockefeller—though it seems probable that the intention in each of these cases was more to deter White from working for anyone else than to employ him as his own top manager. In any case White was, both instinctively and ideologically, more powerfully drawn to Reagan, and at another Chicago meeting of the Hard Core on March 4 and 5, 1967, it transpired that most of his old co-workers agreed with him.

With White's concurrence Reagan let it be known that he would be California's favorite son candidate in 1968, though ostensibly only for the sake of keeping the delegation united for purposes of effective politicking at the convention. But no mere favorite son candidacy could hope to overcome the head of steam Nixon's candidacy was building up as 1967 progressed, and on October 13 White convened the Hard Core for the third time that year—this time at the Dupont Plaza Hotel in Miami, just across Biscayne Bay from the municipal auditorium where the Republicans were planning to hold their convention ten months later. With typical practicality he intended to give his regimental commanders a look at the arena where they would wage their next battle.

Meanwhile, there was a formal decision to be made on who our candidate would be. In a mezzanine conference room at the Dupont Plaza, behind a door bearing the comfortably meaningless sign APEX CO., those present conferred on the afternoon of October 13 and again the next day. At a final session on Sunday morning, the fifteenth, White was authorized to reach final agreement with Reagan's representatives, subject to a more formal "undertaking" to be affirmed in the presence of two or three additional members of the Hard Core.

In mid-November White flew to California to work out the details of the agreement with the Reagan forces, and on December 7 these were confirmed by White and two veteran members of the Hard Core: Dave Nichols and Andy Carter. Now the group could really go to work.

To avoid the (supposedly premature) crossing of the Rubicon that would have been signaled by naming White as Reagan's campaign manager, it was agreed that technically White would simply be retained "independently," by a group of Reagan's longtime friends in California, to "explore the possibility" of a Reagan candidacy. Moreover, White accepted this cautious arrangement with the further understanding that there were strict limitations on the extent to which he would be able to call on Reagan for excursions outside California.

Nevertheless, the deal was struck, and the forces backing Reagan were thereby automatically augmented by the considerable influence and formidable expertise of a large portion of the cohesive group that had engineered the nomination of Barry Goldwater.

To insure the separation of the whole operation from Reagan himself, Reed and White did not even conduct their activities from an office in Sacramento. White, when he was not on the road, could usually be found, innocently enough, in his own longtime Suite 3505 in the Chanin Building on New York's Lexington Avenue, which he had retained as the office of his political consultancy business. Tom Reed, White's colleague and chief contact with his supposed California employers, operated out of a small office on the fifth floor of 47 Kearny Street in San Francisco. (The frosted glass door bore the name of one of the Reed family's agreeably inert oil businesses.) A great many political reporters ransacked Sacramento late in 1967 and through the early months of 1968 in a futile search for "the Reagan presidential campaign headquarters" and came away convinced that there was no such campaign because they could not find its offices. Elementary, my dear Watson: They were elsewhere.

In retrospect, though, it may well be that this extraordinarily hesitant, belated, and almost halfhearted approach to a Reagan candidacy, which reflected Reagan's own ambivalence on the subject, fatally slowed the whole operation, depriving it of the momentum it needed if Nixon was to be bested at the 1968 convention. Theodore White, in his account of the 1968 battle, attributes Reagan's fatal hesitancy to his shock and confusion when a small homosexual clique was discovered in the summer of 1967 in his staff in Sacramento, requiring a major reshuffling of personnel. Clif White, in his own recent account of Reagan's long battle for the presidency,* doubts that the episode had all that much influence on Reagan, and so do I. Reagan's hesitancy may have been unwise, but it had the far better grounds, mentioned earlier: his recognition of the widespread feeling that an ex-actor might not, after less than two years as governor of California, be ready for a presidential nomination and his sensitivity to the belief of many California voters that their governor ought not to go campaigning out of the state.

In addition, Reagan was by now feeling considerable pressure from certain fellow conservatives who were themselves already—perhaps prematurely but nonetheless firmly—pledged to support Nixon in 1968. This was certainly true of Barry Goldwater, who, as already noted, had publicly endorsed Nixon in January 1965. Throughout 1965 and 1966 Goldwater proselytized tirelessly for his favorite, and Reagan's election as governor in November 1966 did nothing to shake Goldwater's allegiance to Nixon. Other leading conservatives were signed up for Nixon by Goldwater during 1967, and members of this group naturally did nothing to encourage Reagan's candidacy—quite the contrary.

* F. Clifton White and William J. Gill, *Why Reagan Won* (Regnery Gateway, 1981).

At the Bohemian Grove in the summer of 1967 Goldwater and Reagan conferred at length. Goldwater came away believing he had obtained Reagan's agreement not to seek the 1968 nomination unless Nixon "stumbled" in his pursuit of it. The recollection of Reagan's backers is rather different and more ambiguous, but the fact is that Reagan, for whatever reason or set of reasons, did hold back from active candidacy until well into 1968.

Chapter VIII

The Blunder of 1968

By early 1968 the rush of conservatives—many of them veterans of the old Goldwater days—to Nixon had become a hemorrhage. Our old friend Peter O'Donnell, who had chaired the Draft Goldwater Committee, was one such, and from a critical state: Texas. John Ashbrook was another. So was Bill Timmons of Tennessee, who had been one of our staunchest Young Republican allies as well as a battler for Goldwater in 1964. To my distress I also learned that Jeremiah Milbank, Jr., the longtime Republican fund raiser whose conservative credentials could be traced all the way back to Robert Taft, would go to Miami Beach as a delegate pledged to Nixon. Even *Human Events* endorsed him.

It was in the U.S. Senate, however, that Reagan in 1968 proved weakest where he ought to have been strongest. Here, unquestionably, the effective agent was Barry Goldwater. Goldwater had been out of the Senate himself since the end of 1964 (though he would be reelected to succeed Carl Hayden in 1968), but he had kept in close contact with his former colleagues and scored some striking successes for Nixon. Most important of all, South Carolina's J. Strom Thurmond became convinced that 1968 was Richard Nixon's year.

In fairness, the conservatives who supported Nixon in 1968 had a powerful case to make for their position. Many were sincerely convinced that Nixon, though not as conservative as Reagan, was conservative "enough"—whatever that might mean. And no wonder: Nixon had taken great care, especially since 1966, to cultivate exactly that impression. It was also true that 1964 was less than four years in the past, and the memory of Goldwater's bitter defeat by Johnson was still keen. America might indeed be trending to the right, and Ronald Reagan was undoubtedly doing a superb job of epitomizing and capitalizing on that trend, but who could be sure that American voters as a whole were ready to go quite that far? Nixon was a critical step or two nearer the (apparent) political center, and many a conservative whose heart was with Ronald Reagan felt that prudence demanded the nomination of the "less extreme" Nixon.

For these and other reasons, the movement of conservatives to Nixon became downright alarming to Reagan and his inner circle through the latter part of 1967 and the early months of 1968. In January, putting aside his concern over what California voters might think, Reagan made a swing around the country, speaking at Republican fund-raising dinners and being, almost everywhere, well received.

On February 28 George Romney, who had failed to excite even much liberal enthusiasm, recognized the inevitable and withdrew as a candidate for the nomination. This left Nelson Rockefeller precisely where he wanted to be, but considerably earlier than he wanted to be there. Most of the important primaries were still ahead, and Republican primaries were one thing Rockefeller always tried to avoid wherever possible. Accordingly, on March 21 he fell back on the strategy he had employed in 1960: proclaiming himself out of the race but in fact positioning himself for a fresh plunge into candidacy once the last primaries were over in early June.

But Reagan's problem was Nixon, not Rockefeller, and by now it was evident to me that some major move would be necessary on Reagan's part to acquire the momentum needed for victory. The problem was discussed at length in a meeting of the Hard Core in St. Louis on March 23 and 24.* Under date of March 25 I circulated the following memorandum to White and Reed, among others:

MEMO TO: Those concerned
FROM: Bill Rusher
DATE: March 25, 1968

I think it may be useful for me to set down in writing, if only for the record, the proposal I made this weekend. My impression

* Tom Reed joined us at this meeting, and the Hard Core members present, in addition to White, Rita Bree, and me, were: Charles Barr, Jerry Harkins (who had been Goldwater co-chairman for Missouri), Ione Harrington, Sam Hay, James Mack (a young midwestern political manager who had also worked with us in 1964), Robert Matthews, William McFadzean, Roger Moore, David Nichols, John Keith Rehmann, John Tope, Tom Van Sickle, and Frank Whetstone. It is a remarkable testimony to the durability of the group that, of the sixteen present at this 1968 meeting, fourteen had attended at least one of our early Goldwater meetings in 1961 and 1962.

was that it generated quite a lot of support, and I urge you to give it your serious consideration.

Our strategy for maximizing Reagan's influence at Miami Beach has always depended upon the assumption that it would be a "brokered" convention. It still seems very likely that this is the kind of convention we will have; but Nixon's apparent long lead ("apparent" to the grass roots, who will be voting in the opinion polls, and probably to the county leadership level of the GOP) makes a stampede a real possibility. I think we must take what steps we can, while there is still time, to prevent it from becoming a reality.

If we are agreed up to that point, let me next say that I do *not* think it is going to be enough to escalate the Reagan movement only imperceptibly, or by such slow and silent methods that it goes substantially unnoticed. However, even if such a sort of escalation were possible, it would merely defeat our necessary objective.

What is needed, I think, is a "big splash"—i.e., an event that will instantly be recognized as ranking with the other major events in the campaign thus far: Romney's withdrawal, Kennedy's entrance and Rockefeller's apparent pullout. I recognize and accept the fact that this event cannot be a declaration of candidacy by Governor Reagan. But I think the form of Rockefeller's pullout provides a pattern which we can and should follow.

Essentially, Rockefeller has said (1) that he is not a candidate, (2) that he is available for the nomination if he is wanted and (3) that he intends to spend his time between now and Miami Beach addressing himself actively to the issues, with a view to exerting a major influence on the platform. Why cannot Governor Reagan say exactly the same thing?

Specifically, why can he not go before a press conference in Sacramento and make some such statement as the following:

"Gentlemen of the press, I have called you together because three recent developments have caused a substantial change in my intentions with respect to my actions during the next four months. First, Senator Kennedy has declared his candidacy for President and entered the California primary. His action brings into sharp focus many of the issues that confront this nation, and as the unopposed favorite son of California for the Republican nomination I would in any case consider it my obligation to outline, in depth and in detail, my differences with Senator Kennedy.

"Second, Governor Rockefeller of New York has reiterated his previous declarations that he is not an active candidate, though he remains available for the nomination if the office seeks the man. That, as you know, has been my own position from the beginning, and it remains my position today. But Governor Rockefeller, in his recent statement, went on to say that he would devote himself, during the next four months, to the discussion and development of the issues, with a view to the manner in which they will be framed by the Republican platform. I welcome his announcement to this effect, though (as you all know) there are many respects in which my own views on the issues of the day differ from those of the Governor of New York. I consider it vital that the Republican delegates at Miami Beach should have the opportunity to hear all sides of these urgent questions.

"Third, as a result of Speaker Unruh's preoccupation with the Kennedy candidacy in the California Democratic primary, we are going to have a recess in the current session of the legislature. I think it is important that the time thus gained be put to the best possible use, not only in shaping the future course of the Democratic Party but in shaping that of the Republican Party as well.

"Accordingly, I have decided to devote as much as possible of the days and months ahead to an active participation in the many-sided dialogue whereby the Republican Party will decide, in Miami Beach, on the best course for itself and for America. I shall do this in a series of policy talks, the first of which will be delivered right here in Sacramento on April 10th. The second will be given in Washington on April 24th, and the remainder, at intervals of approximately two weeks thereafter in cities and on dates of which you will be advised.

"The Republican Party has nothing to fear from a frank discussion of the issues that confront America today. Unless we can clarify our purposes abroad, and bring them into an intelligent balance with our actions, while at the same time coping sensitively with the desperate crisis that confronts us on the home front, our country will have lost its way—perhaps irretrievably. But time is short. I call upon every citizen to join in one common search, one common aspiration: For a Better America. I pledge my own best efforts to that end."

My suggestion—which doesn't look all that bad, I must say, in retrospect—was not adopted, but Attorney General Robert Kennedy's announcement of his candidacy on March 16, coupled with Johnson's dramatic withdrawal from the race on March 31, had the effect of galvanizing Reagan to some degree. Reagan, who thought Kennedy would win the nomination and sincerely believed his election would be a disaster, abandoned his favorite son pose in all but name and hit the road, bidding openly for delegate support. And at 4:00 P.M. on Monday, August 5—scant hours before the convention opened—Reagan officially became a bona fide candidate for the Republican presidential nomination, as distinguished from merely a favorite son.

White's strategy was based on his realization that Nixon's support among the conservatives in many delegations was, to put it charitably, only skin-deep. Many of them were acutely miserable, now that Reagan had declared himself a serious candidate, but were inhibited by the fact that they had pledged their support to Nixon months previously. A large number were locked into delegations bound by the unit rule, or were legally committed to vote for Nixon on the first ballot. *The first ballot:* That was the key. Nixon would be at his strongest on that first ballot. If he could be held short of a majority, his total would shrink on succeeding ballots like a scoop of ice cream in the sun. The way would then be cleared for a final battle between Reagan and Rockefeller, and White was serenely confident as to how that would turn out.

"What might have been" are famous as being the saddest words of tongue or pen, and they are at least in the running for being the most futile as well. The world is forgivably little interested, nowadays, in the fact that Seward came close to defeating Lincoln for the Republican presidential nomination in 1860. But Richard Nixon is no Lincoln, and in view of the unexampled disaster his selection was to prove for his country, his party, and the conservative movement, it deserves to be recorded that his nomination was by no means—as it tends to look in retrospect—either certain or even easy.

In making this point I do not even have the concurrence of President Reagan, who these days is humanly inclined to forget that he did indeed run, and lose to Nixon, in 1968. But in his 1981 book *Why Reagan Won*, Clif White entitled his chapter on the 1968 convention "The Near Miss." And three British reporters (Lewis Chester, Godfrey Hodgson, and Bruce Page) who coauthored a careful report on the 1968 election entitled *An American Melodrama* (Viking, 1969), correctly noted that "Nixon's final majority was agonizingly—almost insultingly—small." What made it so small was the stubborn battle waged by Reagan, Clif White, and the Hard Core.

By the time the convention opened the battle had narrowed down to a struggle for the votes of three southern delegations: Alabama, Mississippi, and Florida. The delegate totals for Nixon, Reagan, and Rockefeller, as reported by the media and in some cases actually believed by important politicians, did not even begin to reflect Reagan's real strength for the reason already mentioned: In many instances a delegate's support for Nixon was extremely fragile. Again and again White was told, "If my vote for Reagan will make the difference, I'll cast it for him. But don't make me walk the plank in my own delegation unless my doing so will truly affect the result." Counting such assurances, Reagan's potential first-ballot total moved tantalizingly upward toward the region that would deny Nixon a first-ballot victory.

All three of the key southern delegations were staunchly conservative, emotionally pro-Reagan, and subject to the unit rule. In Alabama, however, Strom Thurmond and his two key operatives, Harry Dent and Fred Buzhardt, had done their work well: Former Congressman James Martin had persuaded his delegation to endorse Nixon, and it was holding firm. On the day of the balloting White noted a fresh report from CBS News that Nixon's vice presidential choice would be Mark Hatfield of Oregon, one of the most liberal members of the GOP in the Senate. Handing me a floor pass, he instructed me to tell that dismaying news to Jim Martin in the faint hope that it might shake him loose from his commitment. So I plunged out onto the jammed, frantic, floodlit floor of the convention. I passed my old friend and draft-Goldwater colleague Pete O'Donnell with a nod and a rueful grin: He was wearing the badge of a Texas delegate and a saucer-sized Nixon pin. Over there Bill Timmons was leaning against a railing, watching my movements with a Mona Lisa smile—and reporting them to the Nixon command trailer on the walkie-talkie he held ostentatiously in his hand. I waved at him and hurried on. At last, finding Martin, I relayed the Hatfield rumor. Poor Jim sagged and said, "Oh, Lord! If that's true, my delegation will make a lampshade out of me! I'll go check it out." And off he went—to receive, I was certain, the necessary reassurances from Nixon.

Understanding how Mississippi's famously conservative delegation came to be in Nixon's pocket requires us to contemplate a politician exceptionally devious even by the standards of that most devious of professions. Clarke Reed was Republican national committeeman from Mississippi and the leading figure in the party in his state. (It had, at that time, no elected Republican officials.) He was almost automatically the leader of his delegation to the national convention and originally claimed to be, like most of his fellow delegates, firmly pro-Reagan. But the delay in Reagan's proclamation of his wholehearted candidacy had—or so Reed claimed—infected him with doubts, which he proceeded to sow among his delegates. In a caucus before the convention a narrow majority of the delegation had voted to back Nixon, and now Reed was engaged—successfully—in holding it firm. Returning to the Reagan command trailer after my excursion to the convention floor, I passed an adjoining trailer which had been fitted out as a conference room. Someone happened to open the door at that moment, and I caught a glimpse of Reagan talking earnestly, around a long table, to the Mississippi delegates. But Clarke Reed managed to hold them for Nixon.

The last opportunity to make history, therefore, and spare America the agony of Watergate and much else fell to the thirty-four-member Florida delegation. They were in the keeping of Republican State Chairman Bill Murfin, who had leagued himself with Reed and Martin and delivered his delegation to Nixon at the behest of Strom Thurmond. Once again, however, the pressures for Reagan became enormous. White had some fourteen or fifteen solid votes in the delegation, plus hints from still others that they would vote for Reagan and put Florida under a unit rule for the California governor—a thirty-four-vote switch that might well hold Nixon below the crucial first-ballot majority. As with the Mississippians, Reagan met with the Florida delegates personally, and I believe in some cases repeatedly. At a key moment, however, Murfin's nerves briefly gave way under the pressure and he wept a little. Several of Florida's female delegates, it thereupon transpired, couldn't bear to see a man cry. They agreed to stand firm for Nixon—and so, under the unit rule, did Florida's thirty-four all-important votes.

Honorable politician that he is, White quietly released, to

vote for Nixon, the scores of delegates who had bravely offered to risk their political necks for Ronald Reagan "if it would make the difference." It wouldn't make the difference, so why subject them to an unnecessary and perhaps politically crippling ordeal? Unconsummated, too, remained certain larger deals White had struck with some of the convention's leading figures. Only a few people, even today, know precisely how close to victory Reagan came in the 1968 convention.

In 1968 Reagan was only fifty-seven years old and was completing his second year as governor of America's largest state. Nothing in his personality or position then required or received modification to make possible his victory in 1980. Nor can the failure of the 1968 convention to nominate him be attributed with any plausibility to the party's liberals, who had lost control of it in 1964 and were perceptibly weaker still in 1968. The nomination of Richard Nixon that year was the work of conservatives who—let me say it, sadly and perhaps a little bitterly—ought to have known better. At a minimum the nation would have been spared Watergate and the resignation (and executive pardon) of a disgraced president. And in view of the recent "revisionist scholarship" which tells us that, as late as 1972, "the United States was probably in a stronger position in Vietnam . . . than at any previous point in the war,"* it is certainly arguable that Reagan might have brought about a far more satisfactory resolution of that conflict than the disaster Nixon and Ford ultimately presided over in the wake of Watergate. The whole economic history of the 1970s, too, would almost certainly have been different and, in conservative terms, better.

To their everlasting credit, a great many conservatives *did* back Reagan in 1968. *Human Events,* as already noted, supported Nixon, while *National Review* and the American Conservative Union—both sharply divided on the issue internally—equivocated. But Young Americans for Freedom's national board of directors, meeting in Miami Beach, displayed a sounder perception than its elders: Of the board's twenty-one members, nineteen voted to give the organization's endorsement to Ronald Reagan.

* See Fox Butterfield's article "The New Vietnam Scholarship," *New York Times Magazine,* February 13, 1983.

Of course, it can be argued that for whatever reason, Reagan would or might have lost the election in 1968 if the Republicans had nominated him. Certainly a great many conservatives were sincerely afraid that that would be the case. But it is difficult to see why. For one thing, it is far from clear that George Wallace, who won the support of almost 10 million social-conservative voters running on an independent ticket that year, would have persisted in his candidacy if Reagan had announced at some point late in 1967 his own intention to run. There would have been much more than "a dime's worth of difference" between Reagan and Humphrey, and Wallace knew it—and knew that the voters, too, would know it.

But history is history, and the fact is that Richard Nixon was nominated in Miami Beach in 1968. What is important to remember, in tracing the development of modern American conservatism, is that it was conservatives—including Barry Goldwater —who nominated him.

Meanwhile, another development relevant to the growth of the conservative movement was under way. George Wallace, the Democratic governor of Alabama, had reached that office on a traditional southern Democratic platform of explicit racism and had achieved national prominence in June 1963, when he stood, briefly and futilely, at the threshold of the University of Alabama, barring the way of U.S. marshals who had orders to integrate it.

Subsequently Wallace made public appearances all over the country, but now his theme was different. The issue, it seemed, was no longer segregation, or any other formulation of the race question, but the much larger problem of federal intrusion into the lives of individuals and the prerogatives of the several states. During a television panel discussion in which we both participated in Chicago, I saw Wallace stare and point directly into a television camera—a highly professional (and thoroughly unnatural) thing to do—and tell viewers, "This isn't just Alabama's problem. It's *your* problem, and the federal government will be running your lives before long unless it's stopped."

Wallace's liberal opponents long refused, and many still refuse today, to believe that he ever really abandoned the politics of bigotry or that his national campaigns were ever anything but disguised exercises in racism. At the very least they are guilty of being selective in their criticism, for they supported the Democratic party during whole decades in which it was the home of racists far noisier than Wallace, and they gave loyal support to such self-proclaimed converts to the cause of racial tolerance as Supreme Court Justice Hugo Black and Senate Democratic leader Robert Byrd (both former members of the Ku Klux Klan). They even forgave the longtime chairman of the Senate Foreign Relations Committee, Arkansas's J. William Fulbright, for an astonishingly racist voting record in the Senate.

Sincere or not, however, Wallace's antifederal rhetoric and earthy populism soon began attracting support in states where race was far from being a pivotal issue. Adding to his targets the unisex college protesters who were attracting so much attention in the late sixties (" 'Scuse me, sir; I thought you were a girl") and the "pointyhead professors" who taught them, Wallace found himself in near-exclusive possession of issues that resonated among large segments of the U.S. population. These were, by and large, the same social conservatives at whom the Goldwater draft had been aimed: the blue-collar workers, Catholic "ethnics," and lower-middle-class citizens generally, who considered the huge uprush of welfare expenditures under Johnson's Great Society programs an outrageous rip-off, resented the riots staged both by blacks seeking their civil rights and by college students opposing the draft, and feared the perceived decay of the "family values" under the onslaught of drugs, sexual permissiveness, and a widespread loss of religious faith.

Perhaps the most striking evidence of the scope of Wallace's appeal was his success in getting on the ballot as a presidential candidate in all fifty states. No third-party candidate had ever accomplished that feat before. The requirements for ballot status are prescribed, separately for each state, by their legislatures, and in 1968 the laws were a formidably heterogeneous mess, often explicitly designed to make it impossible for any party other than the Republicans and Democrats to get on the ballot at all. Despite all the obstacles, and resorting where necessary to lawsuits to clear obstructions away, Wallace's supporters managed to put their man's name on the ballot in state after state. The new party's name was not everywhere the same, and in some cases Wallace was unable even to run in tandem with his chosen vice presidential running mate, General Curtis LeMay. But when at last the courts invalidated the bitter efforts of Ohio election officials to block a Wallace line on the ballot, the victory was complete: Americans in every state could vote for Wallace if they so desired. Across the battlefield, the success of this effort of the Wallace forces elicited a silent tribute of professional admiration from Clif White.

The 1968 election, therefore, represented an almost perfect example of a contest in which liberals, economic conservatives, and social conservatives each had a candidate on the ballot. The test was not in fact clinically perfect because Nixon was able to retain the loyalty and the votes of many people who were sympathetic to social-conservative concerns but wary of Wallace's racist record or his allegedly leftist performance as a big-spending populist governor. Such reservations ultimately assured Nixon of the support of almost the entire group of conservative activists (myself included) who had backed Reagan in the GOP nomination battle.

Their backing may well have been decisive in November, for Nixon's margin over Humphrey on election day was extremely small. In terms of percentages of the total vote, the figures were: Nixon, 43.4 percent; Humphrey 42.7 percent; Wallace 13.5 percent.

But for all the division in conservative ranks (or, if one prefers, antiliberal ranks), the central lesson of the 1968 election was unmistakable: Something very dramatic had happened to American political sentiment since 1964. A substantial majority of the voters were now responding to conservative appeals of one sort or another. If even most of them could be coalesced in the Republican party (or elsewhere), liberalism's long reign would indeed be over.

Chapter IX

Honeymoon with Nixon

One young observer saw the possibility of uniting conservatives under the Republican banner with crystal clarity. Kevin Phillips, a New Yorker educated at Colgate, Harvard, and the University of Edinburgh, had first attracted attention in political circles in the mid-1960s when, as administrative assistant to Republican Congressman Paul Fino of the Bronx, he composed and circulated some memorandums shrewdly analyzing the shifting voting patterns in New York State. Hired as a high-level assistant by Nixon's 1968 campaign manager, John Mitchell, Phillips extended his analyses to the national level and gradually pulled them into book form, replete with graphs and maps. With Nixon safely elected and himself occupying a post in the Justice Department as a special assistant attorney general under Mitchell, Phillips published the book. Its title, *The Emerging Republican Majority,* boldly proclaimed Phillips's thesis, and its dedication read as follows: "This book is respectfully dedicated to the emerging Republican majority and its two principal architects: President Richard M. Nixon and Attorney General John N. Mitchell."

Unfortunately the two dedicatees were not nearly so far-sighted as their young admirer. There is little evidence that either Nixon or Mitchell took Phillips's thesis seriously during Nixon's first presidential administration or shaped any important political initiatives in its light. But students of political trends recognized the importance of Phillips's book right from the start, and it is not too much to say that every subsequent study of the subject—left, right, or center—is heavily dependent on Phillips's analysis. Almost single-handedly he laid bare and greatly developed the foundations of the political strategy that has dominated the modern conservative movement in the United States.

Phillips was by no means the first person to discover, in certain fragments of the disintegrating Democratic coalition, a fruit-

ful source of recruits to the cause of conservatism. The young
founders of the Conservative party of New York had been doing
extremely well among the Empire State's Catholic "ethnics" and
the Jewish communities of Queens County as early as 1962. Ex-
tending the principle to the national level, Clif White and his
Hard Core had chosen Barry Goldwater as their standard-bearer
precisely because as a man of the Southwest, he could and did appeal powerfully to fast-growing areas of the country that were historically Democratic.

But these moves had been largely instinctive, in response to
political opportunities that able politicians could sense were simply *there*. Moreover, the strategies involved were easily dismissed
by liberal reporters and analysts as mere appeals to bigotry. The
Goldwater draft and campaign in particular were said by liberal
commentators to be based simply on a "southern strategy"—
meaning a cynical scheme to appeal to the votes of white racists
and thereby invade and conquer that old Democratic fiefdom
the Solid South. Such charges not only misrepresented what conservatives had already achieved and might yet achieve but served
to conceal from the liberals themselves what was really happening to the country and their own consequent and very genuine
peril.

Phillips, in a dazzling display of erudition and statistics, demonstrated that the Roosevelt coalition was falling apart like the
one-hoss shay and that several major components of it were susceptible to Republican blandishments of the proper sort. One by
one he analyzed the voting records of every significant demographic bloc and region in the country: in the Northeast the Yan-
kees, the blacks, the Jews, the Catholics, and other "non-Yankees";
in the Deep South the Black Belt, the "Dixie upcountry," and
French Louisiana; in the Outer South the mountains, the Pied-
mont, the Black Belts, the new urban Florida and Texas, the
Southern Plains, and the "Latin Crescent"; in the "Heartland,"
the border states, the Great Lakes, the farm states, the Rocky
Mountain states; and finally, in the Far West, the northern Pacific
coast, the Pacific interior, and—last but scarcely least—southern
California.

In a final chapter, confidently entitled "The Future of American Politics," Phillips drew some portentous conclusions:

The long-range meaning of the political upheaval of 1968 rests on the Republican opportunity to fashion a majority among the 57 per cent of the American electorate which voted to eject the Democratic Party from national power.... The most decisive anti-Democratic voting stream of 1968 was that of the fifteen million or so conservative Democrats who shunned Hubert Humphrey to divide about evenly between Richard Nixon and George Wallace. Such elements stretched from the "Okie" Great Central Valley of California to the mountain towns of Idaho, Florida's space centers, rural South Carolina, Bavarian Minnesota, the Irish sidewalks of New York and the Levittowns of Megalopolis....

Noting that certain blocs and regions—"Megalopolitan silk-stocking voters and Scandinavians from Maine across the Great Lakes to the Pacific"—were trending toward the Democrats, Phillips reviewed the order of battle for what he considered the foreseeable political future:

The upcoming cycle of American politics is likely to match a dominant Republican Party based in the Heartland, South and California against a minority Democratic Party based in the Northeast and the Pacific Northwest (and encompassing Southern as well as Northern Negroes). With such support behind it, the GOP can easily afford to lose the states of Massachusetts, New York and Michigan—and is likely to do so except in landslide years. Together with the District of Columbia, the top ten Humphrey states—Hawaii, Washington, Minnesota, Michigan, West Virginia, New York, Connecticut, Rhode Island, Massachusetts and Maine—should prove to be the core of national Democratic strength....

Unluckily for the Democrats, their major impetus is centered in stagnant Northern industrial states—and within those states, in old decaying cities, in a Yankee countryside that has fewer people than in 1900, and in the most expensive suburbs. Beyond this, in the South and West, the Democrats dominate only two expanding voting blocs—Latins and Negroes. From space-center Florida across the booming Texas plains to the Los Angeles–San Diego suburban corridor, the nation's fastest-growing areas are strongly Republican and conservative. Even in the Northeast, the few rapidly growing suburbs are conservative-trending areas.... Because of this demographic pattern, the South and West are gaining electoral votes and national political power at the expense of the Northeast.

Pulling no punches, Phillips drew his moral: "One of the greatest political myths of the decade—a product of liberal self-interest—is that the Republican Party cannot attain national dominance without mobilizing liberal support in the big cities, appealing to 'liberal' youth, empathizing with 'liberal' urbanization, gaining substantial Negro support and courting the affluent young professional classes of 'suburbia.' The actual demographic and political facts convey a very different message."

At bottom, Phillips's concept of the history and future of American politics envisioned repeated waves of populist sentiment, usually based on the western frontier, overwhelming a series of eastern-based establishments. Modern American liberalism was simply the most recent of these establishments:

> Since the days of Alexander Hamilton and the Federalists, the United States—and the Northeast in particular—has periodically supported a privileged elite, blind to the needs and interests of the large national majority. The corporate welfarists, planners and academicians of the Liberal Establishment are the newest of these elites, and their interests—for one thing, a high and not necessarily too productive rate of government social, educational, scientific and research spending—are as vested as those of Coolidge-Hoover era financiers and industrialists. The great political upheaval of the Nineteen-Sixties is not that of Senator Eugene McCarthy's relatively small group of upper-middle-class and intellectual supporters but a populist revolt of the American masses who have been elevated by prosperity to middle-class status and conservatism. *Their* revolt is against the caste, policies and taxation of the mandarins of Establishment liberalism.

But its time had come: "Now it is Richard Nixon's turn to build a new era on the immense middle-class impetus of Sun Belt and Suburbia. Thus, it is appropriate that much of the emerging Republican majority lies in the top growth states (California, Arizona, Texas and Florida) or new suburbia, while Democratic trends correlate with stability and decay (New England, New York City, Michigan, West Virginia and San Francisco-Berkeley)."

It would be easy to minimize Phillips's achievement, as many critics did, by pointing out how utterly his 1968 heroes, Nixon and Mitchell, failed to grasp and follow the outlines of his strategic vision. But in the long run it was Nixon and Mitchell who were wrong and Phillips who, on the basics, was absolutely right. Events did not take the course he hoped for and predicted, but the course they did take was altogether obedient to his analysis of the underlying imperatives: the defection of large segments of the lower class and lower-middle class from the Roosevelt coalition and the swift growth of strongly conservative new urban and suburban centers in the "Sun Belt" of the South and West. These developments have, quite simply, dominated American politics in the fifteen years since Phillips's book appeared.

There has been no lack of critics or followers trying to contradict Phillips's analysis or shape it to the service of some thesis of their own. Arthur Schlesinger, Jr., consulted by worried liberals as polls in the early 1970s revealed that far more Americans were describing themselves as "conservative" than "liberal," reassuringly declared that the American people might regard themselves as "notionally conservative" but that where their own governmental subsidies were concerned, they could safely be considered "operationally liberal." Richard Scammon and Ben Wattenberg, in articles and a book (*The Real Majority*, Coward-McCann, 1970), warned the Democratic party to address itself to the concerns of a prototypical blue-collar housewife in suburban Dayton, Ohio. In 1975 a young liberal author, Kirkpatrick Sale, sought to interpret Phillips's "Sun Belt" rather differently, arguing that it was inherently as rapacious as the eastern establishment it replaced. A year later Donald I. Warren, a University of Michigan sociologist, published *The Radical Center: Middle Americans and the Politics of Alienation* (Notre Dame), in which he identified a new dissident bloc he called Middle American radicals (or MARs).

I myself, as will be recounted in due course, despaired of ever uniting the new conservative majority under the Republican banner as Phillips had visualized, and—acknowledging my debt to his analysis—called for the formation of a brand-new party. (See my 1975 book, *The Making of the New Majority Party*, published by Sheed & Ward.)

No book can be expected to do the thinking of much more than a decade in political terms, and Phillips himself has since written others that seek to update his analysis and even to improve

on it—books that are invariably stimulating, if short of infallible.*
But his central analysis in *The Emerging Republican Majority* became the Bible of subsequent discussions among thoughtful conservatives as to the essential strategy of their movement, and it
remains highly influential.

Meanwhile, it was now Richard Nixon's turn to have a fling at
governing America, and his approach to that task would necessarily determine the response, and to some extent the future, of the
conservative movement.

The Nixon administration was notable for the scarcity of
movement conservatives in its ranks. Buchanan followed his boss
into the White House as a speechwriter. Huston was named a special assistant to the president, with an office in the Old Executive
Office Building where he carried out various obscure duties. For a
time Reagan's press secretary, Lyn Nofziger, served as Nixon's
deputy assistant for congressional relations. But the higher echelons of the administration were filled with main-line Republican
appointees who, if they ever heard of Phillips's book at all, in most
cases avoided reading it and certainly never dreamed of taking it
seriously.

Those first two years were, nevertheless, as near as Nixon and
conservatives as a whole would ever get to a honeymoon. The
démarche on Red China, the imposition of wage and price controls, and the other measures repellent to conservatives that would
mar the second half of Nixon's first administration were still in the
future. The new president embarked on a massive military and
diplomatic effort to end U.S. involvement in the Vietnam War,
but it was clear that he had no intention of simply cutting and
running. The colleges were in ferment, but that scarcely disaffected conservatives from Nixon; on the contrary, they shared to
the full the disapproval of these antics that characterized a large
segment of public opinion.

It was, in fact, those disturbances of the 1960s, and the emergence of the New Left, that brought into the Republican camp,
and later into cautious alliance with the rest of the conservative
movement, a small but influential group of former leftists and lib-

---

* Cf. *Mediacracy* (Doubleday, 1975); *Post-Conservative America* (Random House, 1982).

erals. New York-based, predominantly Jewish, archly intellectual in their approach to political issues, these were individuals who had emerged from the Marxist milieu of the New York City colleges in the late 1940s and early 1950s: Irving Kristol, Norman Podhoretz, Midge Decter, Nathan Glazer, and Daniel Bell, to name only some of the most prominent. They were the contemporaries, friends, and allies of Irving Howe, Jason Epstein, Philip Rahv, and other leading socialists and social democrats of the period, and their magazine *Commentary*, published by the American Jewish Committee, was the intellectual bellwether of the Jewish anti-Communist left.

But the development during the 1960s of a militant quasi-revolutionary movement in the colleges, dedicated to affirmative action on behalf of America's blacks and often outspokenly sympathetic to the Arab states of the Middle East, shook these people to the core. They were critical of many aspects of American society, but they were certainly not alienated from it or sympathetic to those who were. Slowly *Commentary* swung into a posture of outright opposition to the New Left and (inevitably) began to discover new virtues in American society.

Another magazine prominently associated with this group, and in this case founded expressly to proclaim its views, was Irving Kristol's quarterly the *Public Interest*, launched in 1965. This journal promptly attracted wide attention and respect in moderate-liberal quarters and is still influential. A collection of Kristol's essays, published over a number of years in the 1970s, was called *Two Cheers for Capitalism*—its cautious title nicely summarizing his new position.

By the early 1970s Kristol, Podhoretz, and their publications were squarely in the Republican camp. Within a few years they acquired the name by which, at some cost in personal discomfort, they have become accustomed to being known: the neoconservatives.*

---

* Trying my hand at the popular comic verse form called double-dactyls, I once used that controversial term in a poem about *National Review*'s Rick Brookhiser, who had become a senior editor at only twenty-three:

> Higgledy-piggledy, Richard J. Brookhiser,
> Young senior editor, threatens to fight:
> Hotly denies he's a neo-conservative;
> Swears he's a spring of the paleo-Right.

What made the neoconservatives such important recruits was not their numbers: They speak, at best, for only a segment of Jewish intellectual opinion. (*Commentary*'s circulation is in the neighborhood of 45,000.) Nor, despite their brilliance, was it in any important sense the profundity or perspicuity of their views: The conservative movement, by the 1970s, was fully capable of holding its own in the intellectual arena. But Kristol, Podhoretz, et al. had been the personal friends and allies of the large and influential group of socialist and social democratic intellectuals who have done the heavy thinking for the non-Communist left since the end of World War II, and their defection was felt—and denounced— by these ex-comrades as an event vastly more noteworthy and important than the fact that, say, William Buckley or Russell Kirk had long held a similar opinion.

Politically the neoconservatives unquestionably helped to lead a substantial element of Jewish opinion into the Republican camp during the 1970s, if not earlier. And although this is harder to quantify, it is safe to assume that conservatism also benefited at least indirectly from the influence the neoconservatives exerted on the intelligentsia (in journalism, the academy, and elsewhere), providing access and support that were previously unavailable.

For certain conservatives, however, the later 1960s were less stimulating. These were some of the stronger young personalities who had been drawn into political activism during the heyday of the draft-Goldwater movement and who were unwilling to settle for Nixon Republicanism.

One was a young newspaperman and TV reporter in Milwaukee, Wisconsin: Paul Weyrich, the son of a German immigrant. "I felt deserted," he recalled years later. Already out of college, he was not reached by the recruiters of Young Americans for Freedom, and if there was (improbably) a local chapter of the American Conservative Union in Milwaukee, it failed to attract him. Without altogether realizing it, Paul Weyrich was straining to hear quite another drum.

So was Richard Viguerie, a wiry Texas Catholic who had answered a classified ad in *National Review* in 1961 and landed the job of executive secretary of Young Americans for Freedom. In that post Viguerie learned the critical importance of mailing lists, and in December 1964, in the wake of Goldwater's defeat, he went into the list business for himself. During the late 1960s Viguerie worked steadily to build what would ultimately become the biggest collection of conservative mailing lists in the country. At one time or another he conducted mailings for just about every conservative organization in existence—usually on terms that gave him control of the names and addresses of all who responded. He also worked for quite apolitical organizations (though never for liberals or leftists) and was one of the pioneers of the computerization of mailing lists. Viguerie, too, was basically dissatisfied with late-1960s conservatism: He longed for madder music and stronger wine.

A third figure, first glimpsed in 1960 and also to become significant during the seventies, appears to have lost interest in the conservative movement altogether during most of the 1960s. As president of the Harvard Student Council in 1960 Howard Phillips had been invited to speak for conservative college students at *National Review*'s fifth anniversary dinner party that October, and he subsequently became one of the early national leaders of Young Americans for Freedom. But finding himself on the losing side of one of YAF's early internal battles, Phillips turned to regular Republican politics, and in 1968 conservatives were startled to hear that he had become the manager of Richard Schweiker's successful campaign for a U.S. Senate seat from Pennsylvania. Their surprise was attributable to the fact that Schweiker, as a member of the House, had become known as one of the most liberal Republicans in Congress. Subsequently Phillips held various positions in the Office of Economic Opportunity during the Nixon administration, ultimately becoming its acting director. The OEO had long been a liberal device for funding all sorts of dubious projects, and Phillips slowly came to the conclusion that it ought to be abolished outright. Despite the enthusiastic support of various high administration officials, Phillips lost the ensuing battle with the Democratic Congress over this issue, thanks largely to Nixon's growing weakness as the Watergate scandal broke and spread. But the experience seems to have revived Phillips's conservative fervor and repatriated him to the conservative movement. Like Weyrich and Viguerie, he was soon spoiling for a new fight. In the 1970s they would become the leaders of a new and combative segment of the conservative movement, known as the New Right.

Another and far more prominent political figure whose mood was hardening was Vice President Spiro Agnew. The subsequent scandal over alleged cash contributions paid to Agnew while he was still governor of Maryland and continuing into his vice presidency has too long obscured a true understanding of this thoughtful, complex, and rather likable man.

Agnew was originally a political centrist like Nixon himself. He had first supported Rockefeller for the 1968 nomination but switched to Nixon when Rockefeller, without a word of warning or explanation to Agnew, executed his tactical withdrawal from the nomination race in March.

As a son of Greek immigrants Agnew was perhaps more than ordinarily sensitive to the brutal beating he received at the hands of the liberal media as Nixon's running mate during the 1968 campaign. He had been elected governor of Maryland in 1966, defeating a segregationist Democrat fond of declaring that "a man's home is his castle." But Agnew had noted even then, and resented, a sharp shift in the media's attitude toward him after he called in the leaders of Maryland's black community during race disturbances in 1967 and warned them brusquely that violence would not be tolerated. "Before that," he would later recall, "I could do no wrong. After that, they kept that red [television] eye on me twelve hours a day, trying to find two minutes' worth of something discreditable to put on the evening news." When reporters on his 1968 campaign plane suggested, quite unfairly, that he was guilty of racism for repeating a familiar humorous reference to one reporter as "the fat Jap," Agnew recognized the technique.

Always on the lookout for potential presidential timber and acutely aware that a vice president can sometimes become president overnight, I had made it a point to call on the new vice president in his spacious office in the Old Executive Office Building and get to know him fairly well. For that reason, or perhaps independently, Agnew was also becoming familiar with *National Review*. Over a matter of months he seemed to grow almost visibly in his understanding of, and identification with, the conservative movement. He asked that half a dozen copies of each issue be sent to him at his office, so that he could give them to friends. At least once he phoned me to order a gift subscription for an old friend in Maryland. These could, of course, have been mere gestures designed to cultivate me or the magazine; but I learned from others that Agnew was in fact handing out those half dozen copies, and there were still other signs that this hitherto "inoffensive centrist" (as I described him in an article in *National Review* on December 3, 1968) was becoming a movement conservative in earnest.

Many of Agnew's speeches were now being written by Pat Buchanan, the quondam occupant of Richard Nixon's "conservative desk." Agnew and Buchanan had become friends during the 1968 campaign when Buchanan, after a falling-out with campaign manager Mitchell, had been temporarily demoted to the Agnew entourage. In addition, Nixon himself had long and publicly detested the liberal media, and—judging that the time was now ripe for an attack—he authorized his feisty vice president to launch it. At Des Moines on November 13, 1969, in a speech drafted by Buchanan, Agnew threw down the gauntlet to the news programs of the national television networks:

> Tonight I want to discuss the importance of the television news medium to the American people. No nation depends more on the intelligent judgment of its citizens. No medium has a more profound influence over public opinion. Nowhere in our system are there fewer checks on vast power. So nowhere should there be more conscientious responsibility exercised than by the news media. . . .
>
> The purpose of my remarks tonight is to focus your attention on this little group of men who not only enjoy a right of instant rebuttal to every Presidential address, but more importantly, wield a free hand in selecting, presenting and interpreting the great issues of our nation. . . .
>
> What do Americans know of the men who wield this power? Of the men who produce and direct the network news—the nation knows practically nothing.
>
> Of the commentators, most Americans know little, other than that they reflect an urbane and assured presence, seemingly well informed on every important matter. . . .
>
> The views of this fraternity do not represent the views of America. . . .

As with other American institutions, perhaps it is time that the networks were made more responsive to the views of the nation and more responsible to the people they serve.

I am not asking for government censorship or any other kind of censorship. I am asking whether a form of censorship already exists when the news that forty million Americans receive each night is determined by a handful of men responsible only to their corporate employers and filtered through a handful of commentators who admit to their own set of biases. . . .

Tonight, I have raised questions. I have made no attempt to suggest answers. These answers must come from the media men. They are challenged to turn their critical powers on themselves. They are challenged to direct their energy, talent and conviction toward improving the quality and objectivity of news presentation. They are challenged to structure their own civic ethics to relate their great freedom with their great responsibility.

The reaction of the media was immediate and interesting—immediate (and predictable) in the short run and extremely interesting over the longer haul. Their initial response was to condemn the speech and defy Agnew. He was, they charged, simply and obviously attempting to impose political censorship. Nothing, of course, could have been further from the truth; but the liberals controlled, and in substantial part still control, what is said and written, and therefore to a large extent what is thought, about public events in this country, and their version of the episode has congealed into history as "the time Agnew tried to muzzle the press."

In fact, the Agnew speech had, over the longer run, a striking and readily perceptible result. After Des Moines, the demand for conservative spokesmen—first on television, then on the Op-Ed pages of the nation's newspapers, and finally on speaking platforms—began to grow almost exponentially.

When Agnew rose to speak in Des Moines, there were (just for example) only two widely syndicated conservative columnists in the whole field of American journalism: William F. Buckley, Jr., and James Jackson Kilpatrick. With the exception of Buckley's "Firing Line" (begun in 1966), television was simply a wasteland from the conservative standpoint. Conservatives were doing a bit better on radio, having long since been spotted by talk-show hosts as guarantors of a lively and "controversial" program, and there was even a conservative host or two; but nationally the liberal dominance was secure in radio, too.

Book publishing houses, as well, were largely unwilling to gamble on conservative writers—again with the exception of Buckley. Even Kevin Phillips's seminal *The Emerging Republican Majority* had to be published by Arlington House, a small and avowedly conservative book publisher. The best-selling conservative books of previous years (e.g., Goldwater's *The Conscience of a Conservative* and Phyllis Schlafly's *A Choice Not an Echo*) had to be printed privately or by obscure publishing houses to see daylight at all.

As for the field of professional public speaking, even conservatism's two guaranteed crowd pullers, Buckley and Goldwater, let alone the rest of us, almost invariably had to settle for being the one token conservative on a schedule heavy with such celebrated liberals and/or leftists as Arthur Schlesinger, Jr., John Kenneth Galbraith, Abbie Hoffman, Angela Davis, David Dellinger, Tom Hayden, Bobby Seale, and other well-paid veterans of the college lecture circuit. All of this began to change rapidly after Agnew's Des Moines blast.

I know, because I was one of the happy beneficiaries of this development. During the first season of the "Advocates" television program on PBS, 1969–70, various hapless opponents had been systematically skewered by the show's regular liberal advocate, Howard Miller. Within a year of Agnew's speech, I was employed by the producer, Boston's WGBH-TV, as the regular conservative advocate and during the next few years prevailed on somewhat more than half of my programs, according to the postcard votes of the television audiences. Before that weekly program sputtered to an end in 1974 (the victim of insufficient funding), I was writing a syndicated column, perhaps inevitably titled "The Conservative Advocate," in about a hundred papers from coast to coast, and I could count among my conservative competitors not only Buckley and Kilpatrick but Pat Buchanan, John Lofton, Victor Gold, M. Stanton Evans, and several others.

This increased notoriety as a result of television programs and syndicated columns in turn generated more speaking invitations and even books. No doubt by the early 1970s the conservative movement would have been pounding pretty heavily on the door of the public consciousness in any case, but equally without a doubt Agnew's well-timed blast at TV's bias in November 1969 gave conservatism a handy boost at just the right moment.

As we have seen, during the first half of the 1960s conservatism had been transformed from a purely philosophical movement into a squarely political one, and henceforth its success would be measured not merely by the number of TV and radio talk shows, speaking engagements, columns, and books it generated but by its success at the polls. In 1970 Bill Buckley's brother Jim, some two and a half years Bill's senior, demonstrated that such success was by no means out of the question, even in the liberal state of New York.

James Lane Buckley had taken his first fling at candidacy in 1968, as the Conservative party's candidate against the veteran Senator Jacob Javits, who as usual had the endorsement of both the Republican and Liberal parties. The Democratic candidate was Paul O'Dwyer, and the outcome was a foregone conclusion: Javits was reelected for his third term with 3,269,779 votes on the Republican and Liberal lines. O'Dwyer received 2,150,695 votes, and Buckley garnered a respectable 1,139,402.

But that was merely a *beau geste*—a valiant try at plainly impossible odds. As 1970 dawned, the New York political situation was extraordinarily confused—and highly tempting. The incumbent senator up for reelection that year was Charles Goodell, who had been appointed to the seat by Governor Rockefeller in September 1968 following the assassination of Senator Robert Kennedy. Goodell had been serving his fifth term in the House of Representatives, representing his upstate district ably and on the whole conservatively. In the Senate, however, either because of a sudden sea change in his personal convictions or because he judged that a shift would be essential if he were to win election in his own right in 1970, Goodell swung sharply to the left. It was naturally, therefore, the highest ambition of New York State's Conservative party to defeat him. If, as was likely, the Democrats nominated a liberal candidate, too, liberal New Yorkers might— just might—divide their votes more or less equally between Goodell and the Democrat and enable a really attractive candidate on the Conservative line to win a plurality (which was all that was needed for victory).

I assumed Jim Buckley was still on a business trip to Indonesia when, on April 2, 1970, the phone rang on my desk at *National Review*. It was Jim; he was back, and he came quickly to the point with humorous mock gravity.

"William"—he addressed me—"you are a political seer."

"That is true," I conceded, equally judiciously.

Jim went on to say that the thought of the ultraliberal Goodell's being elected to a further six years in the U.S. Senate was more than he could bear and that he himself was disposed to seek the Conservative party's nomination and run against him, *provided* there was a serious chance of actually winning in November owing to the aforesaid split in the liberal vote. Did I think there was such a chance?

In my opinion there was indeed, and I was hard put to remain outwardly calm as my chat with Jim rambled on to a leisurely conclusion. I told him I would be back in touch with him shortly—and then burned up the phone wires to Clif White.

White was intrigued and sensibly recommended that a poll be taken to find out exactly where New Yorkers stood on the matter of James Buckley and related subjects. The money for the poll was quickly raised, and within a matter of weeks White was analyzing the results. They revealed—to condense somewhat—that the name James Buckley would win the allegiance of about 25 percent of New York voters, no matter who ran against him for the Senate; that another 25 percent were opposed to him, again regardless of the opposition; and that the remaining half of the voters were undecided.

Reading these tea leaves, White pronounced them encouraging. "We can win," he declared confidently—and accepted the post of Jim's campaign chairman.

I was active in helping to flesh out the campaign staff. To serve as campaign director—in effect, as White's chief of staff and undisputed day-to-day boss of the campaign operation—we imported David Jones, a Tennessean then living in Washington, who had won his spurs as one of the principal conservative leaders of YAF, the Young Republican National Federation, and the ACU in the 1960s. In as chief of press liaison went Arnold Steinberg, another former member of YAF's national board. For chairman of the vital Finance Committee we drafted Leon Weil, a stockbroker and Princeton contemporary of mine with whom I had kept in touch over the years in the YR and senior Republican politics of Manhattan's "silk stocking" (i.e., Republican) congressional district.

Campaign headquarters was in an office building at the southwest corner of Madison and Thirty-eighth Street—conveniently near the offices of the Buckley family oil business at Park and Thirty-seventh, not to mention *National Review*'s own premises at Lexington and Thirty-fifth. Here, as spring turned into summer, White and Jones and a staff of a dozen or so planned Jim's itineraries, issued press releases, held press conferences, etc. A *pro forma* request to the Republican State Committee, to permit Buckley to enter the GOP primary against Goodell, elicited only a grim chuckle from the committee. But Nelson Rockefeller himself was again running for governor that year, and his private polls soon told him that Senator Goodell's presence on the Republican ticket was no asset. Lieutenant Governor Malcolm Wilson was therefore reportedly assigned to make sure that the unpopular junior senator did not get close enough to Rockefeller for "photo opportunities" whenever the GOP ticket was for some unavoidable reason all assembled in a single spot.

Down in Washington, Richard Nixon watched the contest with a professional's fascination. He detested Goodell for his swing toward liberalism and was therefore rooting for Buckley, but as the incumbent Republican president Nixon knew there were sharp limitations on what he could do.

His solution to the problem was characteristically devious. One of his aides advised me by phone that the president was scheduled to fly, on Air Force One, out of Westchester County Airport at a certain hour on a particular afternoon. Now, if a group of YAF members or similar types, bearing NIXON & BUCKLEY placards, chanced to be on hand to greet the chief executive, the ranks of the Secret Service would part miraculously, like the waters of the Red Sea before Moses, and they would be allowed close enough to permit photographs of Nixon with the demonstrators and their suggestive placards.

And so it was arranged.

As the campaign rolled on, it became clear that it was a three-way horse race among Goodell, Buckley, and the Democratic nominee, Congressman Richard Ottinger. Of the three, Ottinger came off least well in their tripartite television debates. Goodell was far smoother than Ottinger; but there was no doubt that Buckley's appeal to Republican conservatives was much stronger, and it was, after all, that constituency for which the key battle was being waged. Goodell (who had the Liberal party's endorsement—and Lord knows had earned it) would undoubtedly siphon a good many liberal votes away from Ottinger, but that was almost a favor to us, in view of the Democratic party's usual strength in the state.

On election night (November 3), running into Clif White in a corridor at the Waldorf where the Buckley "victory celebration" was to be held, I assuaged my own nervousness by putting my old friend on the spot: "Is he going to win?"

"Yep. It'll be close, but we're gonna make it," Clif replied.

And so we did: Buckley 2,288,190; Ottinger 2,171,232; Goodell 1,434,472. In a victory speech to his delirious supporters later that night in the Waldorf's Grand Ballroom, Jim defined his role in words he afterward swore he could not remember uttering: "I am the voice of the New Majority!"

Thanks to the size and visibility of the state of New York and the fact that he was the brother of the famous William, it was James Buckley whose campaign and November victory highlighted the year 1970 for conservatives from coast to coast. And—no small point—the names and addresses of the many thousands of conservatives all over the country who contributed to his campaign were duly added to the fast-growing lists being amassed and computerized by conservative list brokers. The movement had come a long way—in articulation and in sheer professionalism—since 1964.

Chapter X

The End of Nixon

By 1971 the Nixon administration was half over, and the honeymoon, or at least truce, that had prevailed between Nixon and the conservatives during his first two years in the White House was in grave peril, as far as many conservatives were concerned. The movement now had its own nationally recognized political leaders such as Reagan (who was reelected governor of California in 1970 by a reduced but still impressive margin of 500,492 votes), Goldwater (who reentered the Senate in 1968), and James Buckley. It had also won the allegiance of Vice President Agnew, and conservatives were enjoying the unaccustomed luxury of speculating as to which among several possibilities they might decide to support for the presidency in 1976—assuming, as they did, that Nixon would be renominated and reelected in 1972. Meanwhile, though, Mr. Nixon was pleasing them less every day.

A rather curious warning shot was fired across Nixon's bow in the August 10, 1971, issue of *National Review*. In a full-page statement headed simply "A DECLARATION," twelve prominent conservatives of the "responsible" variety took the president to task for shortcomings in both domestic and foreign policy:

> We touch only lightly on the failures of Mr. Nixon's Administration domestically. It is a fact that we continue to have inflation and unemployment, excessive taxation and inordinate welfarism. It is also a fact that notwithstanding the reforms he has proposed, and the excellent public servants whose aid he has enlisted, we continue to have an intolerable crime rate, an apathetic court system, and a Supreme Court given in certain matters to ideological abstraction.
>
> These domestic considerations, important as they are, pale into insignificance alongside the tendencies of the Administration in foreign policy. Applauding though we do the President's steadfastness in resisting the great pressures upon him to desert Southeast Asia, we note:

1. His failure to respond to the rapid advance of the Soviet Union into the Mediterranean basin,

2. His failure to warn against the implications of the current policies of the West German government,

3. His overtures to Red China, done in the absence of any public concessions by Red China to American and Western causes,

4. *And above all,* his failure to call public attention to the deteriorated American military position, in conventional and strategic arms, which deterioration, in the absence of immediate and heroic countermeasures, can lead to the loss of our deterrent capability, the satellization of friendly governments near and far, and all that this implies.

Clearing its throat rather portentously, the declaration then went on:

In consideration of this record, the undersigned, who have heretofore generally supported the Nixon Administration, have resolved to suspend our support of the Administration.

We will seek out others who share our misgivings, in order to consult together on the means by which we can most effectively register our protests.

We do not plan at the moment to encourage formal political opposition to President Nixon in the forthcoming primaries, but we propose to keep all options open in the light of political developments in the next months.

We reaffirm our personal admiration and—in the case of those of us who are his friends or who have been befriended by him—our affection for Richard Nixon, and our wholehearted identification with the purposes he has over the years espoused as his own and the Republic's. We consider that our defection is an act of loyalty to the Nixon we supported in 1968.

The signatories were Buckley, Burnham, Meyer, and myself from *National Review,* Allan Ryskind and Tom Winter from *Human Events,* Jeffrey Bell and John Jones (respectively Capitol Hill director and executive director of the ACU), and four individuals from organizations close to the above three: Anthony Harrigan (executive VP of the Southern States Industrial Council), Dan Mahoney (chairman of the New York Conservative party), Neil McCaffrey (president of the Conservative Book Club), and Randal Teague (executive director of YAF).

The idea of merely "suspending" support for Nixon, as a sort of warning, was Jim Burnham's. It had the advantage of making a public splash, without burning all bridges between the statement's cautious signers and the White House. This latter point was quickly noted by various prominent Republican politicians and may have undermined the declaration's intended effect. According to the Associated Press:

> Republican leaders say the defectors will be back because there's no place else for them to go in 1972.
> "Sooner or later, these conservatives are going to look at the alternatives," said Sen. Dole of Kansas, the GOP National Chairman. "They certainly aren't going with any of the Democrats. And there aren't any alternatives on our side. Nixon's the nominee."
> Senator Goldwater of Arizona said he wasn't surprised at conservative dissatisfaction.
> "But I don't believe this is going to amount to much, because when the chips are down, they're going to be with Nixon," Goldwater said. "The alternatives are too frightening."

My own personal and final break with the Nixon administration, like that of many other conservatives, came a few months later over the issue of Taiwan. The island republic had possessed, over the decades since Mao's conquest of the mainland in 1949, no stauncher friend than Richard Nixon. Year after year, while the State Department yearned for détente with Red China, conservative pressures to remain loyal to Taiwan had intimidated Congress after Congress and presidents of both parties, and Nixon had contributed heavily, first as vice president and then in private life, to the success of those pressures.

Then, in the early months of his presidential administration, Nixon moved with characteristic deviousness to reverse his long-standing policy and open the first top-level diplomatic exchanges between Washington and Peking. Henry Kissinger was secretly dispatched to China to confer with Premier Zhou Enlai. A heavily publicized series of Ping-Pong matches between Chinese Communist and American teams was staged, to accustom American public opinion to the new spirit of friendship with these long-execrated enemies.

At the United Nations, which had long panted to admit Red China "as the hart panteth after the water-brooks," these developments were, of course, followed with excited delight. Unfortunately Peking had long made it plain that it would accept membership in the UN only if the Republic of China (the official name of the government on Taiwan) was first expelled. Moreover, the Republic of China held a permanent seat on the Security Council and had steadfastly vetoed every attempt to admit to the UN what it regarded simply as a gang of Communist bandits currently in control of the mainland. This dual dilemma was resolved by the intellectually dishonest expedient of ruling that the question of which set of credentials to accept (as identifying the holder of Chinese membership in the UN) was not an "important" question but merely a "procedural" one and thus not subject to veto. This ruling, however, required the votes of two-thirds of the member nations, and the United States and Taiwan had long managed to keep Peking's support in the General Assembly (where this issue arose) below that critical level.

In October 1971, however, with Kissinger in Peking on yet another visit to his new friends there, the UN's lust for Communist Chinese membership could no longer be contained by such implausible protests as George Bush, our UN ambassador, still managed to utter. The necessary two-thirds of the member nations were assembled. Suggested compromises were swept aside; in the name of "realism" the People's Republic of China was recognized as the holder of China's seat in the UN, including the Security Council; and—presumably in some other name, for it certainly had nothing to do with realism—the equally de facto government of Taiwan, a huge island with a population larger than that of three-quarters of the nations that were expelling it, was denied membership even in the General Assembly.

In February 1972, less than nine months before his scheduled race for reelection, Nixon himself flew to Peking in Air Force One—and contrived to land there, to live coverage by the U.S. television networks, on prime time: 10:00 P.M. in New York, 9:00 P.M. in Chicago, etc. (On the return trip Air Force One was delayed for nine hours in Anchorage to insure that Mr. Nixon's arrival in Washington would occur at an equally favorable moment.)

Nixon and Kissinger had hoped to spare their ex-friends in Taipei the indignity of total expulsion from the UN, but it was, after all, their own policy of détente with Peking that had made it possible—even inevitable. Just how wise that policy was is still not easy to say with confidence. Reportedly Nixon himself regards the détente with Peking as the principal jewel in the notoriously underdecorated diadem of his administration, but the benefits to the United States are hard to perceive. Certainly those visions of Communist Chinese sugarplums that danced in the heads of many a greedy American businessman have gone glimmering: Mainland China is so poor and primitive that not even lavish loans can prepare it for all the things American businessmen are eager to sell it; the economic infrastructure (e.g., the electricity available) simply cannot support them. And Peking's chronic hysterics over our continuing arms trade with Taiwan certainly suggest that we have merely substituted for concern over a flaccid enemy an equal or worse preoccupation with a fat and pouting "friend."

No doubt there are—surely there must be—a few bonuses implicit in the new relationship: scientific and military listening posts in western China, perhaps, to make up for the loss of such facilities along the northern border of Iran. The beauty of such bonuses, as Jay Gould once bragged of a business deal, is that "nothing was lost, save honor."

Well, how important is honor? Bill Buckley, one of the eighty journalists who accompanied Nixon to Peking in February 1972, may have understood the answer to that question better than any of his colleagues (let alone Nixon), for on his return he filed his lonely dissenting opinion, amid the huzzahs, in an article in *National Review:* "We have lost—irretrievably—any remaining sense of moral mission in the world. Mr. Nixon's appetite for a summit conference in Peking transformed the affair from a meeting of diplomatic technicians concerned to examine and illuminate areas of common interest, into a pageant of moral togetherness at which Mr. Nixon managed to give the impression that he was consorting with Marian Anderson, Billy Graham and Albert Schweitzer."

I was surely not the only conservative who, in outrage, had phoned Pat Buchanan at the White House on the morning after the UN's expulsion of Taiwan, the previous October; it cannot have been a happy day for the beleaguered loyalist at Richard Nixon's "conservative desk."

"I am just phoning," I said in my iciest tone, "to say goodbye. And" —as an afterthought occurred to me—"since you are an old friend of mine, to invite you to come with me."

"Yeah?" Pat croaked, nervously but noncommittally. "Where're we going?"

I was not at liberty to disclose, just then, the answer to that question. But there was an answer, and Buchanan—and Nixon— would find out what it was before long.

Among the other conservatives for whom, by late 1971, Nixon's performance in office had become insupportable was my old friend John Ashbrook, then in his sixth term as a Republican congressman from Ohio. It will be recalled that Ashbrook, along with Clif White and myself, had launched the Goldwater draft movement back in 1961. Subsequently Ashbrook, a loner by temperament and preoccupied in any case with his congressional duties, had drifted away from active involvement in the draft organization. But this smiling, heavyset blond remained one of Congress's staunchest conservatives,* and when he succeeded Don Bruce as chairman of the American Conservative Union in 1965, Ashbrook was recognized as perhaps the leading conservative spokesman then on Capitol Hill.

Ashbrook was as disgusted as I was with Nixon's performance in office, especially during 1971, and in the latter half of that year he sounded out various close friends on whether he ought to run against Nixon in the early Republican primaries of 1972—not, of course, in the expectation of winning any of them but simply as a demonstration of the depth of conservative dissatisfaction. I encouraged John as much as possible, pledging not only what financial support I could but, for what it was worth, promising to stump for him in New Hampshire and Florida as well. Other friends, including such significant figures as Meldrim Thomson, who had been a candidate for governor of New Hampshire in 1968 and 1970 and was to win the office in November 1972, likewise promised their help.

Quixotic as Ashbrook's potential presidential candidacy un-

---

* In 1982, when I had the sad duty of speaking at a memorial service in Washington after Ashbrook's tragically early death, I pointed out that his cumulative "ACU rating" (i.e., his rating on key conservative votes), over more than twenty-one years in the House, was 96 percent out of a theoretically possible 100.

doubtedly was, the Nixon forces clearly and profoundly disliked the idea when they learned about it. Nixon wanted no serious defections on his right. Just before the end of 1971, therefore, Buchanan relayed to us, on Nixon's behalf, the following pledges, which were conditioned on Ashbrook's not declaring his candidacy:

1. There would be a "clear signal," early in January, that Agnew was Nixon's choice for renomination as vice president.

2. There would be another "clear signal" that the family assistance plan (Pat Moynihan's baby, which Nixon had adopted and which was anathema to conservatives) would be abandoned.

3. There would be certain specified, though generally modest, increases in the defense budget.

This offer, however, was brushed aside by Ashbrook and his advisers. They recognized it for what it was: an effort to buy off a source of irritation, but no more. On December 29 John Ashbrook announced in a Washington press conference his candidacy for the presidency of the United States.

Our plan was to carry on through the New Hampshire and Florida primaries (on March 7 and 14 respectively), hoping that John's showing in these would be impressive enough to enable us to raise money then for the later primaries—most notably California's, where a large bloc of conservative Republicans was reportedly off the reservation. Lord knows we tried. (I personally spent two days in icy New Hampshire, and another day in far pleasanter Miami, keeping my promise to stump for John.) But the reaction of the voters, under the guidance of the media, was largely one of indifference: Ashbrook got only about 10 percent of the vote in each of the two primaries. Even good conservative friends of ours, knowing that an Ashbrook victory was out of the question, chose to stifle their reservations about Nixon and remain in grace and communion with the White House. To his credit Bill Buckley, upon returning from Nixon's pilgrimage to Peking and deploring it, promptly flew to New Hampshire and pinned on an Ashbrook button as the press cameras clicked, but thereafter *National Review*'s (and Buckley's) enthusiasm for John's candidacy dwindled rapidly.

Somehow, nonetheless, the Ashbrook effort pushed doggedly

on. In California anti-Nixon conservatives did a splendid job of putting John on the primary ballot there by the petition route; but Governor Reagan himself had agreed to head the Nixon slate, so raising money for Ashbrook's effort was almost impossible. Once again Ashbrook won the support of only about 10 percent of the Republicans who voted in the primary—nearly a quarter of a million votes, but still only a negligible proportion. This gave the coup de grâce to John Ashbrook's valiant little protest movement, and from June 1972 forward—coincidentally, the month of Watergate—American conservatives, with varying degrees of reservation, closed ranks behind Nixon.

There were, however, exceptions, and I was one of them. The Democratic party's nomination of George McGovern that July made it difficult, to put it mildly, for a conservative to explain why he would withhold his support from Nixon. But as these pages have testified, I had never trusted the man: had refused even to vote for him in 1960 (writing in the name of Barry Goldwater instead) and had fought energetically against his nomination in 1968. His performance in office, especially after 1970, seemed to me to confirm every reservation I had ever felt concerning him, and in the spring of 1972 I summed up the case against voting for him in an article which I submitted to the editors at *National Review*. I knew, of course, that they disagreed with me (Jeffrey Hart, in fact, was writing speeches for Nixon's "surrogate" campaigners at this time). But I had held since 1957 not only the title of publisher of *National Review* but the rank of a senior editor, and one of the traditional privileges of that rank—of which I have cheerfully availed myself every now and then—is to have one's dissent from a *National Review* editorial position printed in the magazine at page length under the title "The Open Question." That was the privilege I now invoked.

It soon transpired, though, that Bill Buckley was reluctant to honor the tradition in this particular case. He was quietly scandalized by my resolute refusal to support Nixon (after all, good Lord, look at the *alternative!*) and was unwilling to give my apostasy the "bully pulpit" of a page in his magazine. Rather than force the issue, which might simply have played into Nixon's hands, I yielded and arranged to have the article published instead on the

Op-Ed page of the *Los Angeles Times,* where I hoped Mr. Nixon might read it over breakfast at Casa Pacifica. I reprint it herewith, in full and without apologies, in the more genial light of hindsight, when we know the grim price that America, the conservative movement, and the Republican party would all shortly have to pay for their willingness to settle for Richard Nixon:

For conservatives, the presidential election of 1972 is truly the winter of our discontent. Sen. Barry Goldwater's nomination in 1964 turned out to be no mere fluke; it marked a major shift in control of the Republican Party from the Eastern liberals to an aggressively conservative coalition of the South, the Midwest and the West.

And when the party convened again, at Miami Beach in 1968, it was clear that this same coalition was still overwhelmingly dominant. Unfortunately, conservative Republicans were divided that year between Richard Nixon and Ronald Reagan. Fatally, as it turned out, a majority of them opted for Mr. Nixon, believing that he would be easier to elect, and would be adequately conservative once elected. If the formulation had been familiar in 1968, it might have been said that many conservative Republicans changed, that year, from a strategy of ideological "superiority" to one of "sufficiency."

Mr. Nixon's first two years in office were indeed comparatively unobjectionable from a conservative standpoint, and his Supreme Court appointees (to date at least) have indisputably improved the balance of that key body. But, commencing with the year 1971, he has abandoned seriatim almost every other major principle for which American conservatism has stood since the end of the Second World War.

Fiscal sanity and balanced budgets? He has run the United States still deeper into the red, to the tune of $52 billion—not even counting the current fiscal year, which will add at least $27 billion more all by itself. Free-market control of the inflationary forces loosed by those appalling deficits? He has imposed wage and price controls on the economy—just 14 months after telling the nation in a TV broadcast that "Wage and price controls only postpone a day of reckoning. . . . They would do more harm than good."

Loyal support of our anti-Communist allies? He has squarely reversed the policy of his four immediate predecessors on Red China, and led the drive to admit Peking to the United Nations, with disastrous consequences for Taiwan. Uncompromising determination to maintain an adequate defense posture? He has signed with the Soviet Union a treaty which gives the Russians 40% more intercontinental ballistic missiles (1,408 to 1,000) and missile-launching submarines (62 to 44), one-third more submarine-launched ballistic missiles (960 to 710) and a three-fold Soviet advantage in megatonnage of total missile payload. As the *New York Times* exulted editorially in February of this year, "Seldom in Western politics . . . has a national leader so completely turned his back on a lifetime of beliefs to adopt those of his political opponents."

Inevitably, those opponents (the Democrats) have lunged still further to the left, scrounging desperately for support among newly enfranchised voters and freshly mobilized "minorities." Conservatism, for its part, has all but vanished as a force in American politics. Within the Republican Party, and even within its consciously conservative wing, Mr. Nixon's liberal policies have not only failed to elicit serious opposition, but have actually won recruits. (Repeatedly, I have seen letters from the President's conservative defenders, insisting for example that his 180-degree reversal of the American policy on Red China was "long overdue"—a belief they certainly concealed well until he proclaimed the switch). Mr. Nixon, in short, has not only traduced almost all of conservatism's basic principles; he has, for the time being, largely silenced its leaders, confused or seduced a good part of its following and effectively paralyzed the whole conservative movement.

To these and indeed all other criticisms of Mr. Nixon, his apologists have one sovereign answer: "Would you rather have McGovern?"

It is a hard question—which is why the conservative dilemma this November is a real one. Nothing can make George McGovern affirmatively appealing to American conservatives. His original foreign policy was essentially a global bug-out, belatedly modified to provide for the all-out defense of Israel. His domestic program consists, or at least used to consist, of a series of handouts so incontinent that his defenders were reduced to arguing (quite rightly, by the way) that not even a Democratic Congress would ever dream of enacting them into law. His own performance, since he first realized that the new convention rules gave him a serious chance at the nomination, has constituted little less than a headlong flight from these positions and virtually everything else he had previously stood for—giving rise to the suspicion (which I share) that he is actually as devoid of settled principles as Mr. Nixon.

So, for conservatives, the answer to the challenge, "Would you rather have McGovern?" must be No, if we are merely being called upon to acknowledge that, as President, McGovern would very likely advocate policies further to the left than those the President has already embraced, and perhaps even to the left of whatever ugly surprises Mr. Nixon is saving to spring on conservatives in his second term.

But that is far from saying that a McGovern administration would therefore necessarily be worse for America than another four years of Richard Nixon; for the simplistic formulation, "Nixon or McGovern?" fails to take into account the key fact that, under McGovern, conservative opposition to liberal or leftist proposals would be vehement and frequently successful (many would never become law), whereas under Mr. Nixon such opposition is for all practical purposes nonexistent.

Just consider recent history. In the administration of John Kennedy, the American conservative movement grew from the fancy of a coterie to a national force. In that of Lyndon Johnson, it captured the Republican nomination for Barry Goldwater and kept control of the GOP despite Goldwater's subsequent defeat. Under Richard Nixon, it has simply disappeared—and has done so, moreover, not, heaven knows, because Mr. Nixon has been "sufficiently" conservative, but despite his espousal of policies (Red China's U.N. admission, to name only one) that conservative pressure had successfully prevented either Mr. Kennedy or Mr. Johnson from adopting. It is not too much to say that only a Republican President could have carried the day for liberal policies as successfully as Mr. Nixon has.

That is why I have—on this matter alone—disassociated myself from *National Review* and its editors, who have called for Mr. Nixon's reelection. I will not vote for Richard Nixon this November: I believe that conservatism, and therefore America, would on balance be better off—i.e., actually do better, in raw policy terms—under, and in spite of, a President McGovern. At a minimum, we would be compelled to watch the steady disintegration of the American society and either resist it or confess our acquiescence in it, rather than have it shielded from our sight by the comforting but wholly meretricious notion that a vote for Mr. Nixon is somehow a vote against it.

But neither will I vote for Sen. McGovern, even though such a vote would be doubly damaging to Mr. Nixon; for I have no hang-up about a citizen's "obligation to vote" (why vote, in heaven's name, when confined to such a choice?), but I do believe that one's political conduct should be principled, and to vote for McGovern would be tantamount to giving up my principles for my principles.

Rather, I intend to just sit this one out, as far as the Presidency is concerned, and concentrate my efforts on local races. And when, as I fully expect, Mr. Nixon on Election Day reaps the reward of his political flexibility (and his opponent's numerous mistakes) and boots George McGovern from here to Kingdom Come, we conservatives will have to decide whether to hunker down in the GOP and await better days, or seek some other vehicle for salvaging however much of America is left to us.

I realized, as the last paragraph above indicates, that there was no serious doubt in the mind of any thoughtful observer about the outcome in November, and the universal expectation was duly fulfilled: Richard Nixon and Spiro Agnew were reelected overwhelmingly, carrying every state but Massachusetts. Whatever the election implied about the judgment of American conservatives in selecting their standard-bearer, it certainly left no doubt about the strength of their movement.

For the essential significance of the 1972 presidential election lay, of course, in the fact that, for the very first time, the economic conservatives (who formed the traditional core of the GOP) and the social conservatives (in many cases lifelong Democrats, now disaffected from the Roosevelt coalition) voted for the same candidate. In 1968 the economic conservatives, plus some of the social conservatives, had given Nixon a narrow victory over the liberal Democrat, Hubert Humphrey; but George Wallace, running on a third-party ticket, had garnered nearly 10 million votes, virtually all of them social conservatives. In 1972 Wallace (this time running in the Democratic presidential primaries) had been literally shot out of the race by a would-be assassin. Any possibility that his followers would return, that year, to the orthodox Democratic fold was eliminated by the Democrats' nomination of the ultraliberal George McGovern—the high-water mark of New Left influence in American politics. Richard Nixon's overwhelming defeat of McGovern was the clearest possible demonstration, to anyone not willfully blind, that liberalism in 1972 commanded the allegiance of far less than a majority of American voters and that the stability of a precarious but powerful antiliberal coalition of economic and social conservatives was now the dominant fact in American politics.

* * *

One man who at last recognized the existence of a conservative majority as a fact and was prepared to trim his sails accordingly was Richard Nixon himself. Belatedly, but seemingly not too late, he realized the validity of Kevin Phillips's analysis, four years earlier, in *The Emerging Republican Majority*. As Nixon wrote in his own *Memoirs* (Grosset & Dunlap, 1978), crediting McGovern with having precipitated the change (to cover Nixon's own earlier blindness): "McGovern's perverse treatment of the traditional Democratic power blocs that had been the basis of every Democratic presidential victory for the last 40 years had made possible the creation of a New Republican Majority as an electoral force in American politics."

Nixon pointed proudly to the previously Democratic groups that contributed to his 1972 reelection landslide: "Four of these groups—manual workers, Catholics, members of labor union families, and people with only grade-school educations—had never before been in the Republican camp." In his second term, therefore, Nixon went on, "I planned to give expression to the more conservative values and beliefs of the New Majority throughout the country. . . . I intended to revitalize the Republican Party along New Majority lines."

Nixon was not the only major political figure who, as 1972 drew to a close, had his mind on the possibility of a continuing coalition of economic and social conservatives. In the House of Representatives, where the dominance of the Democratic party seemed almost as permanent and unassailable as the Capitol dome itself, it had not escaped notice that if you counted conservatives and liberals instead of Democrats and Republicans, the Nixon landslide of 1972 had produced a narrow but durable conservative majority. What if those conservatives, uniting across party lines, were to organize the House—electing, say, the staunchly conservative Democrat from Louisiana, Joe Waggoner, as speaker and putting conservative Republicans in control of most of the House's key committees? The liberal Democrats, relegated to minority status, would cry, "Treason!," of course, but what could they do?

That such a plan was under serious consideration near the end of 1972 is a simple fact, neither widely reported at the time nor adequately noted since. That the idea was not impossibly visionary is at least suggested by the fact that such "coalitionism" has since been tried, successfully, by bipartisan blocs of determined conservatives in the New Hampshire State Senate and the House of Representatives of New Mexico.

But history had other plans, in their way even more spectacular.

By the early 1970s the number of conservative organizations active on various fronts was increasing almost exponentially, and it is a serious problem for a chronicler to do even rudimentary justice to all of them.

In the publication field the early birds had been joined by the *Alternative* (now the *American Spectator*), an always brash and often sparkling monthly tabloid launched by R. Emmett Tyrrell, Jr., in the 1960s, when he was a graduate student at the University of Indiana, and still published in Bloomington by Tyrrell and a group of his contemporaries. The 1970s saw the birth of Richard Viguerie's feisty *Conservative Digest*, the acknowledged voice of the New Right, and Leopold Tyrmand's erudite *Chronicles of Culture*.

The media themselves were the subject singled out for special attention by Reed Irvine, who incorporated Accuracy in Media and became its board chairman in 1971. Irvine also edits its semimonthly bulletin, the *AIM Report*, begun in 1972. Thanks to AIM, such pillars of the liberal journalistic establishment as the *New York Times*, the *Washington Post*, and CBS's *60 Minutes* have all felt the lash of precise and public criticism when they strayed from accuracy in the pursuit of liberal political objectives.

It was in the early 1970s, too, that Phyllis Schlafly, a remarkable Illinois housewife who had long been active in conservative .causes, began the campaign against the Equal Rights Amendment that will always be associated with her name and that ultimately resulted in ERA's defeat.

One after another, conservative organizations were founded to concentrate on particular subjects. The American-African Affairs Association, of which I served as co-chairman with Max Yergan for ten years, was launched in 1965 to attempt to counter in a small way the steadfastly liberal bias of the African-American Institute and the still harder-left work of the American Committee on Africa. The American-Asian Educational Exchange concentrated on the Far East, with a scholarly emphasis.

Consumer affairs were addressed from a conservative standpoint by Operation Alert, the brainchild of an exceptionally energetic and determined Vietnam War widow, Barbara Keating (now Mrs. Lennarth Edh).* Another woman was the driving force in the chief organization, allied to the conservative movement, concentrating on medical topics: Dr. Elizabeth Whelan, whose American Council on Science and Health drew on a panel of distinguished medical scientists to counter the heavy Naderite influence in this important field.

Issues related to defense were the special concern of John Fisher's American Security Council, while a broader and thoroughly conservative look at global strategic concerns was provided by Frank Barnett's National Strategy Information Center. Barnett, a prewar college English instructor, had watched, as a young U.S. intelligence officer in 1945, the forced repatriation to Russia of the captured members of "Vlasov's Army," the émigré Russian anti-Communist unit that fought beside Germany against Stalin. Many of these unlucky men committed suicide by slashing their wrists with broken bottles rather than face Stalin's vengeance. "I knew then," Barnett once told me, "that I couldn't spend the rest of my life footnoting Chaucer." He has been an active cold warrior since the early 1950s.

On the college front, the Intercollegiate Studies Institute (originally the Intercollegiate Society of Individualists) had also been active in a quiet way since the early 1950s, promoting the doctrine of free enterprise on America's campuses. YAF, of course, had been on the scene since 1960. Now, late in the decade of the seventies, they were joined by the Institute for Educational Affairs, which began by making grants to individual scholars and today is actively encouraging conservative college journalists.

In revulsion against Nixon's performance as president, the early 1970s saw the birth and swift growth of what Kevin Phillips soon labeled the New Right: an interlocking group of relatively youthful conservative activists, distinguishable from many others

* She also found time to be the New York Conservative party's senatorial candidate in 1974.

by their strong sympathy for social-conservative causes (antiabortion, anti-gun control, antibusing, pro-"family") and their eagerness for political action as opposed to pure theorizing. Richard Viguerie was kept busy—and made rich—by his computerized mailing lists of conservative names. Paul Weyrich formed the Committee for the Survival of a Free Congress as the vehicle for his growing involvement in congressional primaries and elections in both parties and all over America. When Congress's constant maladroit meddling in the sensitive field of campaign financing made political action committees the way to go, John T. ("Terry") Dolan created the National Conservative Political Action Committee (NCPAC, pronounced "nikpak") to raise conservative campaign funds and put them where they would do the movement the most good. Meanwhile, to organize the grass roots, Howard Phillips personally visited every one of the country's 435 congressional districts on behalf of his Conservative Caucus.

Despite the allegiance of most blacks to liberal principles and causes, a small but courageous handful of black Americans had always believed and declared that conservatism was the soundest policy for their fellow blacks. During the 1950s and '60s two of the best known were Max Yergan and George Schuyler, both of whom entered the movement through the anti-Communist door. Yergan, a lifelong teacher and expert on Africa, had tangled with Paul Robeson and the pro-Communist element in the Council on African Affairs in the late 1940s. Schuyler, a journalist and newspaper columnist, heaped coals on Communist heads from the vantage point of his column in the *Pittsburgh Courier* and other black newspapers.

In the 1970s perhaps the most prominent black conservatives were two young economists: Dr. Thomas Sowell of UCLA and Dr. Walter Williams of Temple University. Both men saw with special clarity how liberal welfare measures and other types of social legislation were making the condition of black Americans not better but appreciably worse—how, to take just one example, the minimum wage law, by making it unlawful to pay a young black male what his labor is actually worth in economic terms, renders high unemployment among teenage black males absolutely inevitable. Sowell and Williams are both men of high courage and have recognized how rare it is for a black economist to speak up for conservative principles; jokingly they have agreed never to fly on the same plane.

In some ways, however, the most remarkable black conservative of them all is a Philadelphian named Jay Parker. Parker, then a radio talk show host, got his start in the conservative movement as a member of YAF and of its national board in the 1960s. In 1971, when liberal attacks on the FBI began to mount, Parker founded and headed a support organization called Friends of the FBI. In 1978, securely established in his own public relations business in Washington and anxious to work directly on problems affecting his fellow blacks, he founded the Lincoln Institute for Research and Education, and he serves as editor and publisher of its quarterly, *Lincoln Review.*

But if any conservative organization founded in the 1970s deserves pride of place, surely it is the Heritage Foundation. Launched in 1973 by Paul Weyrich, Joseph Coors, and Edwin Feulner, it set out to provide the conservative movement with an aggressive and competent "think tank" that would provide the sort of policy guidance and technical backup facilities that such organizations as the Brookings Institution had long furnished for liberals.

Former Democratic Congressman Ben Blackburn of Georgia was Heritage's board chairman from 1973 to 1982, when he was succeeded by Frank Shakespeare, and Weyrich and Frank Walton served successively as the organization's president until 1977. In that year Feulner, a former administrative assistant to Congressman Phil Crane, assumed the office, and he has held it ever since. With a budget that grew from $250,000 in 1973 to $1,000,000 in 1977 and $9,500,000 in 1983 (compared to $12,000,000 for Brookings), Heritage sponsors a bewildering array of conservative-oriented activities: publishing its own quarterly magazine, *Policy Review;* preparing and distributing about 120 influential *Backgrounder* studies of specific policies and problems every year; sending some fifty academically qualified witnesses from its own staff each year to testify before congressional committees; maintaining a "talent bank" for government personnel and a "resource bank" on issues; etc. In late 1980, as the Reagan transition teams began reaching Washington, Heritage published *Mandate for Leadership,* a 1,093-page, twenty-seven-chapter study of the federal government, analyzing and proposing reforms in every cabinet department and every major agency. Its three thousand policy recommendations were gratefully received by the incoming administration, and nearly two-thirds of them were soon adopted.

At the state level, members of legislatures across the nation organized for conservative action on common or parallel problems through the medium of the American Legislative Exchange Council, founded in 1973. Ten years later its members included some two thousand state legislators around the country, and its national office boasted a million-dollar budget and a staff of ten.

One of the most effective devices for promoting liberal causes has long been the "public interest legal foundation"—in effect, a law firm dedicated to representing liberal litigants in all sorts of private lawsuits, class actions, and miscellaneous legal proceedings having a liberal angle. During the 1970s various young lawyers with more conservative views began creating similar organizations to do battle in the nation's courtrooms for conservative causes. Early on the scene was the Pacific Legal Foundation, formed in 1973, soon followed by the Capitol Legal Foundation, the Washington Legal Foundation, and several others. (From 1977 to 1980 the president and chief legal officer of the Mountain States Legal Foundation in Denver was a young Wyoming lawyer named James Watt.)

Obviously, such activities—whether left or right—cannot be launched or carried on without a certain amount of money. In this respect, incongruous as it may seem at first to someone who has never thought about it, the liberals have historically had far the better of it. Since well before the days of the New Deal, America's colleges and universities have served first as a forcing bed, then as a vast financial, social, and intellectual resource, and now, finally, as a fortress-sanctuary for liberals and liberal causes.

Drawing on academic personnel resources and thus following inevitably in the academy's political footsteps, the large foundations—Ford, Rockefeller, Carnegie, etc.—were next rolled onto line in support of liberalism. When I was associate counsel to the Senate Internal Security Subcommittee in 1956 and 1957 and watching closely the intricate process whereby liberal and leftist causes were funded, it appeared that a major drive would usually first be mounted to have a new liberal project financed by the federal government. More often than not the attempt would be successful. But if by any chance it failed, that was not the end of the story. The project would often simply be funded instead by, for example, the Ford Foundation—old Henry's millions, now wholly under liberal control and available (without the inconvenience of being taxed first, like your income or mine) for the support of liberal causes.

On the conservative side, there was for many years scarcely any financial support worth mentioning. Occasionally some small family foundation with conservative leanings—the Relm Foundation in Ann Arbor or the Volker Fund in California—would make a grant-in-aid of some conservative author or (more rarely) some group of conservative activists. But the lawyers for such foundations were typically terrified of their being accused of noncharitable activities and advised against such involvements; they lacked the imagination and sheer *chutzpah* of the big foundations' more liberal legal advisers.

Here and there a courageous businessman would put his corporation's money where his mouth was. Certainly *National Review* is forever in the debt of Roger Milliken and his family, whose textile corporation (formerly Deering Milliken, now Milliken & Company) has had a full-page color ad in every issue of the magazine almost from the very start and has supplemented that with still other munificent contributions to its support.

But the fact is that the conservative movement was virtually unfunded, save on a purely personal and individual basis, until the Goldwater campaign generated the first large lists of conservatives willing to give money to the cause.

Did the imbalance between liberal and conservative resources matter? You may be sure it did. To take only one example, with which I personally am familiar: While the Young Republican leaders of the early 1950s were trying to decide how they could afford on slender budgets to attend their federation's 1953 national convention in Rapid City, South Dakota, the National Student Association—a campus rival dominated by young democratic socialists and secretly financed by the CIA (and, therefore, at the taxpayers' expense)—was maintaining permanent offices in four capitals of Europe to handle the annual influx of suitably liberal and leftist American college students who were being flown over to attend various conferences, seminars, etc. Which enterprise, do you suppose, appealed more powerfully to the average college student? How could the Young Republicans keep 'em down on the farm after they'd seen Paree?

In the 1970s, however, a few determined and farsighted businessmen with substantial personal resources and (in most cases) their own charitable foundations decided to lend their support to various aspects of the conservative movement. Joseph Coors, as already noted, helped launch the highly influential Heritage Foundation. Coors, a wealthy Colorado brewer, also gave financial support to a large array of other conservative activities, many of them squarely political in nature.

For Richard Scaife of Pittsburgh, on the other hand, one of the heirs of the Mellon family fortune, the areas of greatest emphasis (though by no means the only ones) were defense and foreign affairs. Even in the 1960s his Scaife Foundation had generously supported Frank Barnett's National Strategy Information Center. In the decade of the seventies it expanded its philanthropies to include the Georgetown Center for Strategic and International Studies, among many other conservative organizations.

One of America's wealthiest men, the late John M. Olin, began guiding his Olin Foundation into the field of conservative activities at about the same time. With the help of sound advice from William E. Simon, the former U.S. treasury secretary who sat on its board, the Olin Foundation was soon an important factor in the viability of a whole array of conservative organizations, many shrewdly chosen for their impact in areas not previously covered.

Much the same could be said of the Richardson Foundation, a smaller but intelligently managed foundation created by the heirs of Smith Richardson, the North Carolina chemist who founded the Vick Chemical Company. And to single out these four sources of conservative financing by no means exhausts the list of those that became available as the 1970s progressed. In this as in almost every other respect, the decade of the seventies seemed to be the period in which conservative consciousness and activity acquired critical mass and with it truly explosive potentiality.

The Watergate break-in occurred in June 1972, and the investigation had festered quietly until after Nixon's reelection. At

just that point, however, Watergate—and ironically, Nixon himself—became the focus of resistance to the conservative wave now
so plainly rolling ashore on the beaches of American politics. Now
conservatives would pay the price for their long and inexcusable
indulgence toward this complex, devious, and singularly unsatisfactory leader. The whole rightward progress of American politics, which had been slowed by Nixon's first administration, would
be brought to a halt, temporarily, while Richard Nixon and his liberal enemies between them contrived his downfall.

First, however, one adjustment was required, and it was duly
made. After all, it would scarcely do, from the liberals' standpoint,
if their ancient bête noire were to be toppled from his presidency
only to be replaced by a successor now far more genuinely conservative than he. Several Maryland business felons were found who,
in return for reductions or total remissions of the penalties for tax
evasion and other crimes, were willing to testify that Agnew,
when governor of Maryland, had accepted cash contributions
from them in return for state contracts and even continued the
practice when he became vice president. At least some of these
charges may well have been true, for such contributions were
standard practice in both parties in Maryland for many years, and
Agnew pleaded nolo contendere and resigned as vice president in
November, when formally arraigned on them. But their precise
location on the spectrum of American political misbehavior is
hardly the point, for their significance in the overheated Washington atmosphere of late 1973, as the Watergate scandal moiled on,
was simply that by forcing the resignation of Agnew as vice president, they cleared the way for the final assault on Nixon.

To replace Agnew in the vice presidency, Nixon—who simply couldn't afford a partisan battle on this issue, on top of all the
others he was then waging—nominated a popular, amiable, longtime Republican member of the House of Representatives: Minority Leader Gerald Ford. Congressional courtesy did the rest.
Ford's nomination was ratified in December amid bipartisan
huzzas—and the curtain rose on the final act of the Watergate
melodrama.

I am seldom accused of a lingering weakness for Richard
Nixon. And yet it is a curious fact that at this particular point in

his far-from-inspiring saga, I found myself gravitating gingerly toward his defense. I had, after all, been a lawyer even before I became a conscious conservative, and legal habits of thinking had never died out in me. I could, and did, insist on keeping an open mind about questions of personal guilt and innocence until all the evidence was in—and not only in but persuasive. And the more I looked, purely as a lawyer, at the accumulated evidence against Richard Nixon (I am speaking now of the period *before* the disclosure of the so-called smoking pistol tape, on August 5, 1974), the less impressive it seemed to me.

It was all very well to argue that if (as the mounting evidence amply demonstrated) Haldeman, Ehrlichman, and Mitchell were all involved in the break-in and/or the cover-up, Nixon must have been, too. But "must have been" isn't evidence, as any first-year law student knows, and as the first half of 1974 rolled by, it became apparent that there was a substantial gap between the intensity of the liberals' longing to remove Nixon (which was understandably monumental) and the evidence they had managed to amass to that end. Putting aside my long-standing distaste for Nixon, I cleared my throat and said so.

As it happened, my syndicated column, "The Conservative Advocate," had been launched on August 1, 1973, and by the end of that year it was appearing in nearly a hundred newspapers around the country. In a fair share of these columns I discussed the unfolding Watergate story, almost always from the standpoint of a lawyer trying to assess unemotionally the weight of the evidence. It seemed to me that such anti-Nixon zealots as my old Princeton classmate John Doar, special counsel to the House Judiciary Committee for the investigation of Watergate, were merely confessing the essential hollowness of their case when they urged reporters and other observers to "look at the whole picture" (i.e., rather than the hard evidence)—the familiar cry of the advocate without a provable case; and I said as much. Some of my less observant friends concluded that I had somehow become sentimental about Nixon as I turned fifty. Not so—as I sufficiently demonstrated when the "smoking pistol tape" was at last discovered and disclosed.

To be entirely accurate, not even that tape revealed a truly dreadful misdeed on Nixon's part. It did not, for one thing, even demonstrate that he knew in advance about the break-in. It did, however, make it plain that Nixon had tried, for a period of about two weeks beginning in late June 1972, to dissuade the FBI from tracing the "laundered" money that had been used to pay the break-in team, by inventing a cock-and-bull story that the money had been laundered for legitimate purposes (involving national security) by the CIA. When the CIA declined to go along with this charade, Nixon threw in the sponge and told the FBI to go ahead with its probe. But during those preceding two weeks, Nixon had indubitably engaged in a technical "obstruction of justice"— which is a crime, and a serious one in a public official sworn to uphold the Constitution. One may well wonder how often justice has, equally technically, been "obstructed" by other occupants of the Oval Office, but the law cannot regard that point as exculpatory. Certainly in the Washington atmosphere of August 1974 revelation of such a crime on the part of Richard Nixon could have only one result.

It was therefore almost with a sense of relief that I discharged my legal conscience from its sturdily held post, entitled my column (written for release August 9) "The Evidence Is Conclusive," and joined the almost unanimous chorus then calling for Nixon's resignation or impeachment.

Chapter **XI**

A New Party?

Nixon resigned on August 8, Gerald Ford was duly sworn in as president, and the next important political development, obviously, was going to be President Ford's designation of a new vice president. There was considerable speculation that it might be former Governor Rockefeller (who had stepped down from that office on December 11 the previous year, to give his lieutenant governor and heir apparent, Malcolm Wilson, a good start in the 1974 succession battle), and my friend Clif White flatly predicted as much.

I, however, was confident that it would *not* be Rockefeller and said so to Ed Meese and Mike Deaver of Governor Reagan's staff when I lunched with them at the Sutter Club in Sacramento on August 19. I have since remembered that lunch (and joked about it with Meese) as a spectacular example of how it sometimes doesn't pay to outguess a president of the United States.

My problem, in retrospect, was that it never crossed my mind that I might actually *be* outguessing Ford—might possess, in fact, a sounder notion of where America stood politically, and what was therefore required of him as a Republican president, than he did.

It was perfectly obvious, at least to me, that Nixon's 1972 victory had been (as already discussed) the by-product of a newly forged and distinctly fragile coalition of economic and social conservatives. Victory for the Republican party, at least for the foreseeable future, involved nurturing that coalition and making it permanent. For that purpose, the designation of Nelson Rockefeller—a liberal eastern multimillionaire—as vice president was not only pointless but downright counterproductive. Rockefeller represented virtually everything that antagonized social conservatives, without bringing to the Republican ticket a single new voting bloc or political tendency. His designation could only mean that as far as Ford was concerned, the election of 1976 would see a return by the GOP to the strategy it had pursued, usually without success, prior to 1964: trying to prize from the Democrats a handful of their moderate liberals, to add to the GOP's economic conservatives. The social conservatives either weren't wanted or—more likely, and worse yet—weren't even recognized as a voting bloc that might be lured away from the Democratic fold.

Within a year Ford would be forced to recognize how wildly his designation of Rockefeller as vice president was out of plumb with Republican reality and to distance himself from a Rockefeller bid for nomination as vice president at the Kansas City convention of the GOP in 1976. Without Ford's endorsement—or even with it—Rockefeller could not possibly have won the nomination. Much as Nelson Rockefeller wanted to continue as vice president, he recognized reality more readily than Ford had the year before: On November 3, 1975, Rockefeller announced that he would not seek the vice presidency in 1976.

Meanwhile, as matters stood after Ford's designation of Rockefeller for the vice presidency in August 1974, the conservative movement could only feel that it had been deliberately slapped in the face by the new president. In my column, and even to myself, I tried gamely to argue that by designating Rockefeller as his vice president, Ford was attempting to balance a ticket whereon he conceived of himself as the conservative. But his sheer folly in choosing Rockefeller simply baffled me.

"Why did he do it?" I asked Clif White, incredulously.

"Because it was the easiest thing to do," Clif replied. Obviously Ford could no more afford a long—let alone a losing—battle over the vice presidential designation than Nixon could have, the year before. No doubt it seemed likely that Rockefeller, as the longtime governor of one of the nation's largest states, would evoke as little resistance as anyone Ford might nominate. As for the conservatives, it is clear in retrospect that Ford simply had no comprehension of the seismic forces at work in American politics. Anyway, hadn't Barry Goldwater, in yet another of his mystifying lapses from conservative orthodoxy, declared that Rockefeller would be "acceptable" as vice president?

In point of fact, Rockefeller was to be subjected to heavy going at the hands of the Democrats during his confirmation hearings on Capitol Hill late that year. Much was made of the fact that owing to large deductions, charitable and otherwise, this very symbol of wealth had paid no federal income tax in 1970. Ultimately, however, he was confirmed as vice president—perhaps, as I suggested in my column, because the Democrats were shrewd enough to recognize a Republican handicap when they saw one.

In any event, the latter half of 1974 certainly represented the nadir of the conservative movement's long love affair with the GOP. The Republican party under Ford seemed to be going nowhere that we wanted to go, even though its relatively liberal eastern wing no longer controlled it. No party whose incumbent president could regard the designation of Nelson Rockefeller for the vice presidency as a shrewd move was likely to prove very hospitable to conservatives. Moreover, the Agnew and Nixon resignations had created a stench of criminality which in and of itself would obviously take some years to wear off.

It was, I felt, time to "think anew and act anew." As I warned in my column for September 6, 1974: ". . . if President Ford has indeed been persuaded that he can safely ignore the South and West, in return for electoral votes to be produced by teaming with Rockefeller in the Northeast, conservative Republicans may not consent to sit idly by and watch the Democrats reclaim the South and the Sun Belt. The stage, then, might be set for a new and independent conservative movement in 1976, designed to carry these potentially dominant regions of a changing America."

The congressional elections of 1974, coming so soon after the Watergate scandal and Nixon's resignation, were practically bound to reflect a national swing toward the Democratic party, quite independently of any national trend to the right, and that was in fact the outcome. The Democrats picked up three seats in the Senate, as well as forty-three in the House, and netted a gain of four governorships.

To thoughtful conservatives, therefore, the scene that autumn was dismaying and yet pregnant with possibilities. The conservative movement's long fascination with the equivocal personality of Richard Nixon was over at last. Former Vice President Agnew had resigned in disgrace the previous year. Nixon's own intended choice as his successor, Treasury Secretary John Connally, was under indictment for accepting a bribe on behalf of the nation's milk dealers. (He was later acquitted but remained compromised in the public's eyes to some indeterminate but clearly serious extent.) Senator James Buckley, on whom all eyes and many hopes had been fixed as a possible conservative presidential candidate when he was elected to the Senate in 1970, had in the ensuing four years earned the respect of his colleagues as an able and conscientious member of the Senate but exhibited no flair whatever for generating the kind of publicity that serving as a senator—let alone running for president—requires.

As for Ronald Reagan, he had firmly decided to step down as governor of California in January 1975 rather than seek a third term. But as I learned during my lunch with Meese and Deaver at the Sutter Club in August 1974, Reagan had no intention of retiring altogether from the public scene. It was simply too early to tell what might happen in 1976, and the ex-governor would be maintaining a reasonably high profile, pending developments.

"Hang loose," similarly, was the decision of Clif White's Hard Core, a dozen or so of whose members caucused on the weekend of September 21, 1974, at Charlie Barr's farm near Matteson, Illinois, just south of Chicago. Some of those present believed Ford would run for election in 1976, and that supporting him was the only rational course. A number were waiting, however, to see what Reagan might do in that event. To my surprise, there was even a fair amount of sympathy for the notion that it might be time to start a new party.

The latter, as the autumn went on, became my own settled conviction. On October 12, chatting informally with the members of the national board of directors of Young Americans for Freedom at their meeting at the Commodore Hotel in New York City, I was impressed by their strong interest in the idea of a new party. Four days later, in a plane en route to a speaking engagement in Houston, I roughed out the chapter headings and general subject matter of a book on the topic.

My unconscious mind must have been mulling the idea over for quite a while because once I began work on the manuscript, the book almost "wrote itself." Writing longhand with a fountain pen, on legal-length yellow pads, my fingers almost flew across the pages. It was as if I were simply transcribing a book already written in my mind. By December 26 I had completed the forty-five-thousand-word first draft, contracted for Sheed & Ward (the book publishing house owned by the syndicate that sold my column) to publish a hardcover edition, and arranged to publish a paperback edition myself with the assistance of Jamieson Campaigne, Jr., a member of both the ACU and YAF boards who had gone into publishing with his own imprint.

The Making of the New Majority Party was the title agreed upon, and it emphasized a point I was eager to stress: What I was proposing was not intended to be a "third" party, representing some new force or interest on the political scene, but simply a new vehicle for a particular coalition of existing forces, brought together by their common opposition to the liberals who dominated the Democratic party: the economic and social conservatives.

That the potential for such a coalition existed did not, it seemed to me, admit of much argument: The election of 1968 roughly exemplified, in the votes for Nixon and Wallace, the strength of the two components of the coalition when separated. The election of 1972, in which Nixon carried every state but Massachusetts, demonstrated convincingly the overwhelming power of the same two components when they were united. Virtually every poll taken in the early 1970s showed that substantially more voters thought of themselves as conservative than called themselves liberal. A great deal of sophistical reasoning was being devoted, at the time, to explaining these unsettling statistics away, but I had no doubt of their basic validity. It was simply a matter of uniting the conservatives under one tent.

I was not greatly worried by the fact that economic and social conservatives had their differences—most notably over how much governmental intervention in economic affairs was desirable. (Economic conservatives typically wanted as little as possible; some, though not all, social conservatives favored a fair amount of governmental activity, of a regulatory or even paternalistic type.) I remembered H. L. Mencken's description of the Democratic coalition of southern whites and northern city machines that lasted for nearly a century as "two gangs of natural enemies in a precarious state of symbiosis." If the Democrats could maintain an alliance between coalition elements that disparate, there was certainly nothing inherently impossible about the combination I was proposing.

The real problem, as I saw it, was the failure—indeed, the apparent total unwillingness or perhaps inability—of the Republican party to reach beyond its traditional base of economic conservatives toward the social conservatives. The technique of "co-opting" such discontented blocs is a familiar part of the American political process, and an important one. It was, in fact, the means whereby the two major parties had maintained their dominance for over a century. No third party long survived because either the Democrats or the Republicans always stole its clothes. But somehow the leaders of the GOP (with the important exception of Ronald Reagan) seemed gripped by paralysis at the prospect of reaching out to the formerly Democratic social conservatives.

On closer analysis I thought I could see the obstacle: The small liberal wing of the Republican party could not control it, but it could and did, by threatening to defect to the Democrats (as in 1964), prevent the GOP from making an effective appeal to the social conservatives. The Republican party was forever being scolded by its liberal minority for failing to appeal to "moderate" Democrats and independents (meaning Democrats and independents slightly to the GOP's left), but by that very fact it was being successfully pressured *not* to make a bid for non-Republican conservatives. As far as I could see, there would be no end to this stalemate. Ford's designation of Rockefeller simply reaffirmed the obvious: The GOP would remain locked in its self-defeating posture of appealing only to voters on its left.

The answer, it seemed clear, was a new party: not, I repeat, a "third" party but a party that would be swiftly and inexorably substituted for the GOP as one of the two *major* parties in the bipartisan system of American politics. The idea was to blend two old wines in a new and bigger bottle and in the process establish conservative domination of the American political scene—a domination altogether justified by the conservatives' combined strength—for the foreseeable future. The Democrats, still under liberal control, would remain as the leading opposition party.

In the conviction that the hour called for a new party, I was far from alone. The feisty young activists tossed up by the Goldwater campaign, to whom Kevin Phillips would soon give the name the New Right, were powerfully drawn to the idea precisely because they identified themselves more closely with the social conservatives than with the economic conservatives. Richard Viguerie in particular—now a businessman of independent means, controlling the largest number of computerized conservative mailing lists in the country—was as disaffected from orthodox Republicanism as I was, and we both exercised considerable influence over other conservative activists.

On the other hand, those of us who favored a "new majority party" were under no illusions about the obstacles we faced. "The man with a new idea," as Mark Twain remarked, "is a crank until the idea succeeds." We would be dismissed as visionaries and zealots, and the sheer inertial momentum of the GOP, not to mention the loyalties it evoked and the many actual legal protections it enjoyed, would weigh heavily in its favor.

Only one thing would make the whole project possible: an attractive and believable candidate for the presidency in 1976. I was sure that Reagan was the man and was determined to try to win his consent to my plan. The book would be my selling tool.

Meanwhile, Reagan (whose term as governor would end at midnight on January 5) was preparing to take his own serious look at the 1976 possibilities. Whether Reagan should run for the presidency in 1976 was still an open question in his circle of advisers. Up for more serious consideration, inevitably, was whether, if he did so, he should seek to wrest the Republican nomination from President Ford or run as an independent on a third line. We know, with the proverbial acuity of hindsight, his final decision on this matter, and in retrospect it seems clear that he preferred the Republican route from the start. Certainly Deaver and many of his other advisers did. But it deserves to be recorded that the new-party option was very definitely not excluded for some time. It was far from clear that a successful campaign could be mounted to take the Republican nomination away from an incumbent president, and the concept of a new party was, if daunting, also tempting and glistened with possibilities only dimly perceived.*

Early in January 1975 I flew to the Far East for a trip which

---

* That shrewd politician John Connally, discussing the idea on Bill Buckley's "Firing Line" program in January 1976, evaluated it thus: "If Governor Reagan had said, 'I'm not going into the Republican party; I'm going to lead a third party movement in this country,' I think he could have had an enormous influence not just this year but in the years to come."

kept me abroad for most of the rest of the month. In the course of it I performed various acts of major surgery on the first draft of my book—revising the order of certain sections, etc. An expanded second draft was completed by February 10, and one of the precious typescript copies was promptly dispatched by airmail special delivery to Governor Reagan in California.

My next encounter with the governor took place less than a week later, at the CPAC conference in Washington. Reagan was a regular speaker at these annual affairs, and that year I had the honor of introducing him at the concluding banquet. The time-honored formula "The next president of the United States"—so much more than routine under these circumstances—brought the several hundred conservatives in the ballroom to their feet, roaring their cheers and applause, and Reagan's speech didn't disappoint them. He did not declare his candidacy, but his general inclination was unmistakable. I noted with special satisfaction that he pointedly left technically unanswered a question that he himself bluntly posed: "Is it a third party that we need, or is it a new and revitalized second party, raising a banner of no pale pastels, but bold colors which make it unmistakably clear where we stand on all the issues troubling the people?"

The *New York Times* next day described another paragraph in Reagan's speech as "even more enigmatic": "I do not believe that I have proposed anything that is contrary to what has been Republican principle. It is at the same time the very basis of conservatism. It is time to reassert that principle and raise it to full view. And, if there are those who cannot subscribe to these principles, let us go forward without them."

The media, of course, were well aware of the intentions of those of us who were new-party advocates, and at a press conference on the day of the speech the reporters did their strenuous best to get Reagan to say flatly that he would "rule out" such a course. The Associated Press later reported that "Governor Reagan urged conservatives tonight to unite under the Republican banner and indicated he was cool toward suggestions that he seek the Presidency on a third-party ticket." But the justifying quotation for this assertion was the following equivocal statement by Reagan: "I don't know whether there'll be a third party, but I would hope that the two-party system that has served us so well will continue to do so."

On the whole, I felt that Reagan had kept the door open to the new-party option as steadfastly as it was reasonable to hope he would.

The next afternoon the CPAC conference appointed a Committee on Conservative Alternatives, to evaluate the Republican party and a new party as alternative channels for future conservative political activity. The initial members were: Congressmen John Ashbrook and Robert Bauman, Stan Evans, Ron Docksai, Senator Jesse Helms, Eli Howell, Cy Joly (a Maine veteran of our draft-Goldwater operation), Jim Lyon, Dan Mahoney, Phyllis Schlafly, Bob Walker, Tom Winter, and I.

Later that day I went over to the Madison Hotel to discuss my book manuscript with Reagan. He had received it only a few days earlier and obviously hadn't yet managed to read all of it. But he had certainly dipped into it, for he indicated that his recollection of the events surrounding his 1968 candidacy diverged somewhat from my own.* It had been simply a favorite son affair, he believed, designed to keep the California delegation united. I didn't argue the point strenuously or change the manuscript much. My own recollection of some of Tom Reed's activities out of that little office on 47 Kearny Street in San Francisco, not to mention Clif White's operation at the Deauville in Miami Beach, didn't seem to me altogether congruent with a mere favorite son candidacy. No political figure, I decided, enjoys remembering in fond detail the battles he has lost.

The mid-February CPAC conference made it crystal-clear that the Ford-Rockefeller combination was unacceptable to conservatives, that they looked to Ronald Reagan as their champion in 1976, and that for ten cents they would back him in a new-party effort if necessary. Various leading figures in the GOP now began to respond to this state of affairs.

On February 28 Senator James Buckley brought together at the Martingham Harbourtowne Inn, near St. Michaels, Maryland, some twenty-five people: conservative Republican senators and representatives, plus officials of the Republican National Committee, and various all-purpose conservative activists, including me. I had kept Jim closely informed of my new-party proposal; but he

* See pp. 203–16, supra.

was highly skeptical of its practicality, and the St. Michaels conference was undoubtedly intended to provide an alternative lightning rod for conservative Republican sentiment. The evening was given over to amiable socializing, but when the attendees caucused next morning, opinion was almost unanimous that the Republican party needed a new candidate in 1976. It was also obvious (though unstated) who that candidate ought to be. The new-party option had its advocates, though we were deep in the minority; but there was considerable interest in the idea of some sort of blend of a new organization, capable of appealing strongly to formerly Democratic social conservatives, with elements of the already established machinery of the GOP.

Barry Goldwater did not attend the St. Michaels meeting, but of course, he knew all about the actions of the CPAC conference, and on the very day of the caucus in St. Michaels he sounded a warning against the idea of a new party. Addressing a Young Republican Leadership Conference, he told the YRs that formation of a conservative third party would only split the GOP and "practically insure" its destruction. He warned conservatives against taking a "rule or ruin attitude" and said they should work within both major parties "for the principles in which we believe." Once again the party man in Barry Goldwater was coming out.

By early March it seemed clear that Reagan was eager to run against Ford but was concerned lest he seem divisive in trying to oust an incumbent president of his own party. If he was going to run, his advisers agreed, some sort of Friends of Reagan organization ought to be formed not later than September 1, and the governor ought to make a formal declaration of candidacy around the turn of the year. Even now, however, the new-party option was not entirely "ruled out," as reporters were forever demanding; 1975 had scarcely begun, and no one could foresee what momentum the idea might acquire. I naturally hoped that my forthcoming book—scheduled for publication that June—might generate some.

The spring passed, however, without its acquiring much. CPAC's Committee on Conservative Alternatives (COCA) held its organizing meeting on March 7, chaired by Senator Helms, and created a subcommittee, which I agreed to head, to conduct research into the election laws of the fifty states—research ably carried out by Helms's shrewd young aide John Carbaugh. Early in April, though, I had intimations from friends in California that Reagan was hardening against the new-party option, and I was eager to get out there as promptly as possible to see what I could do. On April 30, bearing a copy of my book, which had at last appeared in print, I had dinner with the governor and Nancy at their home in Pacific Palisades.

I presented the book formally to Nancy, knowing her influence with her husband and hoping desperately that the new-party concept might appeal to her more powerfully than, I now suspected, it appealed to him.

Unfortunately it seemed evident that I was too late. Reagan let me know, gently but quite clearly, that he was disinclined to go the new-party route. He understood perfectly my argument concerning the need for a coalition of economic and social conservatives and agreed with it completely, but he believed that such a coalition could and should be forged under the aegis of the Republican party rather than under the banner of a new party.

"But, Governor," I protested, "the Republicans won't nominate you in 1976!"

"Well, now, that remains to be seen."

"And besides, even if they do, they'll force you to compromise with the liberals by naming a liberal Republican as your vice president."

"No, they won't," Reagan insisted vehemently, and it was impossible to doubt his sincerity. All I could do was hope that circumstances—above all, Ford's locking up of the GOP nomination—would ultimately force Reagan to see the desirability of a new party.

Meanwhile, the question of who would be Reagan's campaign manager for the GOP nomination, if he decided to seek it, was becoming a pressing one. I had begun with the breezy assumption that it would naturally be Clif White again, as in 1968, but my gentle pressures on Reagan and others to enlist Clif's help and advice did not bear fruit. Confronting Reagan's close advisers on the subject directly, I was told that "Clif has his critics as well as friends in the Republican party, you know"—which was true, as it was bound to be of anyone who had been active in Republican politics for nearly a quarter of a century. But I was nonetheless firmly convinced that White was the ablest man Reagan could possibly choose. At last, in response to my pleas to both of them, Reagan and White met for a private dinner at the Madison Hotel in Washington in mid-May.

But Reagan was accompanied (unexpectedly, as far as White was concerned) by John Sears, and according to Clif, the conversation never got far beyond the weather and the baseball season.

Actually Clif had detected the coolness of the Reagan camp toward him long before I did and was convinced that my campaign on his behalf was futile. John Sears's star was rising in the context of a 1976 Reagan campaign, and in due course he was formally named to head it. As for White, vigorously wooed by the Ford forces, he inevitably drifted in that direction.

I had known Sears casually since his years as a Nixon campaign staff member in the late 1960s and regarded him as a reasonably competent political technician but just not in the same league with Clif White. Worse yet, Sears was not in any serious sense a conservative: He was purely and simply a hired manager for Republican candidates for political office, including the presidency. He could and did work for Nixon against Reagan and Rockefeller in 1968; I had no reason to think he couldn't have worked equally well for Rockefeller in 1968 or 1976 if he had been hired to do so. To a limited extent, this very fact benefited Sears and (indirectly) Reagan: The media, detesting conservative ideologues on principle, were fond of Sears precisely because he wasn't one and were willing to do favors for him that they most certainly wouldn't have done for anyone else. As long as Sears remained Reagan's top manager—in 1976 and in the opening stages of the campaign of 1980—he served in this useful capacity as a sort of *apertura a sinistra.*

As the Reagan forces began to zero in on the battle for the Republican nomination, I persisted in pushing for the new-party option. *The Making of the New Majority Party* began hitting the bookstores early in June, and I seized every opportunity offered by television and radio talk-show hosts, dozens of whom I knew personally, to promote the idea. My *National Review* colleagues, most of whom were cool to the whole concept,* loyally printed a substantial excerpt from the book in the May 23 issue and featured it on the cover with the defiant words "A NEW PARTY: Eventually, Why Not Now?" Viguerie ordered 100,000 copies of the paperback edition, to distribute free of charge to people on certain of his key conservative mailing lists.

On June 10 COCA held its second meeting. This time it created a Subcommittee on Independent Conservative Action (with Stan Evans as chairman and Governor Thomson, Congressman Bauman, Eli Howell, and myself as members) to choose in each state the best course to follow, and the best people to look to, if organization of a new party became necessary. There remained, or so it seemed to some of us, a very distinct possibility that if (as we fully expected) Ford ultimately beat back Reagan's challenge, Reagan and the rest of America's serious conservatives would realize at last the futility of staying in the GOP and opt for a new party after all—*if one was then available to them.* At a meeting of COCA on July 30, I advised those present that an independent committee would be formed, subject to all applicable laws, to create in each of the fifty states the possibility of a conservative third choice on the general election ballot in November 1976. My announcement was "duly noted"—and then, for its timid congressional contingent, COCA created at that same meeting a Subcommittee on Conservative Action in the Major Parties.

On August 5, I phoned Governor Reagan to advise him personally of the course I was embarking on. He responded kindly as always, noting that "we have disagreed on this" and expressing the vague hope that if he sought and won the GOP nomination, the machinery I was intent on creating might somehow be useful in winning over social-conservative voters.

Formidable as the obstacles clearly were, I was convinced that a conservative nominee could be placed on the ballot, after the major-party conventions, in every or almost every state (as Wallace had been in 1968) if a serious effort was launched in time—i.e., by the autumn of 1975. An independent committee to make the effort was formed under my chairmanship in a series of complex negotiations during August and September. At first it was

---

* Jeff Hart was an exception. Like me, he was broadly sympathetic to the proposition that economic and social conservatives should be united.

called the Committee for Freedom of Choice; later this was changed to the Committee for the New Majority. Under its auspices, and with the cooperation of a number of other officers and members (notably including Stan Evans, Eli Howell, and such New Right leaders as Richard Viguerie and Howard Phillips), I spent a considerable amount of time from August 1975 to August 1976 helping put the American Independent party on the ballot in as many states as possible. Effective from October 1, George MacKenzie ("Ken") Rast, an able young Florida attorney and conservative activist, became the committee's full-time executive director.

One of Rast's chief assignments was keeping a sharp eye on the legal requirements in each state—a nightmarish job, for every state's laws were unique: Some required a petition drive, some a convention; some insisted that a candidate be specified, others did not; some imposed deadlines as early as February and March, while others more sensibly allowed independent candidacies to be filed as late as September, after both major parties had named their choices.

Money, too, was a problem from the start, despite the generosity of Viguerie and others in a position to make substantial contributions. Worst of all, we suffered from one major disability that had not plagued Wallace's backers in 1968: Although Reagan was our avowed choice, we did not have his consent and therefore could not claim him, in any real sense, as "our" candidate. We could only tell our volunteer workers that the effort ought to be made to prepare for an independent candidacy anyway, so that when the Republicans at last rejected Reagan's bid (as they surely would), there would be a vehicle ready to nominate him or some suitable surrogate.

In the midst of all this activity—activity based on a highly hypothetical series of developments that would unfold, if at all, in rapid succession in the first half of 1976—it occurred to Stan Evans and me that it would be useful to establish direct personal contact with Governor Wallace. Reagan was our candidate, but Wallace's approval of our overall strategy, which very definitely included capturing most of the nearly 10 million votes he had won in 1968, would be useful and might lead us to fresh financial backers. Certainly his opposition was to be avoided if possible.

On August 21, therefore, Stan Evans and I flew to Montgomery, Alabama, for an appointment with Wallace in the governor's office. It lasted about thirty-five minutes, and perhaps naturally our first interest was to see how he looked, four years after the attempted assassination. He was confined to a chair behind his desk but otherwise did not seem notably disabled, let alone disoriented. He heard us out, indicated that he understood our general strategy, and made shrewd comments about various national political figures. But he did not volunteer, nor did we seek, any commitment—it was too early for that sort of thing. He did authorize one of his aides to put us in touch with a possible financial supporter of our project, but several weeks of fruitless phone calls in various directions subsequently convinced me that Wallace and his staff were being approached by others with different notions of how to play the cards in 1976.*

In due course Wallace made a bid for the Democratic nomination, and when it failed, he endorsed Carter perfunctorily.

Meanwhile, as 1975 progressed, it slowly became apparent that Ford could not, in fact, lock up the 1976 nomination. This development, more than anything else, closed the door once and for all on any possibility that Reagan might opt for the new-party course. On November 17 the governor attended *National Review*'s twentieth birthday bash, another splendid dinner for nearly 700 people in the Grand Ballroom of New York's Plaza Hotel, and as the dais guests lined up to greet those attending, I seized the opportunity to make a formal last pitch for the idea. (I reflected that at least Reagan would admire my stubbornness, if not my common sense!) I was aware that his official announcement of his candidacy for the Republican nomination was just a few days away, so my plea was purely for the record.

It received the response I knew it would: Reagan indicated, amiably but clearly, that he was going the Republican route. Years later Jesse Unruh, one of California's leading Democratic politicians, observed that any politician can say no to his enemies, but

* One such, presumably, was Tom Anderson, the archconservative former publisher of *Farm and Ranch* magazine, who commanded the allegiance of various of the 1968 state Wallace parties and ultimately persuaded them to make himself their presidential standard bearer in 1976, under the aegis of the American party. In November, Anderson polled 160,773 votes nationally, or two-tenths of a percent of the total.

that "Ronald Reagan knows how to say No to his friends." I know, ruefully, what he meant. Reagan managed to convey that he appreciated fully the point I was making but simply preferred another route to our common goal. I was deeply skeptical but not at all angry or upset.

The volunteers who worked with us on our new-party drive in state after state were at first recruited from among conservatives known to us because of their prior activity in the draft-Goldwater movement, Young Americans for Freedom, the American Conservative Union, or other conservative organizations. In any given state there was almost always someone I knew who could be approached to organize the necessary petition drive or whatever.*

Careful study of the laws of the fifty states, based on Carbaugh's research and conducted by Rast, yielded the information that the state where we had to act fastest was Nebraska. Under its laws an independent candidate could be placed on the general election ballot in November 1976 only by meeting various exceptionally onerous requirements. Ultimately, however, it became apparent that in the absence of a willing candidate and adequate funds, Nebraska was one of those states in which our volunteers were going to be unable to obtain a place on the ballot. The legal requirements were just too burdensome (unless they could be successfully attacked in the courts on precisely that basis, as former Senator Gene McCarthy's own independent presidential campaign organization, designed to appeal to liberals, was simultaneously trying to do). In many of these states, however, including Nebraska, various independent conservative parties already existed, and these could place a name on the November ballot far more easily than we could. The most spectacular example, of course, was New York, where the Conservative party had only to certify its nominee under the procedures prescribed for legal parties in New York. It was by no means certain that the Conserva-

---

* A notable and in retrospect amusing exception was West Virginia. There was simply no YAF, ACU, or equivalent organization in the state on which to draw. In desperation I turned to Bob Whitaker, a populist friend of mine living in Washington, who I knew had participated in the protests against left-oriented school textbooks in West Virginia's Kanawha County. Bob promised to see whom he could recruit but ultimately had to report failure: "Of my three possibilities, one is running for governor in the Democratic primary; one is running for Congress—also in the Democratic primary—and the third has just been indicted for dropping a bomb from a helicopter."

tive party would agree to fall in with our plan for a third candidate; but there was substantial sentiment on its executive committee for doing so, and its final decision would, of course, depend on the mood of American conservatives at the close of the Republican convention.

In various other states, conservative parties or political groups of less clout and prominence but nonetheless substantial experience (and in some cases an established right to a position on the November ballot) had come into existence to support the Wallace-LeMay ticket of 1968. Now, eight years later, they presented us with a major dilemma. They were, typically, precisely the sort of "fringe" parties we were most eager for our proposed new party *not* to become. The conservatives who controlled them were not unsavory (we kept a rigorous distance from the few such types who tried to make common cause with us), but they were nonetheless to some extent tainted, at least in the public eye, by their 1968 support for Wallace—which was always, and quite wrongly in a race in which the other candidates were Nixon and Humphrey, construed as prima facie evidence of racism. We certainly wanted no such imputation where our new party was concerned, and of course, Ronald Reagan, whom we still longed to nominate, quite rightly wouldn't touch our party with a ten-foot pole if we allowed it.

On the other hand, it seemed to us that simply using, as a vehicle for the nomination and election of Reagan, honorable state conservative organizations that had supported Wallace over Nixon and Humphrey in 1968 could not fairly give rise to any criticism of our party—or of Reagan, if he were ultimately to accept our nomination. As Barry Goldwater had repeatedly said of the support he received, both for the Senate and for the presidency, from members of the John Birch Society, "They're joining me— I'm not joining them."

So gradually, as 1976 progressed, the drive to create an alternative conservative ballot line, for use by Reagan or a surrogate if things went badly at the GOP convention, became a coalition effort with leaders partly recruited by me and my New Right allies from conservative organizations around the country and partly drawn from political organizations descended from the Wallace movement of 1968. The coalition's leaders were not always comfortable with one another, but the mutual conviction that the GOP would again spurn Reagan (as in 1968) was a powerful cement.

For one prominent conservative, the problem was not whether to back Reagan for the Republican nomination or to opt for a new party: He was for Ford. Barry Goldwater, now back in the Senate, no longer had the excuse (not that he ever pleaded it) that he had committed himself elsewhere before he realized that Reagan would run or even that Reagan was too inexperienced to be president. Reagan had now completed two four-year terms as governor of the largest state in the Union, and his candidacy in 1976 had been recognized as a possibility, even a probability, by every political observer from 1968 onward.

Despite this, Goldwater put his important backing firmly behind Ford, officially endorsing him on June 30, 1976. Goldwater has never satisfactorily explained what can only be described, in retrospect, as his long-standing and determined opposition to Reagan's presidential ambitions. Certainly his brief and laconic attempt in *With No Apologies*, his 1979 autobiographical volume, is patently unsatisfactory: "There is a very simple answer. I believed the incumbent would be a stronger candidate. I had seen some indepth polls done by an organization which in the past has always been right. The men in charge of the Reagan campaign had never impressed me as possessing any degree of political skill."

Here, it seems, we are being treated to a reprise of Goldwater's famous preference for pros over amateurs. But with reference to Reagan's 1976 campaign that explanation is preposterous. Sears was the quintessential pro, and the rest of Reagan's political entourage was, by that time, one of the most seasoned in America. An unworthy jealousy then? Perhaps, but one hates to think so. Goldwater probably felt more comfortable among the traditional Republican political types clustered around Ford than he did, despite his Arizona origins, among the loud-shirted westerners surrounding Reagan—not because the former were more "professional" in any serious sense, but because they were (dare it be said?) marginally less conservative.

Barry Goldwater is, as we have said before, a devout economic conservative of the traditional Republican variety, traceable all the way from Mark Hanna to George Bush and well represented by Gerald Ford. But as we have also noted, he was never entirely comfortable with the conservative ideologues who made him their standard-bearer in 1964, and it would scarcely be surprising if he felt less than automatically committed to the new leader to whom so many of them transferred their allegiance in 1968 and again in 1976.

That was the basis of the criticism publicly aimed at Goldwater, by Richard Viguerie and myself, among others, early in 1976. In my column dated February 18 I raised the subject, taking as my text Goldwater's most recent fall from grace:

What are we to make, these days, of Barry Goldwater? The Arizona senator, who has long been one of America's leading conservative spokesmen, recently praised Nelson Rockefeller in terms that make an unintelligible hash of everything Goldwater (or for that matter Rockefeller) has stood for across the years.

The occasion was an interview with Chuck Ashman of KTTV in Los Angeles. Ashman steered the conversation around to Rockefeller, hoping to generate a few sparks. Goldwater, however, suddenly delivered himself of the following astonishing statement:

"I happen to believe that Nelson Rockefeller would be a good president. I wouldn't differ with him much and I would agree with him completely on foreign policy which, after all, is the most important thing we do in this country."

Ashman, no doubt dreaming of the Scoop of the Year, pressed his opportunity:

"You realize, senator, that you may be opening the whole ball of wax for 1976?"

Whereupon Goldwater ploughed doggedly on:

"Yes, I probably am opening the whole ball of wax but I believe Rocky would be a damn good president now that he has ended his liberal drift. I think he'd be fine."

What, then, has come over Barry Goldwater?

Occasionally . . . Goldwater shoots from the hip; it is at least possible that he hated himself the morning after that interview in Los Angeles.

But it is more likely, I am sorry to say, that Goldwater's grip on conservative principles just isn't (and perhaps never was) the absolutely dependable thing we believe it to be. After all, he endorsed Nixon for the Republican nomination in 1968, brutally undercutting Ronald Reagan's authentically conservative bid. It is an open secret that Goldwater is in Ford's camp today, ready to endorse him (again, over Reagan) when it will do the most good. He said publicly in November 1974 that Rockefeller would be "acceptable" to him as Ford's choice for Vice President. And now he proclaims that Rockefeller "would be a damn good president"! Every dog is entitled to one bite, they say—but four?

Such criticism of his true-blue conservatism apparently wounded Goldwater more than I supposed it would (or intended that it should), for Mary McGrory was soon quoting the salty senator, in her own ultraliberal political column, as referring to Richard Viguerie and me as "those sons of bitches." Luckily Goldwater's animadversions, like Arizona thunderstorms, blow over as rapidly as they roar up, and peace and amity have since been restored on the Goldwater front, at least as far as I am concerned.

Up to this point I had not considered my column, launched by United Press Syndicate in August 1973, as in any serious conflict with my personal political activities. The column, after all, was forthrightly entitled "The Conservative Advocate," and in it I never made any bones whatever about my own political preferences. Nor was there anything in the least mysterious about my political activities. My own private condemnation was (and still is) reserved for those political commentators—and there were, and are, plenty of them—who have personal preferences quite as strong as mine but choose *not* to proclaim them. And of course, a sharp distinction must also be drawn between political *commentators,* as a category, and political *reporters,* whose job is to report political developments without adding any personal comments or emphases whatever.

At the same time I did feel, as time went on, that there was a potential conflict between my role as a political columnist or commentator and my chairmanship of the Committee for the New Majority. I was not seriously afraid, for the reasons mentioned above, that my chairmanship might somehow result in misleading the readers of my columns but rather that my position as a columnist might somehow—unfairly, and against the wishes of the newspapers who ran the columns—be used to enhance the prestige of the committee. In April 1976, therefore, I relinquished the committee's chairmanship to Lester Logue, a Texas conservative who had been one of the movement's most loyal backers, while making it plain that I did not intend to cease my political activities as such.

I attended the Republican National Convention in Kansas City from August 15 to 19. The American Independent party had grimly scheduled its own convention to be held in Chicago beginning the following Wednesday, August 25. The events at the two were clearly going to be linked.

On Monday, the sixteenth, the Republican convention was addressed by three major figures: Landon, Goldwater, and Rockefeller. I could not help reflecting wryly how much, and yet how differently, those three had affected my life: Alf Landon (then eighty-nine), whose 1936 defeat by Roosevelt had fueled my youthful determination to work for Republican victory; Barry Goldwater, whose 1964 nomination I had struggled for and savored with all its implications; and Nelson Rockefeller, the Adversary, whom conservatives had at last managed to sideline. What, I wondered, would be the next chapter in the story, and what political figure would symbolize it?

At Kansas City Clif White, whose services had been rejected by Reagan, accepted President Ford's invitation to serve as de facto manager of the Ford convention campaign. In a trailer outside the Kemper Arena not unlike the ones from which he had quarterbacked Goldwater's nomination at San Francisco's Cow Palace in 1964 and Reagan's unsuccessful bid at Miami Beach's Municipal Auditorium in 1968, White now piloted Ford's candidacy through the obstacles posed by the Reagan candidacy. A few feet away, in a similar trailer, our mutual friend Andy Carter of New Mexico, a loyal member of the Hard Core from its earliest days, performed much the same function for Reagan. (John Sears, Reagan's official manager, stayed aloof from the Reagan trailer operation, preferring to concentrate on problems of strategy.) There was an inevitable poignancy about the turn of fate that led two old friends, even cronies, to two trailers in Kansas City where they would now do battle for rival presidential candidates. But there was good humor and enduring mutual affection, too—and not a little quiet pride that both wings of the Republican party were now turning, for their convention expertise, to graduates of the fondly remembered draft-Goldwater movement.

Most of the other members of the Hard Core present in Kansas City in 1976 gave their loyalty to Reagan. Frank Whetstone and Roger Moore, in particular, had important assignments. I, too, of course, was rooting for Reagan, but without much hope.

As we now know, Reagan's challenge to Ford was an impressive one and failed only by the narrowest of margins. After a disappointing start in the New Hampshire primary, Reagan came back with surprising power in North Carolina and by late July was tantalizingly close to the majority needed for nomination. In a two-horse race, however, there is little room for surprise: The other votes—a narrow but sufficient majority—belonged to Ford. Some bold stroke was called for, and Reagan agreed to John Sears's rather desperate proposal: On July 26 Reagan announced his choice for the vice presidency—Senator Richard Schweiker, a Pennsylvanian with a reputation as a liberal Republican—and invited Ford to do likewise.

Given the circumstances, it was an acceptable gamble. Schweiker might be able to shake loose a few Pennsylvania delegates, and meanwhile, any choice Ford announced, or even his refusal to announce one, might cause severe disruptions in the Ford camp.

I was giving a speech across the Bay from San Francisco at a luncheon three days after Reagan's announcement when I was summoned to the phone for a call from Reagan himself. He was plainly trying to reassure his conservative supporters, some of whom had been badly upset by his choice of Schweiker.* I told him I thought a conservative Republican presidential nominee practically *had* to nominate a relatively liberal running mate, to "balance the ticket." I also reminded him that a year earlier, at dinner in his home in Los Angeles, I had predicted that he himself would have to do exactly that, if by any chance he got the presidential nomination. But Reagan went on to argue, convincingly as

---

* One important Reagan backer, Representative Philip Crane of Illinois, broke with Reagan over the Schweiker choice, and the rupture was never subsequently healed.

usual, that Schweiker was not as liberal as he was cracked up to be. I was glad to hear it.

A few days before the Republican convention opened, a bold move in another quarter briefly diverted the attention of both the Ford and Reagan camps from their grim concentration on each other. A source close to Senator James Buckley of New York managed to attract heavy journalistic notice by refusing to deny that Buckley was considering offering himself as an alternative presidential choice in case the convention could not decide between the two closely matched front-runners.

I happened to be in Florida on a speaking engagement when this news broke, and I was promptly descended on, via telephone, by my friends in both the Reagan and Ford headquarters, each of which darkly suspected the other of being behind the Buckley story in some sort of deep Machiavellian maneuver.

Actually I was not at that time in particularly close touch with Senator Buckley, despite the assumption of my friends that I could readily find out what was going on. I knew, however, that Buckley was in considerable trouble in his reelection bid, even though he had been a loyal member of the GOP caucus in the Senate and would receive not only the Conservative party's nomination this time but, without much trouble, the Republican party's as well.*

The political management of Jim Buckley's affairs had largely devolved on Len Saffir, a former journalist who was now his administrative assistant, and I was soon able to establish that Saffir was the source of the rumor about Jim's alleged presidential ambitions. That did little to solve the problem of its authenticity, though, and I was unable to reach Jim directly. When I did finally encounter him, as we were both collecting our baggage on arrival at the Kansas City airport, he was modestly deprecatory about the idea but slyly fell short of repudiating it altogether.

I concluded—correctly, as it transpired—that the whole thing was simply a maneuver to gain a little badly needed publicity for New York's junior senator in preparation for his reelection

---

* He was in fact defeated for reelection that November by Daniel Patrick Moynihan, who had narrowly bested Bella Abzug in the Democratic primary. If Abzug had won the nomination instead, Buckley would undoubtedly have beaten her easily.

bid and so advised my friends in the Ford and Reagan camps. They growled and resumed their fierce mutual concentration.

Ford refused, wisely, to be drawn into naming his vice presidential choice in advance of his own nomination, and the Reagan forces sought to make the issue one of principle, offering an amendment to the convention's rules to make such disclosure compulsory. The wisdom of this change in the rules was debatable at best, but the vote on whether to adopt it had little to do with its merits, whatever they may have been. The vote on "rule 16-c"— the proposed amendment—swiftly became a test vote on the relative strengths of the Ford and Reagan forces and was recognized as such by both sides. When the amendment was rejected, 1,180 to 1,069, everyone knew that Ford would win the nomination.

Oddly enough, Reagan's defeat in the 1976 convention was attributable, in not inconsiderable part, to the very man who had so skillfully played his nemesis in 1968: Clarke Reed, that curiously counterproductive "conservative" from Mississippi. This time, as before, Reed (Mississippi's longtime Republican national committeeman) had begun—as any Mississippi Republican practically had to—by proclaiming his undying devotion to the Reagan cause. But again, as in 1968, he confessed to feeling undermined in that devotion at the last minute by events beyond his control: in this case Reagan's designation of Schweiker as his vice presidential running mate. Apparently Reed's passionate conservatism, which had never prevented him from being a good personal friend of Nelson Rockefeller's and had sturdily survived Reed's support of Nixon over Reagan in 1968, was too pure and precious a thing to endure the presence of a liberal allegedly as abandoned as Schweiker on the Reagan ticket. So, as the convention voted on 16c, Reed walked out on Reagan once again, taking a purblind majority of his fellow Mississippi delegates—and, under the unit rule, the rest of them as well— with him.

After it was all over and Ford had been nominated, something—dare we suppose a stricken conscience?—impelled Reed to walk up to Reagan in public and declare, in tears, "Governor, I've made the worst mistake of my life." (Well, the second worst anyway—after 1968.) Reagan merely patted him on the shoulder and replied, "That's all right, Clarke." Personally I felt the occasion called for . . . something else.

Ford's choice of Senator Dole for the vice presidency, to succeed Nelson Rockefeller, sufficiently indicated Ford's narrow conception of the Republican party. It simply reaffirmed the GOP's suicidal unwillingness, under "moderate" management, to appeal strongly to formerly Democratic social conservatives. As James Reston remarked dryly of the Ford-Dole ticket, it would run strongly all the way from Grand Rapids to Topeka.

Ford's nomination shifted the spotlight, at least in the world of conservatism, to the forthcoming convention of our new American Independent party at the Conrad Hilton in Chicago. We had not managed to duplicate Wallace's 1968 feat of getting on the ballot in all fifty states, but by mid-August we were already assured of a ballot position in about thirty-six, and if any halfway plausible candidate were to accept our nomination at Chicago, it seemed likely that the surge of enthusiasm for him would carry us onto the ballot in five or six more.

I therefore spent much of the intervening week phoning leading conservatives, starting with Reagan, to see if one of them would accept the offer of our presidential nomination—a nomination that would assure such a nominee at the very least an important role in the 1976 election, with perhaps even greater potentialities in 1980. For federal law provided that any party receiving even 5 percent of the popular votes in a presidential election would receive several million dollars for its campaign four years later. Larger percentages would produce correspondingly larger federal subsidies.

Reagan, whom I of course called first, was cordial as always but—as I anticipated—declined our offer. He had been put, by the media and others, in a position where he had been compelled to pledge that if defeated for the Republican nomination, he would support the GOP convention's choice. Connally, Helms, and Governor Meldrim Thomson of New Hampshire similarly declined our invitation, with appropriate expressions of appreciation for the thought. (Helms had waged a successful battle to modify the platform draft in various conservative directions and may have felt inhibited on that account, among others.) One prominent conservative member of the House of Representatives mulled over the possibility of accepting our nomination for about forty-eight hours, leading me to hope briefly that he would indeed make the plunge, but at last he decided, with obvious regret, to pass up the chance.

Our failure to persuade any really plausible candidate to accept the nomination of the American Independent party robbed the whole new-party effort of its central purpose. Worse yet, it had the disastrous effect of putting its nomination up for grabs by the more extreme pro-Wallace elements at our convention, who had been willing (though in some cases reluctantly so) to go along with the nomination of Reagan, say, or Helms, but who would be delighted to choose some standard-bearer closer to their hearts' desire if no bigger name was available. Rather than let the convention go by default to some unacceptable candidate, I persuaded Robert Morris, my old chief counsel at the Senate Internal Security Subcommittee who was now president of the University of Dallas, to seek the American Independent party's presidential nomination, and Richard Viguerie teamed with Morris as his vice presidential running mate. A majority of the delegates, however—tempted by visions of millions of federal dollars for a fresh try in 1980 if only they could poll 5 percent in 1976—were in a mood for what they imagined was stronger medicine. It soon became apparent that they were prepared to give the party's nomination to former Governor Lester Maddox of Georgia, a notorious racist. Before that sad moment arrived, Morris, Viguerie, and I, and most of the delegates loyal to our vision of a new, conservative, and responsible national political party, had withdrawn from the convention and made preparations to leave Chicago.

One immediate result of our withdrawal was a rapid shrinkage in the number of states in which the American Independent party was able to put its candidates on the general election ballot. New York's Conservative party, for example, which had observers at the convention (several of whom voted as delegates from New York, though not as official representatives of the Conservative party), might have endorsed an important national conservative but would have no truck with extremists. And the same was true of a number of other state organizations.

As a result of this, as well as of its own intrinsic weaknesses, the American Independent party ticket of Lester Maddox and William Dyke failed to win that 5 percent of the total vote in November which was essential to qualify it as a continuing participant in presidential elections and a recipient of federal campaign funds in 1980. It received instead 170,531 votes out of 81,555,889 cast, or two-tenths of 1 percent, and with that whimper breathed its last.

This thoroughly miserable end to our 1976 experiment with a new party—an effort into which many good and earnest people had thrown themselves for over a year—naturally lent itself to the drawing of all sorts of conclusions, many of them wrong.

For me personally, the most painful—though mercifully also the most transient—aspect of the immediately ensuing weeks was a fair amount of good-natured ribbing by conservative friends of mine who had predicted all along that the project would fail. I had known very well, however, the odds against success and had taken the gamble with my eyes wide open. If 1976 had been the year a new major party appeared on the national scene (as the Republican party itself had done, swiftly eclipsing the Whigs, in 1856), we would have been hailed as prophets. Since the attempt failed, we were fair game for scoffers and critics.

It would be merely foolish, however, not to acknowledge that 1976 demonstrated anew the imposing staying power of the two major parties. They are not immortal by a long shot, but they are wonderfully durable, and I have never heard the reason put better, oddly enough, than by a shrewd Chinese student of American affairs on the far side of the Pacific Ocean.

While visiting Taipei in January 1975, I discussed the idea of a new party with my old friend Fred Chien, who at the time was director of the Government Information Office of the (Nationalist) Republic of China on Taiwan. Chien, who is one of the brightest younger officials in the service of Free China,* holds the degree of Doctor of Philosophy in political science from Yale University, his specialty being American politics. He listened to me sympathetically but then shook his head.

* He is currently its unofficial ambassador in Washington.

"Bill," he said, "I'm afraid your idea won't work. Americans are so used to voting for either the Republicans or the Democrats that the idea of voting for any other party strikes them as vaguely unpatriotic."

I disagreed at the time, of course. I assumed that any party as conservative as the one I contemplated—one that would surely draw liberal fire for its alleged "superpatriotism"—could hardly seem, however vaguely, un-American. But old habits die hard, and the Republican party, for all its forty-five-year record of almost unbroken defeat in its efforts to control Congress and the recent disasters represented by Agnew and Nixon, wasn't ready to die.

Characteristically, however, it wasn't ready to win either. The Democrats, meeting in New York from July 12 to 15, nominated Georgia Governor Jimmy Carter for president. It was a shrewd move on their part, even if we credit Carter's own adroit campaign and a large quantity of sheer luck for his victory. For the analysis on which our new party concept was based, and which Ronald Reagan considered the key to Republican victory, was still correct: There was an antiliberal majority in the country, consisting of traditionally Republican economic conservatives and formerly Democratic social conservatives. A Democratic victory in 1976, therefore, depended on preventing these blocs from coalescing again, as they had done for Nixon in 1972. The obvious solution was to repatriate at least some of the social conservatives to their Democratic homeland. And that is precisely what Carter with his southern Baptist, "born-again" Christian, anti-Washington credentials managed to do.

Chapter **XII**

Consolidating the New Majority

It is, of course, ridiculous to speak of Jimmy Carter as "conservative" in any but the most relative sense. But in politics positions *are* relative, and in 1976 Jimmy Carter was, with the exception of George Wallace, *relatively* the most conservative candidate seeking the Democratic nomination. He recognized this by choosing Senator Walter Mondale as his vice presidential running mate, in an obvious effort to balance the ticket. (Mondale was the political and ideological protégé of Mr. Liberalism himself, the dying Hubert Humphrey.)

In November 1976 Carter held on to most of the key blocs still represented in the traditional Democratic coalition. He did exceptionally well among black voters, even for a Democrat, improving on George McGovern's 1972 score by a percentage point or two (probably because Carter was a Baptist), and for this reason it was widely declared after Carter narrowly defeated Gerald Ford on November 2 that the black vote had "made the difference." Of course, in any election that is won by a narrow margin (in this case 40,830,763 for Carter to 39,147,793 for Ford) it is possible to say that any sizable bloc that voted for the winner "made the difference." But there is no question whatever that the bloc that swung most dramatically from Republican in 1972 to Democrat in 1976 was composed of white social conservatives.

This swing was demonstrated brilliantly by Kevin Phillips in an analysis he published in his excellent newsletter *American Political Report* in 1977. Phillips identified the county, in each of twenty key states, where the Republican vote had fallen off most heavily between 1972 and 1976. As he noted, "they are *all* rural or small town WASP areas." He listed them as follows:

State	Most-shifting County	1972 GOP%	1976 GOP%	Shift	Intrastate Geographic-Demographic Description
N.J.	Cumberland	59%	42%	−17	South Jersey rural–small town°
Pa.	Greene	57	38	−19	SW Pa. Appalachian WASP°
Md.	Dorchester	76	51	−25	Chesapeake Bay small town–rural°
W.Va.	Wyoming	64	32	−32	Southern poor white coal area°
Va.	Franklin	67	35	−32	Rural Appalachian–Southside°
N.C.	Columbus	72	23	−49	SE coastal poor white°
Ky.	Marshall	60	27	−33	SW "Little Dixie"°
Tenn.	Lake	68	23	−45	West Tennessee rural white
Ala.	Lawrence	66	18	−48	Tennessee Valley white rural°
Miss.	Tippah	88	31	−57	Poor white NE foothills°
Fla.	Holmes	93	37	−56	NW Panhandle "Cracker" Country°
Texas	Delta	62	21	−41	East Texas–Sulphur River Delta
Okla.	Atoka	74	25	−49	SE farm-coal area (poor white)°
Mo.	Dunklin	68	32	−36	SE "Boot" rural area°
Ill.	Massac	70	45	−25	"Little Egypt" poor white°
Ind.	Owen	70	48	−22	Southern Indiana rural WASP°
Ohio	Meigs	71	48	−23	Ohio River–Appalachian°
Iowa	Ringgold	69	46	−23	South Iowa WASP (poor farms)°

°Asterisk indicates this was also state's general region of *worst* GOP decline.

Commenting on these dramatic figures, Phillips went on to say:

> In contrast to Nixon-Agnew ability to woo low- and low-middle-income white voters with a mix of social conservatism, economic activism and cultural anti-establishment postures, Gerald Ford had little rapport with these voters—and their heavy shift was the key to his loss. From South Jersey and Appalachian Pennsylvania west through the Ohio Valley to Kansas and down to New Mexico's "Little Texas," this Southern-tinged low-income and low-middle-income white vote probably accounts for 15% of the U.S. total. And our estimate is that among such voters, the GOP presidential vote slipped from 70% in 1972 to 30% in 1976. Such slippage among a 15%-of-the-country voting group would be enough to turn a 54% national victory into a 48% loss.

The most important lesson of 1976, therefore, was that the Republican party's soundest strategy was to nominate a candidate capable of uniting economic and social conservatives in an anti-liberal coalition. If it failed to do so—if it insisted, as in 1976, on naming a presidential candidate who appealed only to economic conservatives—it would lose to a Democrat capable of repatriating even a portion of the social conservatives.

And that, in turn, meant that perhaps the idea of a new party, designed expressly as a vehicle for a coalition of social and economic conservatives, was neither dead nor inherently impractical but merely premature. As matters stood in the wake of Ford's defeat by Carter in November 1976, everything depended on whether in 1980 the GOP would see this formula for victory under its nose and act accordingly.

Personally I was not optimistic. At the time of the 1976 Republican convention and for a few weeks afterward the public and private remarks of leading GOP conservatives suggested that if Carter defeated Ford, there would be an early and major post-election push either to capture the GOP for conservative principles or even, conceivably, to form a new party after all. But despite Ford's defeat, the longed-for push failed to develop, and gradually I accepted the fact that it would not do so. The Republican party, it appeared, was quite content to ignore the national antiliberal majority and keep right on losing.

In December 1976 I found occasion to be in Los Angeles and called on Governor Reagan in the Wilshire Boulevard PR offices of his former aides Mike Deaver and Pete Hannaford, out of which he now worked. Over lunch nearby we discussed the events of 1976. I also tried to sound him out on the subject of 1980, but didn't get far: "It's too early to say." It seemed clear that he simply, and rightly, had made no decision yet. Significantly, however, in a speech in Washington on January 15, 1977, Reagan called on his fellow conservatives to stay in the GOP and "start acting to bring about the great conservative majority party we know is waiting to be created"—simultaneously keeping the door open and signaling his continued allegiance to the GOP.

My own feeling was that even if Reagan decided to run in 1980, his age (which would then be sixty-nine) might well prove a problem in voters' minds. But 1980 seemed, in any case, very far away. For the ten-thousandth time I wished the GOP had nominated him in 1968, when he was only fifty-seven.

If the prospects for a new party were at a historic low after our Chicago fiasco, and if the Republican party simply wasn't interested and couldn't *get* interested in a serious effort to unite and represent America's by now husky antiliberal majority, what alternatives remained? I could think of only one, and it scarcely seemed very promising: the Democratic party.

And yet the Democratic party has represented many things to many men in the course of its long history, and as we have seen, its 1976 convention made an unmistakable turn to the (relative) right in nominating Carter. Carter's subsequent victory in November was, as Kevin Phillips demonstrated, attributable largely to his success in winning back many white lower-middle-class voters (blue collars, "ethnics," etc.) who had voted Republican in 1972. If I knew this and understood its implications, presumably there were Democratic politicians capable of reaching the same conclusion. Some of them might be close enough to Carter—perhaps in his Georgia entourage—to influence his future course in a conservative direction. If so, I wanted them to know that there were conservatives prepared to respond.

I put my problem to a well-connected Democratic friend. His first impulse was to arrange an introduction for me to Charles Kirbo, Carter's close friend and political *éminence grise*. On second thought he changed his mind (with what consequences for the longer-range future we will never know) and said he would set up an appointment with Bert Lance instead.

There were already hand-sized clouds on Lance's horizon when I called on Carter's budget director and crony in his office in the Old Executive Office Building on July 13, 1977. But I certainly had no inkling that Lance's political downfall was likely or even more than remotely possible, and we had a friendly talk. I told him frankly that there were votes in it for the Democratic party if it moved to the right, as the country was clearly doing, and that I thought it would be a good idea to set up a line of communications, for input and output, pending further developments. He listened carefully, did not take issue with my central point, and suggested amiably that we keep in touch.

It was, however, to be my last meeting with Lance as well as my first. On September 21 he was forced to resign under indictment for various alleged malfeasances in connection with his banking interests. (He was later acquitted, after a jury trial.) Meanwhile, Carter was piling up a record in office that withered my fragile hopes of a more conservative Democratic party, so I didn't even bother to pursue the Kirbo possibility.

In my own sphere of activities, therefore, the prospects for effective conservative political action were by 1978 looking distinctly bleak. But elsewhere, quite outside my purview, an encouraging development of the first importance was taking place.

Participation of religious leaders and their followers in political activity is certainly nothing new in this country—witness that "noble experiment" Prohibition. But in the decade of the 1960s the politically active clerics had been almost uniformly liberal. William Sloane Coffin, Jr., Yale's outspoken chaplain, had completed his transition from CIA agent in the Korean War to one of the most vociferous opponents of America's involvement in Vietnam. And of course the Reverend Martin Luther King, Jr., was, until his assassination in April 1968, unquestionably the leading advocate of expanded and enforced civil rights for his fellow blacks.

The idea that such clearly political activities on the part of clergymen somehow violated the famous constitutional separation of church and state did not, I think it is fair to say, even occur to liberals at the time. Nor can I recall that conservatives, to the extent that they disagreed with specific views or tactics of either Coffin or King, ever made much of that particular objection. Similarly, the 1983 statement of America's Roman Catholic bishops on U.S. nuclear policy escaped criticism on that score.

It was, oddly enough, Jimmy Carter who in 1976 took the first step toward mobilizing politically a very different religious constituency: the Baptist and generally evangelical Christian whites from whom he himself sprang. Carter let it be known that in 1967, at a time of deep despair in his personal and political life, he had undergone a religious experience which he described in the conventional evangelical phrase as being "born again"—reborn into a more confident, more assertive Christianity. There is no reason to doubt the sincerity of Carter's statements on this subject or the impact of the experience on his subsequent life.

Nor do I see on what grounds Carter can properly be condemned for alluding to it in his campaigns. Voters are entitled to know what sort of goods they are buying, and if being a "born-again Christian" evokes support from other born-again Christians, how is that distinguishable from, say, Jacob Javits's long grip on the "Jewish vote" in New York—or, for that matter, Mario Cuomo's indisputable appeal for Italo-Americans? Carter's success (already mentioned, p. 292 supra) in repatriating a large number of social-conservative voters to the Democratic party in 1976 was unquestionably owing, in large part, to the power of his appeal to such voters as a fellow evangelical Christian.

It was not merely a matter of social identification. The identification was *presumed*, rightly or wrongly, to carry with it a community of views on certain questions directly relevant to the particular religious commitment: support for the sanctity of marriage and the "family values" in general; opposition to abortion; opposition to the use of drugs (and perhaps even alcohol); concern over the growth of pornography and sexual promiscuity; etc. And these in turn will be recognized as among the cardinal issues motivating social conservatives politically from the 1960s forward.

Jimmy Carter was the first American politician at the national level in modern times to make a deliberate appeal to the social conservatives (or at least to the born-again Christians among them) in a successful bid for the presidency. George Wallace's appeal in 1968 had been deliberate but not successful; Richard Nixon's (in 1972) was successful but was not so much deliberate, or at any rate forthright, as typically indirect: he welcomed the social conservatives' votes without, thanks to McGovern's extreme liberalism, much needing to bid for their support. (In his memoirs, as we have seen [p. 251, supra], Nixon declared his intention to make the bid more explicit thereafter; but Watergate intervened, so the trick remained untried.) Ronald Reagan would make the social conservative constituency his own in 1980.

But the born-again Christians whom Carter repatriated to the Democratic party in 1976 were a relatively disorganized, inchoate bloc—far from the militant "religious right" that mobilized its millions for Reagan in 1980. What happened to bring this new and consciously conservative force into being? Who organized it and led the resulting organizations?

Liberals will be interested to know that at least according to Richard Viguerie, who observed and aided this development from its inception, the precipitating factor was a proposed Internal

Revenue ruling (later withdrawn and hence never actually promulgated) under which any private school founded after *Brown* v. *Board of Education* would have the burden of proving, on pain of losing its tax-exempt status, that it was *not* founded to avoid that landmark desegregation ruling.

Whatever the reason, the off-year elections of 1978 saw the religious right organized for political action for the first time since Prohibition. Antiabortion voters were particularly well mobilized and accounted for the defeat of Senator Richard Clark (D., Iowa). But Catholics dominated the antiabortion battle, whereas evangelical Protestants were the largest segment (though not the only one) in the newly developing religious right. Under the Reverend Jerry Falwell the Moral Majority (the name of his organization—often confused with the religious right as a whole) conducted campaigns to register many citizens who had not previously voted at all and saw to it that they and other evangelicals voted for candidates committed to their values. Roughly analogous political efforts were also being conducted in the late 1970s by such other conservative pastors as Dr. James Robinson, Dr. Pat Robertson, Dr. Jim Bakker, etc.

Is there, as such critics as Norman Lear have charged, something inherently wrong about such activities? Certainly, as already noted, political activity on the part of clerics and their mobilized religious constituencies is as American as apple pie. But the critics of the religious right advance a particular objection which, at least superficially, seems to go further. It is often stated roughly as follows: "I don't mind them having those views; I just object to them trying to impose their own moral values on others."

That focuses the question on what, precisely, the religious right is perceived to be doing and whether this is, in fact, something new and legitimately objectionable.

All political movements seek, in a sense, to "impose their views on others." Anyone who lobbies for higher taxes, or for unilateral disarmament, or for reimposition of the draft, or for the death penalty is certainly trying to meddle actively in the lives of some or all of his fellow citizens. The only thing that makes the political activities of the religious right seem different somehow is the fact that the issues that concern them are typically issues on which their opinion is directly and visibly derived from some *moral* position. They oppose abortion because they believe it involves the taking of innocent human life—and that this is against God's commandment. They oppose premarital sex and homosexuality, and therefore tend to oppose municipal ordinances facilitating these "life-styles," because they believe that these, too, are in violation of God's decrees.

But is such a rationale really any different from that of the liberal who favors increasing taxes to subsidize food stamps for the poor and justifies this exaction on grounds of "compassion"? Such a person is certainly appealing to some obligation on society's part, if not at bottom religious, then at least ethical, to act sympathetically and charitably toward the unfortunates in our midst. Is he not, then, "seeking to impose his own moral [or ethical] attitude on others"?

Or what about the laws requiring a father to provide child support? If a liberal can perceive and enforce a father's obligation to support a child he has helped bring into the world, why can't a religious conservative perceive—and equally seek by the political process to enforce—a mother's obligation not to destroy a life she is sheltering in her body? Different people easily reach different conclusions about the ethical or religious imperatives in the two situations, but it is hard to see why supporting one law constitutes imposition of a moral view and supporting the other doesn't.

My own guess is that what makes the critics of the religious right obscurely uncomfortable about its views is not that it "tries to impose them on others" (it doesn't, save by the perfectly legitimate processes of evangelism and ordinary political lobbying) but that it harbors moral views at all—i.e., takes morality seriously, as a guide to personal conduct. Many Americans, and not merely liberals by a long shot, tend to deal with morality in very gingerly fashion—keeping it at a comfortable distance, applying it in extremely abstract ways, and taking swift refuge in a pious "refusal to judge" whenever a moral issue is raised in a concrete manner or context.

In any event, by 1980 the religious right had been brought fully on line as a member of the political coalition sustaining the conservative movement. It is far from representing politically, in and of itself, a "majority" of the American electorate, despite the claim implicit in the catchy title of Jerry Falwell's organization.

But it is a new, distinct, and powerful force on the national political scene and will unquestionably continue to make its influence felt in both local and national elections henceforth.

Another political development of the late 1970s deserves notice here as among the factors contributing to the national conservative victory in 1980. That was what might be called the institutionalized backlash of the drive to ratify the Panama Canal treaties.

Support for the treaties was bipartisan and impressive. Former Presidents Nixon and Ford both endorsed President Carter's successful completion of the initiative they had respectively originated and carried forward. Former Secretary of State Kissinger, himself deeply committed to the project, likewise strongly urged ratification. Almost without exception the principal instrumentalities whereby public opinion is generated—the major television networks' news programs, the two major newsmagazines, the two leading national newspapers—spoke favorably of the treaties. It did not escape notice that the banking lobby, which was later to prove its puissance by forcing Congress to repeal the withholding of interest payments even though both President Reagan and Speaker O'Neill favored it, was energetic in the campaign for ratification—because (or so critics charged) certain large banks were holding Panamanian government IOUs that could not possibly be redeemed unless canal revenues became available to Panama. Even Bill Buckley, impressed by Kissinger's arguments and others', joined the protreaty forces and took James Burnham with him (although *National Review* kept a fairly low profile on the subject, out of respect for the opposing views of other senior editors).

The campaign to drum up popular support for the treaties (which would progressively give Panama control of the canal over a period of two decades) went on for a year while the Senate bided its time, awaiting creation of a national atmosphere in which it could ratify the treaties at a bearable political cost. And yet it is a remarkable fact that the American public, which had begun that year opposed to the treaties by a margin of two to one, ended it, at least according to some polls, still opposed to them.

The opposition to the treaties was led (outside the Senate) by

the national conservative movement, with only a handful of notable exceptions: Buckley and Burnham as aforesaid, plus George
Will (if he is to be counted as a conservative) and for some curious
reason the late John Wayne. For the rest, the conservative movement was singularly unified on this subject, with Ronald Reagan as
its chief spokesman. In an expanded version of "Firing Line" aired
live on January 13, 1978, Buckley, Burnham, and Will debated
Reagan, Pat Buchanan, and Dr. Roger Fontaine on the issue.

Who won the debate is still a matter of dispute, but there is
very little doubt which side profited most in the long run from the
controversy. The treaty was ultimately ratified on April 18, 1978,
by an agonizingly narrow margin (68 to 32—with 67 votes, or
two-thirds of the Senate's total membership, required to prevail)—demonstrating, depending on one's point of view, either
that the Senate still had the moral and intellectual resources to resist raucous jingoistic demagoguery or that in a pinch, where
really large business interests are involved, the Senate will truckle
to them regardless of the manifest and overwhelming desire of the
American people to the contrary.

But the largest single net benefit to any of the warring parties,
as a result of the whole affair, was undoubtedly the massive accre-
tion of new names acquired by conservative mailing-list entrepre-
neurs like Richard Viguerie. Viguerie himself estimates that the
campaign to petition the Senate not to ratify the treaties yielded
the names and addresses of some half million additional voters
who could later be approached on behalf of related conservative
causes (e.g., Reagan's 1980 presidential campaign). Of such defeats
are brighter tomorrows born.

By 1979 the conservative movement had come to the climax
of its long march from the depths of impotence and near anonymity in the early 1950s. It had spent the decade of the fifties defining
and organizing itself; during the sixties it had moved resolutely
into politics, elaborating a mass base and developing political
spokesmen of national rank; in the seventies, with evidence of a
national antiliberal majority on every hand, it had wrestled with
the problem of how to build an enduring conservative coalition to
govern America. Now, as the 1980 election approached, the answer to that question gradually became apparent in the personality and political strategy of Ronald Reagan.

There is little point in recounting here in detail Reagan's 1980 campaign and ultimate victory. They were fully covered in the media. Moreover, I was not in especially close touch with his 1980 campaign, partly because I did not feel all that comfortable with his resolutely nonideological campaign manager, John Sears. By the time Sears was dismissed as Reagan's manager, late on the afternoon of the day of the New Hampshire primary, Reagan's basic campaign organization was well in place, and I was more than content to watch it from my front-row seat at *National Review*.

I did have one private concern: the so-called age issue. Reagan has always had the good fortune to look ten or fifteen years younger than his biological age, and from my own observations of the man I personally had no doubt whatever that he would be up to the presidency both physically and mentally. But he would, at his inauguration, be less than a month short of his seventieth birthday—the oldest president in our history—and I was uncertain how deeply this might concern the voters at large. Accordingly, I kept in close touch with Rich Williamson, the campaign manager for Illinois Congressman Phil Crane, who had declared his own candidacy for the Republican presidential nomination in August 1978—the first candidate to announce formally. (Reagan waited till November 13, 1979.) Crane, a youthful conservative with a Ph.D. in history, a splendid voting record, and the distinction of being the chairman of the American Conservative Union, was of course competing directly with Reagan for the support of conservative Republicans and stood no chance whatever, even of influencing the result, *unless* something—e.g., a serious emergence of the age issue—went radically wrong with the Reagan campaign.

The New Hampshire primary, which Reagan won handily against the whole field of his rivals (the final tally gave Reagan 49.6 percent, Bush 22.7 percent, Baker 12.1 percent, Anderson 9.8 percent, Crane 1.8 percent, and Connally 1.5 percent), told me, however, that to the Republican voters of New Hampshire at least, the age issue was simply a nonstarter. And there was no reason to suppose that New Hampshire Republicans differed in this respect from other Republicans or from Americans in general. I therefore promptly stopped worrying about the age issue and watched with satisfaction as Reagan rolled up victory after victory in binding primaries. By late May he had locked up the Republican presidential nomination. The convention in Detroit, unlike its many predecessors in the days when favorite sons and local bosses could withhold key blocs of votes for bargaining purposes, would be merely a "media event," enlivened (if at all) only by Reagan's disclosure of his choice for the vice presidency.

I went to Detroit for the coronation. Although it was mathematically impossible for Reagan to lose, there were still lots of other things that could go wrong, and the Reagan managers (Bill Casey, who had succeeded Sears, and Senator Paul Laxalt of Nevada, Reagan's closest friend in the Senate) took care to avoid them all. Waiving Clif White's brief deviation from orthodox Reaganism in 1976, they wisely asked Clif, who knew more about the running of conventions than anybody else, to take charge of that important phase of the overall operation. Clif chuckled when a trailer was duly parked just outside the Joe Louis Arena, from which he and his regional aides were to operate. There was plenty of office space inside the Arena that would have served just as well or better, but habit was too strong: Ever since 1964 at the Cow Palace in San Francisco, convention floor operations for presidential candidates had been directed from trailers parked outside, and by golly, there would be a trailer for Reagan in Detroit.

The selection of the vice presidential candidate did indeed provide the convention with its dash of excitement, and a curious business it was.

At the bottom of the matter lay a fundamental problem: Reagan, who took the choice of a vice president seriously and was determined that the designee should be someone who could be counted on to continue his outspokenly conservative policies if he should ever have to assume the presidency, apparently lacked confidence that George Bush possessed that vital qualification and perhaps others as well.

Bush, though bested by Reagan in the primaries, was incontestably the second strongest candidate for the presidential nomination, with the second largest bloc of delegate votes (253 to Reagan's 1,580). Moreover, Bush's support came largely from the ancient core of the Republican party: its business-dominated, relatively liberal eastern wing—economic conservatives who deeply believed that budgets should be balanced and who resonated in close harmony when Bush denounced as "voodoo economics" the supply-side economic theories that Reagan had embraced.

Perhaps Reagan remembered my 1975 prediction that if he stayed with the GOP and won its nomination, he would be forced in any case to choose a relative liberal as his running mate, to "balance the ticket." At the time Reagan had sworn he would do no such thing, but perhaps he also remembered my gentle taunt in 1976 when he chose Schweiker. If so, he would have been surprised to learn that at Detroit I was perfectly comfortable with the idea of Bush as vice president. A balanced ticket seemed to me desirable if the party was to be united for the campaign, and I certainly didn't consider Bush very far to the left.

More likely, however, Reagan simply wanted a vice president who shared his views and measured up to the job, and harbored serious doubts as to whether Bush did. In any event, there were soon rumors of earnest discussions in Reagan's suite high up in Detroit's Renaissance Plaza Hotel, and former President Ford was among those seen to enter and leave. If later accounts are to be credited, negotiations got under way between Ford and Reagan representatives (the former led by Henry Kissinger, who had long been a passionate Reagan foe and who as late as March tried desperately to get Ford to enter the nomination race). Apparently Reagan was thinking of offering the vice presidential nomination to Ford, and the negotiations concerned what areas would be Ford's responsibility if he were nominated and elected vice president.

Rumors to these and almost all other conceivable effects swept the convention hall on Wednesday evening, July 16, while the preliminary speakers and rituals of a national political convention droned on. If Reagan was indeed going to offer the vice presidential nomination to Ford, I personally thought it was a very bad idea. What to do with ex-presidents is a difficult enough problem in any case. To make one vice president, and therefore necessarily subordinate to his successor in the Oval Office, seemed to me to offer well-nigh endless opportunities for discord, not least thanks to the mischief-making propensities of the White House press corps. I had to admire Reagan's calm assumption that he could dominate in such a situation, but I wondered—and worried.

In preferring Bush to Ford for the vice presidency, incidentally, I found myself at odds with a good many of my fellow conservatives. As a "moderate" Republican, Bush was, after all, a longtime denizen of the enemy camp, and conservatives are not notoriously fond of such compromise tactics as ticket balancing. I was alarmed, though, at their apparent indifference to the danger represented by Ford, who was every bit as much a moderate Republican as Bush. Moreover, as a former president he would, it seemed to me, have an infinitely greater temptation and ability to wage guerrilla warfare within the new administration.

But there was no time or opportunity to convey my misgivings to Reagan or even to Clif White in his trailer. Luckily the crisis resolved itself when Ford, being interviewed by Walter Cronkite on television as the Reagans watched in their suite, allowed Cronkite to coax him into an admission that under the arrangements then being negotiated, he would in effect be "co-president." That apparently set off the warning bells at last in Reagan's mind: The negotiations collapsed, Reagan designated Bush for the vice presidential nomination despite his doubts, and I returned to New York a much relieved man.

The Democratic convention in New York City in mid-August simply confirmed, to my mind, the analysis I had made four years earlier: In strictly relative terms, Carter was still perceived by his fellow Democrats as deriving from the party's conservative wing, and many of them simply couldn't stand it. Their champion was Ted Kennedy, and he was the convention's emotional favorite. But like Reagan, Carter had locked up his nomination well in advance by winning enough binding primaries, and presidential muscle prevailed over sentiment at Madison Square Garden.

Since my own apartment is only a few blocks northeast of the Garden, I equipped myself with press credentials and dropped over one evening. I was rewarded by the sight of Vice President Mondale rhetorically asking three thousand delegates and alternates, most of them dependent on government for their livelihood in one way or another, "Can we *afford* four years of Ronald Reagan?"—and being answered with a passionate and unanimous *"NO-O-O!"*

Another observer of the Democratic convention was my old friend Clif White, who came to town, took a hotel suite, laid in a suitable supply of refreshments and cheese niblets, and played host to a steady stream of newsmen and political cronies. I hadn't known it before, but it is quite customary for each party to have a low-profile observer or two on hand when its rival is meeting, just to keep an eye on things.

The campaign itself warmed up as usual after Labor Day. I was soon convinced by the polls that the voters were eager to get rid of Carter if at all possible (not because they disliked him but because the poor man almost totally lacked the essential qualities of leadership) but were anxious first to reassure themselves about Reagan's essential soundness. Insofar as the candidates' policies concerned the voters, most of them probably leaned toward Reagan's (remaining, however—a point my friends sometimes overlooked—only "moderately" conservative). But the media had regaled them with stories depicting Ronald Reagan as a wild man who would dearly love to get his finger on the button of nuclear war, and many Americans were forgivably disposed to spend as long as possible making sure that that accusation was false.

That was why, like Clif White and certain others at the Arlington headquarters of the campaign, where opinion was divided on this subject, I favored the general idea of a debate between Reagan and Carter. It was the earliest national manifestation of the now-familiar argument "Let Reagan be Reagan." The slogan justified itself brilliantly when the debate was at last held late in the campaign (October 28), and Dick Wirthlin's polls tested its effect on undecided voters.

The impact was almost seismic. A vast television audience had at last watched Reagan under obvious pressure and liked very much what they saw: not a wild man, or a bumbler, or a senile movie star, but a warm, thoughtful, and manifestly self-possessed human being with a gift of gentle humor. During the single week of campaigning that remained, each report from my friends in Arlington was better than its predecessor. By the weekend before election day we knew that Ronald Reagan would be elected president of the United States. It was quite a feeling.

What we didn't know, and in fact never dreamed, was that the GOP would also carry the Senate. In mid-October, nervous over press reports indicating a decline in the prospects of certain key senatorial candidates, I had phoned Paul Weyrich to see what he could tell me. Weyrich, who was far and away the ablest nuts-and-bolts political operator in the conservative movement, with his fingers deep in scores of congressional campaigns, dismayed me by confirming the press reports. His own pollsters, he said, were reporting a steady falloff in support for almost every senatorial candidate who was being heavily backed by the conservative movement. He simply couldn't understand it.

Reagan's victory, therefore, was made substantially sweeter when the returns made it plain that the Republicans would control the Senate. Arriving at a New York television studio about 11:00 P.M. on election night, to be interviewed as a conservative spokesman on the day's spectacular events, I saw economist Alan Greenspan, formerly chairman of President Nixon's Council of Economic Advisers, across the room, undergoing similar questioning. The crowd and the general pandemonium between us prevented me from going over to him, but we exchanged smiles and waves.

It seemed apparent to me that the election returns brilliantly vindicated the basic proposition—implied by the three immediately preceding presidential elections—that there was a solid conservative majority in the country, but that it possessed both economic and social components and that both had to be appealed to successfully if a conservative victory was to be achieved. Reagan had insisted to me in 1975 that this could be accomplished within and through the Republican party. I gravely doubted it and had felt vindicated by the convention and election results of 1976. Now it was Reagan who was vindicated—certainly at least for the time being.

The other spectacular winners that evening were my feisty friends on the New Right—men like Richard Viguerie and Paul Weyrich, who had labored through the 1970s to amass and deploy the mailing lists that played such a dramatic role in defeating liberal senators like Church, McGovern, Nelson, Magnuson, and Durkin. Even the House of Representatives, though remaining nominally under Democratic control, would be far more responsive now to conservative pressures.

Less than forty-eight hours later, as I was watching a taped rerun of the president-elect's first press conference on the television set in my Manhattan apartment, the phone rang at about 8:00 P.M.

"Hello?"

"Bill Rusher?" It was a man's voice, carefully neutral.

"Yes?" I replied inquiringly.

"Ronald Reagan."

I was so astonished that I literally stood up, as one is expected by protocol to do when the president of the United States enters the room. I later learned from a newspaper dispatch that Reagan had spent several hours that Thursday phoning old friends, presumably enjoying their shock on discovering that the caller was the president-elect. If so, he certainly got his money's worth out of me!

Reagan's election, despite all that had happened to the country in the previous twenty years, still managed to catch a good many liberals by surprise. They were simply the victims of their own excellent propaganda. Arthur Schlesinger, Jr., for one (who had breezily dismissed the conservative stirrings of the 1950s as merely "the ethical afterglow of feudalism" and had explained away the opinion polls of the 1970s with the reassurance that Americans might be "notionally conservative" but that they remained "operationally liberal") confessed himself astonished at the resurgence: "No intellectual phenomenon has been more surprising in recent years than the revival in the United States of conservatism as a respectable social philosophy."

Max Lerner, however, a more discerning observer with a long background as a liberal commentator, reproached Schlesinger for his obtuseness: "Conservatism gave plenty of notice, if the liberals had kept their eyes and ears open." In a perceptive column entitled "The Earthquake," Lerner assessed what had happened:

> No greater upheaval in American politics has occurred for a half-century, since Franklin Roosevelt's victory over Herbert Hoover in 1932. The reach and depth of the Reagan sweep belie the current wisdom that it came only as a protest vote against Jimmy Carter and inflation.
>
> Ronald Reagan's triumph was too convulsive to be confined

within so narrow an analysis. It expressed a wide range of discontents, not only with the economy but with foreign and defense policies, with taxes, welfare and social policies, and the entire climate of ideas. It expressed, along with the discontents, some deep, pent-up social angers.

This wasn't a tremor. It was an earthquake. It was long preparing. It represents a long-range retreat from the liberalism of the New Deal welfare state. Early in the campaign I wrote of the support for Reagan as a sign of the ending of the long affair between Americans and traditional liberalism. Reagan is a symbol of the closure of the liberal dream. . . .

Something like a class revolution has been taking place. Since the violent 1960s, the middle-middle and lower-middle classes have been seething with social resentments over the runaway changes in the culture. They, too, were part of the American dream—they had worked and scrimped, fashioned a trade or small business, built a house, raised a family. They felt threatened by the forces that seemed intent on taking this away from them.

This time the Populist revolt was led by the conservatives. Economic distress is only part of the story. Also part of it are the reawakened religious impulse and the concern about the work ethic and about the endangered values system.

Even European reporters and commentators, who had long uncritically accepted the assurances of American liberals such as Schlesinger that conservatism was a negligible phenomenon in American politics—a flash in the pan, attributable largely to the homespun western charm of Barry Goldwater's personality—at last got the message. The reception room at *National Review* suddenly seemed full of Belgian television commentators and Italian newspaper reporters, all curious to know more about "thees consairvatisme." We enlightened them as best we could.

There were, of course, plenty of observers ready to argue that the American people in 1980 voted not for Reagan but simply against Carter and that, therefore, Reagan's election was not a mandate for anything at all. Such people have the problem of explaining why, in that case, half a dozen prominent liberals were also carried feetfirst, that November, out of the U.S. Senate. I would not, however, dispute the contention that all election results are to some extent ambiguous. I have always pitied the

American voter, who must go into a voting booth once every four years, pull a single lever, and *by that act* register his views concerning the candidates and the issues and on how the country's basic problems, both foreign and domestic, should be handled for the next four years. For that very reason I take issue with those fellow conservatives of mine who breezily assume that Ronald Reagan's election was a clear mandate to enact into law the entire conservative agenda or even the entire Republican platform of 1980, let alone to repeal every act of government that some conservative has in the past seen fit to criticize. Fortunately Ronald Reagan is far too wise a man to make such a mistake.

Although the 1980 election was almost certainly a watershed—not in the sense of establishing the GOP as the dominant party (for that remains to be determined, in part by the GOP's own future decisions) but in the sense that America moved collectively to the right, definitively ending liberalism's long reign in the political sphere—it should not be forgotten that liberalism remains dominant in the media, in academia, and among the American intelligentsia in general. This situation, too, is in process of change, certainly of modification. It is even probable that there is simply a cultural lag involved, comparable to others we have seen in American history. This would hardly be the first time that political developments have outrun, or even contradicted, the views of the intellectual establishment. But for conservatives in these fields there is certainly plenty of work still to be done.

Since this account of the growth of the conservative movement, climaxed by its victory at the polls in 1980, is bound to be painful to any liberal who has pressed on thus far, let me add one other analgesic admission. It is decreed in the very nature of things, and certainly in the nature of politics, that every end is in some sense a beginning, and vice versa. To be born, someone has said, is to die a little. Similarly, to win politically is to begin the long process of losing, and to lose is to lay the first foundation for ultimate victory.

I am not suggesting that modern American conservatism and liberalism are merely two sides of the same coin, which fate flips alternately forever. On the contrary, I believe that modern conservatism is the wisest political formulation yet achieved of the truths man has learned about himself in relation to his social environment, and I am inclined to think that liberalism of what might be called the Teddy Kennedy sort is so shallow and evanescent a phenomenon that it will probably (quite unlike the more serious left) not revive in our politics at all. But at the purely partisan level and at the deeper levels of intellectual and social dominance, the systole and diastole that characterize all living phenomena will go on. I have no doubt that Reagan's victory, and conservatism's, have lit fires of combative determination in many a youthful breast not at all unlike the one that Franklin Roosevelt's 1936 landslide ignited in the thirteen-year-old whose mother happened to come from Alf Landon's hometown in Kansas.

But whatever the 1980 election can reasonably be argued to have meant and whatever ups and downs the Republican party or the conservative movement may experience in the future, Reagan's victory can be said to mark the point at which the conservative movement achieved a political maturity equal to the intellectual maturity it already possessed. In one sense, it just doesn't matter whether conservatism wins or loses some particular future election: The point is that conservatism is unmistakably *on the playing field* at last, as one of the two major contestants. It has numerous candidates for public office eager to expound its views; it has seasoned political managers ready to manage their campaigns; it has formidable research institutions developing its analyses of every conceivable issue; it has "public interest" lawyers testing its contentions in the courts; it has columnists, radio and television commentators, and authors of all sorts, pleading its causes; and slowly but steadily young conservative journalists and academicians, in growing numbers that cannot be resisted forever, are entering and rising through those long-hostile ranks. Contemplating the generation of young conservatives that is coming along after my own, I am sometimes reminded of Ripley's dramatic formulation for the growth of the population of China: If the Chinese people were to march, four abreast, past a given point, they would march on forever.

Chapter XIII

The Reagan Administration —and Beyond

Since this book is essentially an account of the growth of the American conservative movement, as viewed from my own personal vantage point over a period of nearly thirty years, a detailed analysis of the events of the Reagan administration would be gratuitous and inappropriate. But certain developments taking place in that administration are a necessary part of the story I have to tell. The conservative movement largely produced the Reagan administration. Inevitably the Reagan administration has profoundly influenced, and to some extent reshaped, the conservative movement.

When Ronald Reagan was inaugurated as president on January 20, 1981, the conventional wisdom in Washington was that the job would tame the man in short order. As a candidate, most pundits agreed, Reagan had talked a pretty tough conservative game. But running for the presidency is one thing; actually *being* president is quite another. The pressures are enormous, the available options are often few and painful, and the neophyte chief executive soon discovers the limitations under which his much execrated predecessor labored. Within six months or a year at most Reagan was bound to break the hearts of the conservatives who had backed him so enthusiastically and become just one more centrist president, trudging dutifully back and forth between right center and left center as inexorable circumstances dictated. That was certainly the scenario lovingly anticipated by the resident gurus of the capital.

It hasn't worked out quite that way. Ronald Reagan lives in the real world—which is to say, he is well aware that in politics it is often necessary to compromise. As governor of California, contending with a legislature in which both houses were Democrat-controlled, he honed his own instinctive skills in the high political art of give-and-take. But for my part at any rate, I have been truly amazed at how briskly, how resiliently, and withal how persistently he has done battle for the causes for which he campaigned—and, I might add, in general how successfully.

My expectations for a Reagan presidency were reasonably high, but they were conditioned by my unhappy recollections of the Eisenhower and Nixon administrations. Eisenhower, it seemed to me, had simply let down our side—settling for a stalemate in Korea, letting off the liberals with scarcely a wrist slap for their long acquiescence in Communist penetrations of important segments of American society, ignoring major foreign policy opportunities in the Middle East and Hungary in the interests of his own reelection campaign, and, finally, giving Khrushchev a wholly unnecessary propaganda coup by squiring him around the United States in 1959.

There had been no organized conservative movement, in the political sense, during Dwight Eisenhower's eight-year administration, so perhaps he can be forgiven for failing to respond to conservative demands, let alone for failing to formulate them. But what can be said for Richard Nixon? He was well aware of the conservative movement, considered it an essential element of any Republican victory, and sought to win its support and keep it on his side. But as long as he was in the White House, he never once indicated that he regarded conservatism as anything but one more medium-sized piece on the chessboard of his calculating mind. "We are all Keynesians now," he could wisecrack—and mean it, insofar as he was capable of meaning anything. From Taiwan to wage and price controls, he seemed almost to enjoy traducing every conservative position with which he had come to be identified in the course of a quarter of a century in politics.

I certainly did not expect to see Ronald Reagan accord conservatives, or conservatism, similar treatment. But I was ruefully aware of the scenario described earlier, and I fully expected that Reagan in office would be a substantially diminished version of Reagan the crusading campaigner.

Nor was I alone in that expectation. Lovingly counting o'er the obstacles facing the new president, the liberal columnist Tom Wicker put it this way:

> The stubborn layers of Federal bureaucracy that await Mr.
> Reagan on Jan. 20 are as thick and resilient as those that greeted

Mr. Carter four years ago, and often smothered him thereafter. Similarly, the numerous aggressive interests represented by sophisticated lobbies in Washington will remain as adept as ever at preventing what they do not want to happen—teachers, for example, in protecting the new Department of Education, or almost any group in protecting *its* appropriation from a President in search of "waste and extravagance."

As he seeks his promised cuts, moreover, Mr. Reagan will find that large and growing "entitlement" programs absorb about 75 percent of the Federal budget without even going through the appropriations process. And the intractable problems with which Mr. Carter grappled—stagflation, productivity decline, the drain on Social Security trust funds, energy costs, decaying cities—are still intractable.

Reagan's impact on Washington—above all, his spectacular success in pushing his tax-cutting program through the Democrat-controlled House of Representatives in the first year of his term— is now history. To me at any rate, his efforts to cut the domestic budget or at least to reduce the rate of its expansion, to prune the junglelike regulatory undergrowth, and to rebuild the nation's defenses deserved almost equal praise. Reagan did not always get his way, but he got it an impressively large proportion of the time, and the triumphant declarations of his foes, including those in the media, that he had suffered some stinging defeat (as in the autumn 1982 battle over funds for the MX missile) often proved premature. Like a skillful club boxer, Reagan moved into the attack, landed his punches, backed off, shifted his weight, parried, and attacked again. I came to feel that I was watching a protagonist who knew precisely what he wanted, enjoyed battling for it, and firmly intended to get it in the long run. Conservatism, it seemed to me, not only had never had a finer champion in the White House but, in the light of the odds in politics, could rarely if ever expect to be quite so lucky again.

Not all conservatives agreed with me. The New Right in particular—as fiercely combative as ever—was on record before Reagan's term was half over as loudly dissatisfied with his performance. As far as I could see, it was simply the old question of whether the glass was half full or half empty. Point to Reagan's strenuous and successful battle to reduce income tax rates, and they would reply quite accurately that counting Social Security withholding increases already mandated, the average American's total tax payments would actually *rise* in Reagan's second year. Point to his efforts to reduce domestic spending, and they would argue correctly that many of the "reductions" were not, in absolute terms, reductions at all but merely reductions *in the rate of increase.* And so on, through an elaborate litany of complaints.

It should be noted, though, in fairness to both sides, that the New Right's reservations about Reagan are not exactly new. In 1976 Richard Viguerie, in addition to participating in our joint effort to provide a third line on the ballot in case the GOP failed to nominate a conservative, financed an unsuccessful attempt to run up a respectable score for John Connally as a write-in candidate against Reagan in the New Hampshire Republican primary. And in the early stages of the 1980 campaign Viguerie once again preferred Connally, and perhaps others, to Reagan. Presumably Reagan is aware of this and keeps it in mind as New Right criticism rains down on his head.

The rest of the conservative community is much less critical of Reagan's performance in office—though it quite properly reserves and frequently exercises the right to disagree with him on particular policies, appointments, etc. But in general, even when the disagreements are sharpest, personal relations between Reagan and members of the conservative community remain warm. Again and again he has used the prerogatives of the presidency to shed a little welcome luster on worthy conservative figures and institutions—the sort of official or semiofficial recognition that liberals long considered the reward of their manifest merits and reserved almost exclusively for themselves and their favorites.

Thus on February 21, 1983, the president attended a large reception held in Washington by *National Review* and proclaimed it "my favorite magazine." Two days later James Burnham and Clare Boothe Luce were among the distinguished citizens on whom he bestowed the Medal of Freedom at a White House lunch. Three days earlier he had given the major address at the concluding banquet of the annual Conservative Political Action Committee conference in Washington—the eighth time in ten years that he had done so. Two and a half months later, returning from California to Washington, he stopped in Ashland, Ohio—

where no incumbent president had ever been before—to address a fund-raising dinner for a Memorial Center at Ashland College in honor of the late Congressman John Ashbrook.*

Despite individual reservations about this or that, it would appear that Ronald Reagan's affection for the conservative movement is very definitely requited. When the 700 people attending the aforementioned CPAC conference were polled, 88 percent of those responding affirmed that they wanted Reagan to run for re-election.

Quite aside from the matter of Reagan's personal support for conservative principles, policies, and institutions, the conservative movement was bound to be affected by the extent to which Reagan appointed identifiable and resolute conservatives to public office. Here the reviews, as far as conservatives go, are distinctly mixed.

I happen to be in a position to testify personally to the earnestness of Reagan's early efforts to recruit qualified conservatives for appointments in his administration. But I had no already drawn-up list of Reagan enthusiasts qualified for office and eager for appointment, nor did anybody else I knew. To start with myself, I had already advised Reagan, prior to the election, that other commitments (including the commitment to write this book, which has consumed all my small supply of spare time for two years) would preclude me from seeking any job, either full or part time. Most of my contemporaries in the conservative movement were in much the same position—men and women with established careers that demanded their full-time attention, who had, moreover, reached an age at which going to Washington to work in somebody else's administration had lost the charm it might have possessed if they were still in their thirties or forties.

Searches for qualified individuals were, of course, going on all over Washington and the country in the weeks and months after Reagan's election, but the process was slow and uncoordinated. According to one subsequent account, Reagan asked his "kitchen cabinet"—a group of conservative businessmen from California who had been his friends and business advisers for many years—to

---

* Ashbrook died unexpectedly at fifty-three, in May 1982, of a massive gastric hemorrhage, while campaigning for the Senate seat of Ohio Democrat Howard Metzenbaum.

oversee informally various aspects of the transition process, and they briskly parceled out assignments roughly corresponding to the major governmental departments and agencies. But unfortunately no one in the kitchen cabinet concerned himself expressly with the problem of recruitment per se. This oversight was finally corrected in February 1981, when, reportedly at the instigation of Lyn Nofziger, the members of the kitchen cabinet protested to Reagan that not enough true-blue conservatives were making their way into the administration. By then, however, the whole top echelon of government posts had been filled. The conservatives who were appointed in and after February in response to this belated complaint were therefore necessarily assigned to lesser jobs.

Reagan, in other words, had to make his way through November and December 1980 and January 1981 with only short and inadequate lists of conservatives submitted by personal friends, while the pressures of time and politics were forcing him to make major personnel choices from among the serious possibilities before him—not all of them, by any means, notably conservative.

The essential problem was that appointees to high government office are normally, and to some extent rightly, drawn from the ranks of those who have at some time held lesser government positions—and there were, of course, almost no movement conservatives with any prior experience in government. A column of mine, written in late January 1981, summed up the dilemma in terms of the selection of someone to fill the (imaginary) post of secretary of the marines, and my Washington sources assure me that the situation described in my parody was so typical that I am emboldened to reprint it here:

> The conservative activists whose efforts contributed so substantially to the nomination and election of Ronald Reagan complain that they are being passed over in the staffing of his administration. Are they right, and if so what can be done about it?
>
> By and large they are right, and unfortunately very little can be done about it.
>
> Let me illustrate the problem with a hypothetical case that I suspect is fairly typical. You are President Reagan, and you must choose between two candidates for the post of Secretary of the Marines, both of whom are being strenuously pushed by their supporters.

One is J. Parmalee Butterthorpe III, of the Pennsylvania Main Line Butterthorpes. He is 45, a graduate of Princeton University and Yale Law School, and a registered Republican of vaguely centrist views who supported his friend George Bush up till the convention last year. After a number of years in private law practice in Philadelphia (during which he married the favorite cousin of Senator Heinz), Butterthorpe served as Assistant Secretary of the Marines under Presidents Nixon and Ford. When Carter was elected, Butterthorpe retired from Government and resumed his law practice, becoming one of the principal attorneys for General Motors. He did not completely lose touch with government, however, for in 1978 Mr. Carter named him as one of three official U.S. representatives at the inauguration of President Babel Bongo-bongo of Lower Volta. He is not, or at any rate not any longer, a member of any private club that excludes women, blacks, or Jews. Accompanying the Butterthorpe résumé are glowing letters of endorsement from Vice President Bush, Senator Heinz, the president of General Motors, and (of all people) Barry Goldwater, who owed Heinz a favor.

The other candidate for the job is Fred Bezirk, 34, of Hushpuppy, Nebraska. Bezirk attended Hushpuppy High and Rockford College, graduating from the latter with honors. At Rockford he founded and became the first president of a chapter of Young Americans for Freedom, later rising to YAF's national Board. He has been passionately interested in politics since the age of 16, when he joined the Draft Goldwater movement, and was a Young Republican for Reagan at the 1968 convention in Miami Beach. He was a Reagan delegate from Nebraska at the convention in Kansas City in 1976, and last year was Reagan's Western Nebraska chairman. Bezirk is vice president of his father's grain storage business, a devout Methodist, an outspoken conservative, and himself a former Marine, having served with distinction in Vietnam. He is married to his childhood sweetheart, and is a cousin by marriage of the president of the Atchison, Topeka and Santa Fe Railroad. A letter of endorsement from the latter, plus one from Bezirk's Congressman and one from Senator Jesse Helms, accompany his résumé.

Which would you pick, if you were Reagan?

Maybe I have tilted the pinball machine a little in the above hypothetical case, but not much. There is a category of people, of whom Butterthorpe is typical, who have spent their lives carefully positioning themselves to rise higher no matter who is president. They are well connected; they have avoided taking any stand that

could possibly offend anybody; and they have accumulated all sorts
of Brownie points along the way. Then there is quite a different sort
of person, typified by Bezirk. These are the people who care, and
care deeply. They got interested in politics because they couldn't
stand what they saw happening to their country. They have often
had an ear torn off, figuratively speaking, in the course of nearly
two decades fighting for Barry Goldwater and Ronald Reagan.
They have no government experience, if only because nobody they
supported was ever elected to anything, or had any jobs to pass out
if he was.

Which shall it be—Butterthorpe or Bezirk? President Reagan
hesitates: His heart is with Bezirk. But Butterthorpe is older, more
broadly educated and experienced—and after all he served in a
high post in that very department once before. Then too, it isn't a
job in which one's shade of Republicanism greatly matters. And
Senator Heinz will be so grateful. . . .

All hail Secretary Butterthorpe!

Obviously, in the long run the only solution to the problem is
to appoint to the lower echelons of government conservatives who
will later be available and qualified for promotion to the high
posts. And not the least important achievement of Ronald Reagan
as president is that he has done precisely that. Future conservative
administrations will thus have a pool of talented conservatives
with government experience to draw on—a resource unavailable
to Reagan himself when he took office.

But will there *be* any future conservative administrations? I
have already made clear my confidence that the conservative
movement has achieved maturity, and will continue henceforth to
play an important role in the politics of our era. Conservative
analyses of social, economic, and political problems are now too
numerous, too incisive, and too widely disseminated to be disregarded, and they will inevitably have proponents active in the political process.

Precisely what form that activity will take, though, depends
in large part on a major decision the Republican party must make
when Ronald Reagan at last steps down as president. Enough has
been said to underscore my own conviction that the conservative
majority in this country can be sure of winning a presidential
election only when it is united—i.e., when, as in 1972 and 1980, its

economic and social components are both appealed to success-fully. As long as Reagan is the party's leader, that essential strate-gic precondition will be understood and fulfilled. But what will be the inclination of the first Republican national convention that doesn't have Ronald Reagan to nominate? Will it insist upon choosing a standard-bearer who genuinely understands the abso-lute necessity for the coalition? Or will it revert to the type of purely economic-conservative Republicanism that lost, with the exception of Eisenhower's two personal triumphs, every presiden-tial election from 1932 through 1960?

To ask that question is not to make a veiled allusion to the present short list of possible post-Reagan presidential nominees. For their merits are not all that unevenly distributed. Jack Kemp, who is widely regarded as the favorite of movement conservatives and who most certainly understands the importance of the social-conservative component of the conservative coalition, has not yet established himself as fully *presidentabile*—partly because of his narrow and unsatisfactory base as a member of the House of Rep-resentatives. And George Bush, who as Reagan's vice president may be said to have the inside track to succeed him but inherits a heavy burden of conservative distrust because he hails from the economic-conservative core of the GOP and draws much of his strength from its relatively liberal eastern wing, could be seen not long ago on the cover page of the Reverend Jerry Falwell's *Moral Majority Report*. These and other possible nominees all seem at least potentially capable of making the bid for coalition support that alone can put a conservative candidate comfortably over the top, but whether any given one of them would do so—or will even be given the chance—remains to be seen.

If the Republican party rejects the coalition strategy, it is en-tirely possible that the right will split, with economic conserva-tives remaining predominantly loyal to the GOP and social conservatives moving toward some form of independent activity or even, if the Democrats are smart or lucky, back for a time into their ancestral party (as in 1976).

But these are mere speculations, and in any case they do not seriously modify the essential reality, which is that conservatism cannot and will not be denied indefinitely the influence on Ameri-can society that is dictated by its inherent strength.

* * *

Every political movement that has a beginning must necessarily have an end, and as predicted earlier, the dynamism of the modern conservative movement will in due course exhaust itself—much as an ocean wave, seen from an airplane, forms in response to the pressures around it, curves upward and crests, then subsides into the sea from which it sprang, making its last contribution to the shape and momentum of the next wave.

But conservatism itself, properly understood, is a prescription for political activity based on a profound analysis of the nature of man and of human society, and as such it transcends, and will of course survive, both the particular movement we have discussed and that movement's necessary end. In our day it has been the task of conservatives to proclaim the imperative of human freedom, to nurture the traditional values of our civilization, and to summon the West to the defense of both that freedom and those values against the formidable challenge of communism. Those tasks are by no means completed, but it is now at least possible to feel that they are in the hands of a movement capable of completing them.

Many conservatives will think that I am being unduly optimistic to assume that the present struggle will end successfully from the conservative standpoint. The moral capital of the West has been heavily overdrawn, and its more prosperous sectors have been overrun, as prosperous sectors always are, by external elements far more concerned with consumption than with creation or construction. Standards have declined, or even disintegrated, and many of the stigmata of a mature civilization in process of decay are all too visible. But it is the West we are dealing with, and we are dealing with it, moreover, not in a historical vacuum but in the context of certain specific challenges.

The challenge posed by twentieth-century liberalism, which played so long and so dominant a role in American politics, may prove less menacing in the future than its impressive past might lead one to expect. There are, of course, apologists for liberalism who will argue that it was never really tried. Witness Washington correspondent Elizabeth Drew's defense of governmental activism, in an article in the *New Yorker* not long after Reagan's election:

While certain politicians and other people are wont to make broad statements to the effect that federal programs don't "work," they are actually referring to the social programs of the sixties, which have had mixed results. The problem, to be somewhat general about it, was that there was excessive ambition, a sense of unreality, in regard to what could be accomplished; that there is now an overload and an underrelating of programs; and that in fact the experiment of the sixties was very short-lived. It did not really begin until after the middle of the decade, and soon ran into the competing claims of a war. By 1969, a new Administration, headed by a man who had campaigned against the programs, was in office. Two things are needed, according to the most dispassionate thinkers: an unsentimental sorting out of what is efficacious and what is not, and more rational organization and management of the government's efforts.

But Irving Kristol seemed closer to the mark when he pronounced the following epitaph for his former faith: "What we call liberalism has enacted its agenda; it's falling apart. The good fight has been fought and won, only the victory is ambiguous. Certain things didn't respond as they were supposed to. Crime is worse; education is in trouble. These things are important to people, and liberals have no philosophy to guide or inspire anybody."

Liberals have no philosophy: That is their fatal weakness— one not shared, incidentally, with the harder left. "Liberals and reactionaries do not understand politics," Peter Drucker once observed; "conservatives and radicals do." Conservatives and radicals have both thought deeply about the nature of man and society, reached firm (though opposite) conclusions on the subject, and formulated social policies congruent with their conclusions. Both can be upended temporarily by reactionaries bent on reviving some defunct but fondly remembered social order or by liberals who have managed to assemble an electoral majority for some transiently popular social vision. But in such adversities both can derive nourishment from roots deep in the soil of political philosophy, and that is why the final conflict—*la lutte finale* of communism's international hymn—will not be between liberals and reactionaries, or between reactionaries and radicals, or even between liberals and conservatives, but between conservatives and radicals.

For the moment the opposition to the conservative movement—liberal and harder left alike—has retreated into its twin Alpine redoubts: the media and the academy. These, therefore, are likely to be the scene of conservatism's next battles and almost certainly in that order.

We are always tempted to imagine that current trends will continue into the indefinite future and therefore visualize that future as the one thing it most certainly will *not* be: a featureless projection of the past. Many observers of the American society believe that its essential dividing line today is no longer the familiar one between the haves and have-nots that gave rise to the old liberal agenda, but a new one between the older, orthodox, producing segments of the society and a new segment, born of high technology and reaching toward self-awareness, status, and power as something very like a new class in the Marxist sense.* This is what Kevin Phillips has called the Knowledge Industry, and others the verbalizers: an amalgam consisting of major elements of the media, the foundations, the research institutes, the governmental and corporate bureaucracies, and the academy.

The advent and power drive of this new class (if that is what it proves to be) have been partially masked by the fact that it has adopted, as a device for recruiting allies and combating its chosen foe, much of the old liberal agenda of the have-nots. But this is deceptive. As *National Review* has remarked editorially, " 'The poor' must be understood in a special sense, as potential clients for the redistributive ministrations of the New Class, the middlemen of social justice. Analytically, 'the poor,' as a concept, legitimates the power-grab of the New Class middlemen in the same sense as 'the proletariat' legitimates the power-grab of the Leninists."

The old liberal nostrums—above all, those relying on the salvific powers of big government—have been tried too recently and too extensively, and have failed too spectacularly, to command enthusiastic support today, even from many who were once proud to march under the banner of liberalism. Governmental intervention, especially in its newer forms (e.g., pollution control), is henceforth

* See, e.g., B. Bruce-Briggs, ed., *The New Class?* (Transaction Books, 1979), and Phillips, *Mediacracy*, loc. cit.

more likely to be employed principally as a means of hamstringing the hitherto dominant producing class, while the new class of verbalizers tries to establish, through its grip on the realm of ideas, a rival and ultimately superior center of power.

We have already seen the development in Washington of a corps of verbalizers, based in the media, in certain "think tanks," and in the more secure echelons of the bureaucracy, which wages war on presidential administrations not to its liking. The score in this contest, which has been going on since the assassination of John Kennedy, is running heavily against the presidents. But Ronald Reagan has done rather better than his predecessors, precisely because of his prowess as the Great Communicator—i.e., by virtue of his ability, as a verbalizer on behalf of the older social classes, to compete with the new class effectively on its own terms.

This clash between the producers and the verbalizers may well provide the principal grist of domestic controversy in the United States for the remainder of this century. It is not at all unlikely that political leadership among the verbalizers will be provided by able spokesmen derived from the ranks of television personalities—by far the best-known and best-liked Americans of our day. Of course, as the example of Ronald Reagan suggests, that will be a game at which two can play.

At a somewhat longer remove, there is one other battle that the conservative movement must fight and win. As the media will be the battleground of the first, the academy will be the arena of the second. It will be the most important and most difficult battle of them all.

As we noted at the outset of this volume, the conservative movement, like any social movement, has both intellectual and political aspects. Necessarily the former precede the latter: Thought precedes action, laying the foundation and justification for it. This can and does occur in both small and large ways. At the small end of the spectrum, some sort of platform, however nominal, is ordinarily considered necessary to almost any political campaign. (Even a mob is inspired by a slogan.) At the other end, a world view almost implies a political order based upon it.

The Judaeo-Christian world view was the intellectual precursor and foundation of Western civilization. In the Renaissance this world view underwent modification in the direction of "humanism." The ensuing Reformation and Counterreformation resulted in two political dispensations: a Catholic, hierarchical, and still essentially supranational dispensation which remained dominant in the Latin areas of Christian Europe and a Protestant, individualist, and intensely nationalistic dispensation which quickly overran northern Europe, Britain, and (in the eighteenth century) the Atlantic rim, including what was to become the United States.

In the late eighteenth century a new major development, stemming from the Renaissance, took place in both the Catholic and Protestant sectors of the Western world. Modern science, making its debut, gave rise to the conviction on the part of many serious thinkers that mankind could dispense with God altogether: that "pure reason" was the proper guide to conduct and that by its light alone the human race could henceforth find its way. This great development, closely associated with that vast influx of knowledge called the Enlightenment, promptly had the inevitable political consequences: Many of the new societies that happened just then to be emerging from absolutism or shaking off its last shackles (including the United States) left open under their constitutional arrangements the relation of mankind to God. Either no church was established, as in the United States, or the established church was required to coexist with other religions and with freethinkers professing no religion whatever.

The past two centuries, therefore, have been an era in which many of the children of the eighteenth-century Enlightenment have sought to guide mankind solely by the lights of science—or, more broadly, "pure reason." Freedom of religion has been permitted almost everywhere, save in the new and relentlessly totalitarian societies of the Marxist-Leninist variety. But in the West, including the United States, the result of religion's indeterminate status has been the near-total secularization of both the society and the culture.

Once again political consequences have been speedily forthcoming. In nation after nation of the Western world, in direct proportion to the impact of these developments, the whole tone and texture of the social order have been altered. Hedonism, reflected in such phenomena as drugs and sexual promiscuity, has soared and received wide legislative sanction. Criminality, no longer impeded by moral fetters and thus now inhibited only by laws once enacted largely to codify powerful moral prescriptions, has grown by leaps and bounds. The social will to defend against external perils has weakened almost to the point of inanition.

Let us call it coincidence that at this juncture a remarkable man—an exile from the Soviet Union, a Nobel Prize-winning author, a convert to Russian Orthodox Christianity—rose to address the commencement convocation at Harvard on June 8, 1978. Alexander Solzhenitsyn spoke in Russian, but his words resonated throughout the world. Nothing he said was entirely new, but everything—the occasion, the subject, above all the origins and history of the speaker—conduced to give his address an impact which, though felt immediately, has not even yet been fully appreciated. In those perhaps forty minutes, Alexander Solzhenitsyn defined for the next era of human history the intellectual agenda of Western man:

> The mistake must be at the root, at the very basis of human thinking in the past centuries. I refer to the prevailing Western view of the world which was first born during the Renaissance and found its political expression starting in the period of the Enlightenment. It became the basis for government and social science and could be defined as rationalistic humanism or humanistic autonomy: the proclaimed and enforced autonomy of man from any higher force above him. It could also be called anthropocentricity, with man seen as the center of everything that exists....

Solzhenitsyn went on to describe how the Middle Ages had become "an intolerable despotic repression of man's physical nature in favor of the spiritual one." This overemphasis had been succeeded, however, by one even worse: a "new way of thinking" which "based modern Western civilization on the dangerous trend toward worshipping man and his material needs.... That provided access for evil, of which in our days there is a free and constant flow."

It took two hundred years for this development to end in "total liberation ... from the moral heritage of Christian centuries, with their great reserves of mercy and sacrifice." But today the divorce is complete:

> The West ended up by truly enforcing human rights, sometimes even excessively, but man's sense of responsibility to God and society grew dimmer and dimmer.... All the glorified technologi-

cal achievements of Progress, including the conquest of outer space, do not redeem the twentieth century's moral poverty, which no one could imagine even as late as in the nineteenth century. . . .

I am referring to the calamity of a despiritualized and irreligious humanistic consciousness.

After a crisp analysis of the disaster into which a selfish humanism has led mankind, Solzhenitsyn boldly pointed the way toward recovery:

It would be retrogression to attach oneself today to the ossified formulas of the Enlightenment. Social dogmatism leaves us completely helpless before the trials of our time.

Even if we are spared destruction by war, our lives will have to change if we want to save life from self-destruction. We cannot avoid revising the fundamental definitions of human life and human society. Is it true that man is above everything? Is there no Higher Spirit above him? Is it right that man's life and society's activities have to be determined by material expansion in the first place? Is it permissible to promote such expansion to the detriment of our spiritual integrity?

If the world has not come to its end, it has approached a major turn in history, equal in importance to the turn from the Middle Ages to the Renaissance. It will exact from us a spiritual upsurge, we shall have to rise to a new height of vision, to a new level of life where our physical nature will not be cursed as in the Middle Ages, but, even more importantly, our spiritual being will not be trampled upon as in the Modern Era.

This ascension will be similar to climbing onto the next anthropological stage. No one on earth has any way left but—upward.

What Solzhenitsyn is saying here is so breathtaking that we may forgive the *New York Times* for the astonishment with which, the next day, it found itself editorially defending the Enlightenment—an intellectual breakthrough it had not seriously expected to be called upon to defend. For that is precisely what Solzhenitsyn is demanding: the rethinking of the Enlightenment—a true reintegration, after two centuries, of the Judaeo-Christian heritage into the ongoing moral, intellectual, and political tradition of the West. It is not a step backward that he contemplates but a step forward and upward—a whole new stage in the spiritual progress of mankind.

Such a development, if it occurs at all, will necessarily take decades—very probably the better part of a century. One important early step will almost surely be a deeper reconciliation of religious imperatives and demonstrable economic laws than has yet been achieved. Others will preoccupy the genius of many thinkers and in all likelihood result in new political dispensations not readily recognizable to twentieth-century man.

But there are signs on every hand, for those able to interpret them, that "pure reason" is tiring in its long pursuit of objective truth and that it may at last be preparing to acknowledge the existence of what Christians call God. In the arcane world of subatomic physics, for example, science is apparently approaching its last frontier: a strange twilight realm where particles seemingly both do and do not exist, where "matter" and "energy" are both describable only as mathematical formulae, where "time" dwindles to a mere perspective from which we see reality. In 1977 Berkeley physicist Henry Pierce Stapp asserted that "Everything we know about nature is in accord with the idea that the fundamental processes of nature lie outside space-time but generate events that can be located in space-time."

Compare that with the following passage from C. S. Lewis's *Miracles*, written thirty years earlier: ". . . it is probable that Nature is not really in Time and almost certain that God is not. Time is probably (like perspective) the mode of our perception. . . . To [God] all the physical events and all the human acts are present in an eternal Now."

Thus do the physicists of the late twentieth century seem to be approaching insights achieved, intuitively rather than scientifically, by the metaphysicians of the fourth and thirteenth.

Certainly it is no longer news that mankind-without-God is in difficulties. Dr. Colin W. Williams recently put it this way: "The way of 'religious establishment,' in which unity is imposed on the community from above, is no longer viable. But the path of secularism, which seeks to leave behind the divisive conflicts of revealed religion by moving into the world of autonomous reason, has also proved bankrupt." Perhaps Dr. Williams, who is a former dean of Yale Divinity School, may be dismissed as biased. But it is a piquant touch that his paper in which the quoted statement appears was written for, and published by, the Aspen Institute for Humanistic Studies.

It may well be that in the intellectual and political realization of Solzhenitsyn's vision the American conservative movement will find, in the rest of this century and the opening decades of the twenty-first, its most challenging assignment and its last and most important achievement. Certainly nothing else it could accomplish would contribute so substantially to the betterment of mankind. As always, the intellectual achievement would promptly bring in its train important political consequences—including the final victory of Western Judaeo-Christian society over that misbegotten child of the Enlightenment, communism. For that, after all, is what communism at bottom is: a determined attempt to understand, organize, and direct the history and progress of mankind without reference to, or recognition of, the spiritual dimension in human nature. It is precisely because conservatism recognizes and makes due allowance for that dimension that it takes issue with communism at a level simply not reached by liberalism. And that is also why, if mankind is ultimately to be spared communism's world dominion, conservatism will be the means of its deliverance.

Beyond that happy day, the American conservative movement as we have known it will gradually lose its identity in the forward sweep of history, as the waves of human progress, rolling forever westward around the world, wash at last against the far shores of the Pacific, and mankind draws ever closer to its high but unknowable destiny.

Index